Unconfined

UNCONFINED

LESSONS FROM PRISON AND THE JOURNEY OF BEING SET FREE

LILY TAYLOR

NASHVILLE

NEW YORK • LONDON • MELBOURNE • VANCOUVER

Unconfined

Lessons from Prison and the Journey of Being Set Free

Published in New York, New York, by Morgan James Publishing. Morgan James is a trademark of Morgan James, LLC. www.MorganJamesPublishing.com

ISBN 9781631952999 paperback
ISBN 9781631953002 eBook
Library of Congress Control Number: 2020944138

Cover Design by:
Jonathan Lewis

Interior Design by:
Christopher Kirk
www.GFSstudio.com

Edited by:
James Pence

Morgan James is a proud partner of Habitat for Humanity Peninsula and Greater Williamsburg. Partners in building since 2006.

Get involved today! Visit
MorganJamesPublishing.com/giving-back

Foreword

"**I** didn't think that could ever happen to me!"

You hear these words all the time when people are interviewed after a tragedy. Most of us will walk through life believing the really bad stuff we see on TV and read about on the internet only happens to other people, never to us. All too often we lull ourselves into forgetting that the comfort of normalcy we cling to can disappear in the blink of an eye.

And, what if it does?

How do you respond when the secure walls of your comfortable life come crashing down around you, only to see them replaced with prison bars, both physically and emotionally?

Lily Taylor and her family endured nearly a decade of this very thing. From living the American dream, to the harsh reality of finding yourself on the wrong side of the Federal Justice system, they quickly discovered that no one is immune to tragedy.

Through the pages of the book you now hold in your hand, Lily takes you on her family's journey alongside her son, Stephen, who was given all the world had to offer and threw it away in an escalating series of poor decisions. Stephen's bad choices ultimately led to a place no one ever expected him to be—federal prison.

"I didn't think we could ever end up here!"

What most never realize is that when one person goes to prison, they take their family with them. Although their loved ones aren't sentenced to a government detention center bodily, they're trapped in a prison they carry with them wherever they go. From incessant fear, overwhelming anxiety, financial burdens and crippling self-doubt, the impact on loved ones is catastrophic.

Unfortunately, once we find ourselves down in the darkest depths of suffering, we can begin to feel like there's no more hope. But that's when the spark often ignites.

You see, light cannot exist without darkness. And for some of us, the darkness needs to be all-consuming before we start looking for a ray of hope.

The light keeps shining in the dark, and darkness has never put it out. (John 1:5 CEV)

Maybe you have someone in your family who's gone through prison or maybe someone you love is headed down the road that leads there. Maybe *you* are on that trajectory right now and need to figure out how to hit the brakes before it's too late. If any of these things rings true, don't put this book down until you've read the whole thing.

Pastor Bil Cornelius, Lead Pastor, Church Unlimited
Church Unlimited is a multi-site, 15,000-member church
and humble *God Behind Bars* partner

Preface

The events in this book are based on a true story. The names and the order of some of the events have been changed to protect the innocent—and the guilty. If you picked up this book because you have a connection to someone in prison, you are not alone. The incarceration rate of the United States of America is the highest in the world. One in thirty-two adult Americans are under some sort of criminal justice control—either incarcerated, on probation, or on parole. Despite the large percentage of the population affected, the number of people sharing their story is relatively small. The aim of this book is to add to the number of people who are being set free, both in body and in spirit. If you or someone you love is confined, either by prison bars, or by addiction, mental illness, or another type of bondage, *do not lose heart*. As you will see in the pages to follow, God has the power to make all things new.

"*Then I will make up to you for the years that the swarming locust has eaten.*"[1]

---

1   Joel 2:25-32 (NASB)

PART I

RIPTIDE

CHAPTER 1

Stephen – 2003

Stephen Taylor stood in the middle of a bad decision and planned to see it through to the end. He took a sip of hot coffee and edged the hotel curtains back for a view of the parking lot below. Puddles of water from an overnight drizzle shimmered on the blacktop and twinkled on cars as the hot Texas sun wooed their moisture into the atmosphere. He had been watching their small, rented moving van all night and all morning and had seen no sign of law enforcement. Not much was stirring in any direction except a few Dallas commuters headed to work on the tireless freeway one block behind the hotel.

His partner Tom was not answering his cell phone and that made Stephen angry and anxious. They used disposable, prepaid cell phones so that their calls could not be traced. They were staying at one hotel but parked the van at a hotel next door. That way, they could keep watch and if the van were somehow discovered, abort the mission.

Stephen glanced out the window for the fifth time in as many minutes. He knew it was time to move the rented U-Haul.

Where is Tom? And why isn't he answering?

Now Stephen was worried. He wanted to go pound on Tom's hotel room door, but his mind was racing. Was it a setup? Stephen paced the floor. For all he knew,

3

the Feds had already arrested Tom, and were just waiting to nab him as soon as he left his hotel room.

He took a Xanax and washed it down with a cold beer from the refrigerator. He would have to pass a drug test when he returned to El Paso, but the Xanax would not show up. His employer would be looking for traces of marijuana—right now he had access to 1,000 kilos. There was an insatiable market for the potent product, but Stephen was not tempted to steal any of it. His drug of choice was alcohol.

In a few minutes, the pill and the beer did their job, and he walked next door and woke Tom, who had overslept. He planned to dock Tom's pay substantially for the error but would not tell him until payday. It was time to get this shipment to the customer.

Stephen paid the hotel bill with cash, taking a few minutes to flirt with the young college student at the front desk, and they were on their way. Tom drove the U-Haul and Stephen followed in a separate watch car. They pulled out of the North Dallas hotel parking lot and headed for Tennessee.

Stephen had made this trip before.

***

If there is a career path to becoming a drug trafficker, Stephen stumbled on it from a side road. He was the only child from an affluent family, with parents and grandparents who dreamed of him attending the University of Texas. His maternal grandparents, Henry and Lila Mayfield, had been UT supporters and season-ticket holders for forty years. Lila came from Texas oil money and her inheritance afforded them a prosperous lifestyle. One beneficiary of their largesse was their only grand-child: the blue-eyed, auburn-haired, Stephen Mayfield Taylor.

Stephen's parents split up when he was four. For that reason, Stephen spent many of his formative years with Henry and Lila, who liked to take him to dinner with their friends and display him like a trophy. Henry, a high school principal, was exacting and stern with his teaching staff, but overly indulgent with his only grandson. At seven, Stephen could order anything he wanted from a restaurant menu, even if it wasn't appropriate for a child. Most seven-year-olds wouldn't order shrimp cocktail or baked Alaska, but Stephen often ordered the most exotic item on the menu.

When he was not at the Mayfields, he lived with his father, Skip. This was not his choice. He preferred the freedom and exhilarating chaos of his mother's house over the structure and discipline of his dad's. He never saw her at any of his little league games, but she took him on glamorous and exotic trips from time to time that none of his friends could even imagine.

Routine, however, fit perfectly with Skip's disposition. Everything ran on schedule at his house. Dinner at six. Bath by eight. Bed by nine. Whites washed only with whites, and dark colors with their companions. Socks stayed neatly folded with their partners in the sock drawer. Every Saturday was filled with chores, and Sunday was consumed with church and lunch with Skip's parents, who also doted on their only grandchild, although with less excess.

Stephen excelled at football, basketball, and surfing. As a teenager, he spent many long days surfing off Padre Island, the long barrier island that hugs the Texas coastline. Stephen's skin grew dark and his hair bleached golden in the sun while he and his friends watched the horizon, hoping to catch even larger whitecaps that accompany the frequent tropical storms that visit the barrier island.

In the summer between eighth and ninth grade, the tide of Stephen's life began to turn. A school friend's parents—both nurses—offered to pay him good money to score some weed for a party. This might have presented a problem for the average eighth grader, but not for Stephen. His mother had gotten him a summer job busing tables at a Mexican restaurant owned by a friend. Stephen struck up a friendship with one of the cooks at the restaurant, a nineteen-year-old man who drove an expensive truck that Stephen had admired. The cook had tried to sell Stephen weed once before, but Stephen didn't have the money. But when presented with the opportunity to make some money from his school friend's parents, he took the cook up on his offer. The following week his new clients were willing to pay more—this time for cocaine—and Stephen was in business.

Before he was old enough to shave, the temptation of easy money was dragging this fresh-faced surfer away from the shore like a riptide. When the cruel tide released him fourteen years later, he was far from the place where he stepped in.

CHAPTER 2

Skip – June 2004

Skip Taylor pulled into the driveway of his upscale brick home in the Hill Country near San Antonio, Texas. He shut off the engine and listened to the tick, click, clunk of the hot metal cooling down. He always parked his truck in the garage, but he liked to let it cool in the driveway before pulling it in so that the condensation from the vehicle's air conditioner would not drip onto the clean garage floor.

Skip opened the garage door with the programmable button on the control panel of his truck. He kept his garage and home very tidy. He did not believe in letting things get dirty or cluttered. Skip believed everything should have a place, and that place should be logical and improve the function of the item. Skip's tools were neatly arranged inside shiny, red toolboxes and hanging from hooks and containers on the wall.

Skip had always used tools to make a living. Today, those tools were spreadsheets and financial operations software, but in his twenties he had earned a living as an electrician. He had learned his trade as an apprentice, working at a large petrochemical refinery. His technical skills and mathematical ability had gotten him noticed by a supervisor at the plant who thought that he would make an excellent accountant. Thanks to an employer-sponsored tuition assistance program, that prediction became a reality. But he never lost his first love for instruments and mechanical things. The right tool could extend a man's own strength and effectiveness. With a good pair of Channellock pliers, for example, he could apply ten times the torque on a stubborn bolt. In those early days he had been lean and strong, using his strength and agility to get the job done faster than most of his peers, often doing his job at the top of a telephone pole or a tall smokestack.

Skip glanced at his tools wistfully as he entered the house from the garage. He walked into his office and placed his briefcase down. This room was his favorite place in the whole house. The hand-scraped wood floors and supple leather chairs complemented his fine oak desk. Not everyone liked the taxidermy wildlife mounts on the wall, but they were badges of honor to Skip. Whitetail deer, axis deer, antelope, aoudad rams, poised forever in statuesque repose. Each trophy represented an exciting trip that he had taken and a challenge he had overcome. To glance at them brought back fond memories of woods, campfires, hiking, stalking game, friends, and the pride of his expert marksmanship.

He stopped in the expansive kitchen for a moment and grabbed a bottle of water from the fridge. He drank the water, enjoying the distant view from the tall windows in his living room, then continued through the bedroom to sit on the leather bench in his closet and remove his polished leather work shoes. Skip placed them side by side in the open spot on a Scandinavian wire-shelving unit he had installed in his closet. He always noticed a man's shoes. He thought a man with well-cared-for shoes probably conducted his business transactions with professionalism.

He stripped off his starched, pressed business shirt and slacks and placed them in the hamper designated for dry cleaning, then fished out some neatly folded athletic clothes from their drawers and put them on for a jog. He moved to the bench at the foot of his bed and laced up his new, high-tech running shoes. Passing the full-length mirror on his way out of the bedroom he considered his physique. Not too bad for a fifty-something man. A bit soft around the middle, perhaps, but his broad shoulders and strong arms helped mitigate this flaw. All those years of hard, physical work still showed in his arms. He grasped a door jam and pressed his chest in close, stretching out his tight hamstring muscles.

Before he stepped out to begin his run, Skip dropped to his knees. He had prayed the same prayer every day for the last four years. "Lord, wherever Stephen is, whatever he is doing, please watch over and protect him. Please keep him alive one more day."

Skip exited the house through the back door, which was inside the garage, and locked it behind him. Stephen had always teased him about locking that door. But Skip's father had taught him to lock up precious items.

Guns in the gun safe.

Tools in the tool chest.

Emotions locked safely in the heart.

Skip put the key in his pocket and let down the overhead electric garage door using the electronic keypad he had installed himself on the exterior of the garage. He jogged down the hill from the top where his house was perched, thinking about the one area of his life that was not neat and tidy: his relationship with his son, Stephen.

CHAPTER 3

May 2001 – Stephen

Stephen was living in Austin when his speculative commercial activities went to the next level. Not overnight, but surreptitiously, like the way the Pedernales River swells when there has been rain upcountry. The river can be deceptively deadly. Sunbathers downstream near Austin, where the weather is fine, can be caught off guard and swept away by water that rises quietly without warning, from a rain far upriver. Stephen didn't know it yet, but he was about to be swept away.

He was twenty years old and should be a junior in college. That was the path his family wanted him to take. When his grades started to fall off in his freshman year of high school, his grandparents, trying to salvage their dream of his attending the university they had chosen for him, insisted that he be sent off to an expensive private boarding school. But school was difficult for Stephen. The material just didn't stick with him. He often survived his courses by paying a classmate to help him do homework and write papers. Sometimes he bartered for this service with marijuana, which he brought back to boarding school after each school break.

Stephen wanted to be an entrepreneur and be his own boss. He had tried often to get his grandparents to finance his ideas, but the answer was always the same: finish college first. Unable to raise the capital to finance a particularly bold and promising business idea, he decided to fall back on his old standby: selling marijuana. There was constant demand and the profit margin was large.

He and two trusted friends set up a grow factory in a rented house in East Austin. They put plastic sheets on the windows, changed the locks, purchased some hydroponic gardening supplies, and soon had a small marijuana crop growing. Each man planned to sell his share of the product and keep the profit. Just days before the designated harvest date, all their carefully cultivated plants were stolen in the night. Stephen was out of luck and money.

It was at that time his friend Claire introduced him to Chris, an acquaintance of hers. Chris always had money and picked up the tab at restaurants and bars. When the two men had been hanging out for about two months, Chris introduced Stephen to a friend of his named Marco.

Stephen clicked with Marco right away. He had all the trappings of a successful businessman. The BMW. The Rolex. The great-fitting clothes and contagious confidence. Stephen liked Marco even more when he learned that Marco had bypassed college to become an entrepreneur. After college, Marco had moved to Dallas to take a job with Texas Instruments. But instead of slowly working his way up through the large company, Marco quit his job and started a string of cellphone stores with a business partner. It was obviously the right decision. Instead of the grind of the nine-to-five office job, Marco owned a business that apparently ran itself.

On several occasions after their initial meeting, Marco invited Stephen to join him for a day of golfing or boating. Stephen was enamored with Marco's lifestyle and wanted to soak up as much knowledge as he could from his new friend. Instead of just talking about women and Longhorn football, Stephen asked Marco copious questions about the operation of the cellphone stores.

One day as they were steering Marco's beautiful ski boat around Lake Travis, Marco asked Stephen if he wanted to become involved with the business—by making a special delivery of some products to Tennessee. Without needing to be told, Stephen understood it involved something illegal, most likely drugs.

Suddenly, Stephen understood why a wealthy businessman would take an interest in him. The last eight weeks had been an interview. Stephen also realized the cellphone stores were a small part of Marco's business, probably a front to launder drug money.

Stephen wondered if Marco chose him because of his savvy business sense or because he seemed like someone low on options. He decided it was the former and said yes. Besides, he would not have to see or handle the drugs, just drive the rented van from point A to point B. Someone else would take care of loading and unloading.

Dreaming about the payoff was easy; driving the van was terrifying. So anxious to get home and disassociate himself from the van, Stephen drove the twenty-eight-hour round trip straight, stopping only briefly to refuel and use the restroom. As promised, when Marco greeted him upon his return, he handed Stephen a fat envelope containing $20,000 cash.

The payoff was huge, but most went to pay off past-due rent and other debts. And the job had exacted an emotional toll. Stephen was feeling the riptide pull him back into a lifestyle he wanted to leave behind. Knowing that he might not have the strength to say no in the future, Stephen contacted Marco and told him he wasn't interested in doing another job.

"That's cool," said Marco. "I understand. It's all good. We're still friends."

A few weeks later, however, Stephen ran into Marco at a dinner party at a beautiful home near Austin. They struck up a conversation over ribs and pinto beans around the large granite island in the kitchen. After dinner, they wandered out onto the big wooden deck in the backyard to drink Shiner Bocks and smoke cigars. They stood under a giant oak tree growing out of the middle of the deck. The homeowners had strung twinkling white lights around the trunk and every limb so that the majesty of its size could be fully appreciated in the dark.

"I thought you did a great job with that opportunity in Tennessee," said Marco. "I could sure use you to do one more project. The buyer is a good customer and I don't want to keep him waiting. I'll pay you fifteen thousand to make another van delivery."

Stephen took a swallow of his beer to buy time. He stared into the twinkling branches, for a moment searching for a reason to say no. He didn't want to be involved in this scheme, but with that kind of money he could invest in one of his own business ideas.

"Look, Stephen, the handwriting is on the wall. You know that cannabis is going to be legal in the next few years," Marco said. "It's medicinal. It's natural. And it's not addicting. We are positioning ourselves to take advantage of the industry when it opens. We are just like any pharmaceutical company that produces a beneficial product and creates an infrastructure, distribution, and marketing program in advance of FDA approval. This is actually a smart business to be in."

The chance to be part of a business start-up was what Stephen dreamed of most of all. It seemed so much less threatening, when described in these terms. And he was sure he could *save* some of the money this time.

He said he'd think about it—at least that's what he thought he'd said.

Two days later the doorbell rang and there stood his old buddy Chris.

"Hey, what's up?" said Stephen, slightly embarrassed that he was wearing sweats and Chris was wearing chinos and a fitted shirt. Then he noticed the padded envelope in Chris's hand.

"Marco wanted me to drop this off to you. You must have made a good impression," said Chris.

Stephen didn't immediately reach for the envelope, hoping there was still a way to resist.

"Everything you need to know is in the envelope. I gotta run. We can catch up later," Chris held out the envelope, and this time Stephen took it.

Inside was a pre-paid cellphone, a map, a professionally typed itinerary, and an airplane ticket. Stephen's instructions were to fly to El Paso and pick up the van, which would be parked at a strip center adjacent to one of the cellphone stores.

He put the packet on his kitchen counter and thought about it for two days. He practiced ways to turn down the job. But, he didn't have a better plan or a good excuse for saying no. He had already spent most of the money from the first job.

As if he were sleepwalking, Stephen boarded the plane and flew to El Paso. But when the plane touched down, he woke from his trance and realized he was very scared. He was in a strange city without any safety net. He had to get out of this.

He rehearsed his speech for the entire twenty-five-minute taxi ride and, when he arrived at the store, called Marco on his pre-paid phone.

Ditching the pleasantries, Marco said, "Hi. I'm glad you got here. Let me tell you where to go next."

Stephen interrupted, "Marco, I can't do this. This isn't for me. I am going to leave the cash in an envelope with your name on it at the store and head home."

After a long pause, Marco said, "Well, I'm a bit disappointed because you seem like a guy I can trust. I put a $5,000 down payment for the job in your hand and you brought it back to me, so that says something. My people really like you. I'm not ready to give up on you quite yet. I'll tell you what, this really isn't a good time to back out. I'm in town. In fact, I'm close by. Wait there, and I'll go with you to make this drop off. We can discuss it face-to-face." Marco hung up without giving Stephen a chance to object.

Stephen didn't really have a better plan, and besides, he didn't even have enough money to buy a plane ticket home if he returned Marco's down payment. Marco drove up in about ten minutes in a shiny, new Mercedes sedan.

He really must have been close by.

Marco pulled up beside Stephen and rolled down the window. "Get in."

"Where are we going?"

"To meet someone who can change your mind about me."

Stephen shoved his fearful thoughts into a back corner of his brain and climbed in the car. They stayed there until he saw they were approaching the International Bridge to Mexico.

Mexico? Stephen thought. *No one even knows where I am. If something happens to me here, my family will never know what happened to me.*

But what could he do? Jump out of the car and run?

Stephen and Marco chatted amiably as the scenery grew mountainous and forested.

"We're going to meet a woman in Chihuahua," Marco said. "She works for a friend of my father; a man who changed my life."

Marco described how after college he had gotten an entry-level job and worked hard at it, putting in nine-hour days and doing other jobs on the side.

"I married my college sweetheart and we scrimped and saved and bought a little house. About the time I thought I had acquired something in life, my wife divorced me and took half of everything I'd worked for, including my 401(k)."

Marco looked at Stephen. "There are very few ways to really make the life you want. You can go to college and get a job and claw your way up the ladder, and when you're fifty—if you're lucky—you'll have something. But you'll be too old to enjoy it." He paused. "Or you can hitch your star to me and I will make you rich. You're just the guy I need to oversee part of my operation."

Stephen forgot the rebuttal that he had practiced. Marco was driving a Mercedes. And he had delivered $20,000 to Stephen just a few weeks ago. Stephen's mind wandered back to all the respectable people he had scored weed for while he was in high school. Doctors. Nurses. Attorneys. Real estate agents. Everyone wanted it, but no one wanted to be the one to get it. In those days, he had bought nice clothes and financed fun escapades with his little side job. Apparently, there was a lot more money to be made higher up the distribution chain. It didn't have to be his job forever—just until he saved enough money to start a legitimate business of his own.

When they arrived in Chihuahua, they pulled up to a home that looked a bit like a Spanish mission. It had a tall, rock wall around the compound and lush grounds. A peacock strutted across the driveway behind a gate. Marco entered a code and the gate rolled open. When Marco and Stephen approached the thick, wooden front door, it opened. A tiny, old woman stood there. She stared at Stephen for a long moment and Marco said nothing. A moment later, she said, "Well, come in then," in Spanish.

As they walked down a beautiful hallway, Stephen admired the tile floors, high ceilings and beautiful art. It reminded him of his grandparents' home. Marco, who had been so chatty in the car, didn't say a word. They entered a library that looked out over a swimming pool with a waterfall, and a view of mountains in the distance.

The old woman and Marco exchanged sharp words, entirely in Spanish. Stephen spoke Spanish, but he assumed neither of the other two people in the room knew that. The old woman disparaged him, and Marco defended him. Stephen felt a surge of pride as Marco described him as trustworthy and smart. Marco suggested that Stephen was worthy of being absolved of the serious offense of failure to make the delivery, and that he was smart enough to perform other important services.

It began to dawn on Stephen just how badly this could have gone. But for Marco defending him right now, his very life could have been in jeopardy. Instead, his friend was putting his own credibility on the line for him. Stephen could not completely understand why Marco was willing to do that, but a sense of loyalty and devotion was building in him with every word. And within the span of ten minutes, Stephen's situation had gone from a possibility too bad to imagine, to getting a promotion.

The old woman's name was Esperanza. Stephen knew that the name meant *hope* in English, and no person could have looked less like her namesake. Her words did not match her outward appearance either. She looked like a peasant, with unkempt hair, no makeup and weathered skin that reminded Stephen of tree bark. But she spoke eloquently, with an Old-World, poetic style. Stephen surmised that she might be the owner of this palatial mansion, instead of the housekeeper she appeared to be.

Esperanza had obviously lived a hard life. In what way Stephen could not yet guess, but she wore it on the outside like a grand patina. After a long pause in the conversation, she leaned her head back and looked them both over as if she were studying them through reading glasses. Pursing her lips so that a net of little bow-strings formed around her lips, she said in perfect English, "He will man the safe house, or his services will be terminated."

Stephen let out a breath of relief, tipping off everyone in the room that he had understood the conversation and the consequences. He had never had a reason to speak Spanish with Marco.

Esperanza and Marco both turned and looked at him. No one said anything, but Esperanza gave Marco the tiniest disapproving glance with her lashes.

For the first time since Stephen had known him, Marco looked like he was unsure how to respond. So, Stephen took a risk and said in formal and respectful Spanish, "*Puedes cuantar con migo.*" You can count on me.

She raised one eyebrow slightly and nodded almost imperceptibly to Marco. Marco spoke back with just his eyes, and the moment was over.

Something changed inside of Stephen in that moment. He went from feeling like a fraud who had never made anything out of his potential, to the trusted confidant of a star on the rise. He learned that his duties would include renting a house on the U.S. side of the border where bulk product from Mexico could be brought to be repackaged. He was given authority and financing to rent storage units and procure moving vans and props. Stephen told Esperanza that day that her faith in Marco's recommendation was not misplaced, and that he would not let them down. And it was not long before it became obvious to everyone in the organization that Stephen had a knack for logistics.

To keep the peace at home, Stephen told his parents and grandparents that he had gotten a job with a cellphone franchise in El Paso through a friend he met in boarding school. When he showed up for Thanksgiving dinner in a new truck, everyone was amazed at the reversal of his work ethic.

And in fact, Stephen was working hard and enjoying his job. He especially liked that Marco considered him a key employee and continued to send ever-increasing business to Stephen at the safe house. In fact, Stephen showed great resourcefulness for this work. His talents for disguising marijuana for transport earned him exciting trips to exotic resorts in Mexico and paid him well.

He made a good impression early in his assignment when he decked out one truck to look like a legitimate construction contractor, hiding drugs in rolls of insulation. Another time, he purchased appliances and concealed drugs inside some of the appliance boxes, while the boxes closest to the tailgate contained legitimate washers, dryers, and ovens. Stephen also hired drivers likely to avoid suspicion: older, Anglo men who looked more like painters and roughnecks than drug traffickers. Stephen sometimes traveled in a separate vehicle several cars ahead of the delivery van to relay back the presence of law enforcement. On more than one occasion, his specially packaged delivery trucks had gotten pulled over for a traffic violation but escaped without a search, due to Stephen's cargo subterfuge and driver training.

Just when he was settling into the job and feeling good about the rewards, Stephen received a phone call from Marco that changed everything. He picked up the phone in good spirits. "Hey, boss. What's up?"

"I have something to tell you and I need to tell you in person. I'm coming over."

"Now?"

"Yes. Who is at your house?"

"Just me."

"Good. Keep it that way. I'll be right over."

When Marco arrived, he looked like he hadn't slept in days. Ordinarily, Marco looked so polished that it took Stephen by surprise. Marco wasted no time with small talk.

"My boss, Jorge, is dead. He was murdered in Juarez, Mexico."

Stephen was so shocked he didn't say anything for a long moment. Then he filled the silence. "Do we know who did it?"

"Yes. But I can't talk about it to you. It could put you in danger. But if you don't know, you'll be safe. Does that make sense?"

Stephen took a deep breath and tried to take it all in. "What happens now?"

"I'll take Jorge's place. I notified Esperanza last night. I had to act fast, or else other cartels would take our business. And I'm considering grooming you to take my place."

Stephen nodded his head slowly but said nothing. The pervasive fear that had floated on the edges of his daily consciousness punched through the barrier around his heart like a sledgehammer. It was the first time Stephen had allowed himself to consider the danger that surrounded him. It was like he hadn't noticed the sharks circling in the ocean, but now he could smell their pelagic, deadly breath.

CHAPTER 4

Stephen – April 2003

I t made sense that Marco stepped up to take over Jorge's business. Marco knew the suppliers, the buyers, and the successful distribution channels. But it was a bit of a surprise that Marco wanted Stephen to move up with him. He still occasionally entertained the thought that Marco would let him leave the business when he wanted to, but he left the question unasked.

On a cool night in April, Stephen was on a delivery haul, driving the *watch* car. He now earned $25,000 for supervising each delivery, instead of $10,000 per month to supervise the safe house.

Stephen could have saved some money and kept a lower profile by staying at an inexpensive hotel, but he preferred luxury. This night it was the Wyndham Anatole in Dallas, Texas. He was living like a rock star, and his dreams of owning his own business were slipping into memory.

After an expensive and indulgent evening with a beautiful girl that he often hooked up with when he was in Dallas, Stephen stood alone, looking at the lights of downtown Dallas wondering why he was so unhappy. He had traveled widely and seen many beautiful places and people, but despite the money in his pocket and the posh surroundings, something deep inside ached to turn around and go back home.

He swirled the honey-colored whiskey over the ice in his glass and thought about the little house on Padre Island that he had shared with his dad, just the two of them. That house had always been full of friends. All the neighborhood kids congregated there.

Stephen glanced up from his thoughts and stared at the glittery skyline of Big D. The shiny gold of his Rolex watch reflected in the window glass like one of the city lights.

Why did Dad always let so many kids hang out there?

Stephen remembered that Skip appeared stressed when the house was full of noisy kids. As a single father, it was probably a struggle to supply all the soft drinks and snacks his friends had consumed. Perhaps his dad had tried to fill the vacuum left by his mother's departure by allowing all the neighborhood kids to congregate there?

Many of Stephen's friends lived with single mothers, and they thought it was cool that Stephen lived with his dad. The fact that they lived on an island and fished every day after school sounded to others like it must be so cool. But Skip wasn't like most other dads. He was present and watchful. It had always annoyed Stephen how Skip never quite let him out of his sight. Even when Stephen and his friends were fishing or surfing or just roaming the island, Skip stayed in touch with the other parents and was constantly checking up on them.

Stephen desperately wanted to be rid of his dad back then. He wanted to chase after all the things his dad wanted to keep him from experiencing. He wanted to be like his beautiful, ebullient mother. He wanted to leave.

Now Stephen found himself in a situation where he had all the money and material possessions that he could manage, but he had no one he could share it with. He had plenty of female companionship, shallow acquaintances he kept at a distance. The few people who cared about him were smart enough to have suspicions. His parents and grandparents peppered him with so many questions about the cellphone business when he tried to visit, that he quit visiting. His web of lies was threatening to strangle all his relationships.

In the luxury suite, with a drink in hand and $30,000 in a secret compartment in his car, the hollow feeling in his gut and the tremor in his hand told him it was time for a different life. It was D-Day. He felt Disillusioned. Disappointed. And Done. He'd thought that he could make a new family with this daring group of businesspeople who seemed to value his talent. Their praise had made him feel special in a way that he'd never felt at home. But now he realized that as each day passed making stronger ties to this new family, the further he had become from his real family. Soon, he would not be able to go back. He was standing on the brink of all-in. Or was there a way out? He wasn't sure.

CHAPTER 5

Stephen – May 2005

Stephen lay on a float in the neighborhood swimming pool of his lady love, Kylee. His tan skin was shiny with coconut-smelling sunscreen, and dark sunglasses protected his bloodshot eyes from the searing Austin summer sun. Freckles covered his broad shoulders. He never liked them much, but women always did, so he used the good UV protection lotion, mostly on his face, to keep from peeling.

Kylee's four-year-old son, Ian, was sitting in the baby pool with blue plastic swim floats strapped on his small brown arms. Many children Ian's age splashed and played in the pool, but he was still too cautious and afraid to get in the big pool.

Stephen used his hands and feet to keep the float strategically positioned so he could keep an eye on Ian while balancing his beer with the hand that wasn't paddling. He was very fond of the boy, and the feeling seemed to be mutual.

Ian was emotionally delayed in some ways, probably because of his unstable upbringing. To support them both, Kylee had tried her hand at quite a few jobs. She had the skills to be an excellent administrative assistant but found waitressing more lucrative. Unfortunately, few daycare centers were open at night, and Kylee had often been forced to leave Ian with friends to go to work. She brought along his favorite video game console wherever she had to leave him, and Ian was an ace at all the games.

Kylee was a stunner. She had been waiting tables at a gentlemen's club when Stephen first met her. He drank much more than he had intended to that night because he wanted to keep her coming back to the table so he could flirt with her. She was prettier than any of the sexy girls on the stage. She had perfect olive skin; wide, dark eyes; and perfect lips.

Those lips.

They were full and plump around her snow-white teeth.

Kylee had a slim, athletic build that attracted Stephen. Her hair was a splash of soft curls, and she wore a ribbon to keep them out of her face.

Because he was drunk, Stephen had asked her if her eyelashes were real. He had never seen eyelashes that long. She was young, but he was slightly younger, at twenty-five. He had a wad of cash in his pocket, something Kylee found very intriguing. He didn't mention he had obtained it from selling a small amount of marijuana to a bunch of college kids,

Stephen went home with her that night, and they began a torrid, crazy, difficult love affair.

During one of their many break-ups, Stephen had met Marco and moved to El Paso. For a short time, Stephen and Kylee reconciled, and Kylee moved to El Paso to be with him. For the better part of a year she enjoyed living in a comfortable house, driving the car he'd bought for her, going to movies, and other benefits of Stephen's income.

As a girl growing up in a small Texas town with five siblings, Kylee had never had much to call her own. But when she found a cellphone in the pocket of his jeans, loaded with pictures of other girls, she left in a flurry of tears and returned to Austin.

Stephen tried not to miss her or to want her, but he did. After his meltdown in Dallas, he had packed up and left El Paso quickly and returned to Austin. He left a well-practiced message on Marco's voicemail and hoped for the best. He had hoped to reconnect with Kylee but never had the guts to call her. Almost a year after their split, they met again serendipitously.

Stephen had spent the day tubing down the Guadalupe River, an entertainment staple of Central Texas. The Guadalupe is a cold, clear, spring-fed river that courses over a bone-white, rocky bottom through central Texas. Cat-like, the river steers clear of the mud and dirt of Texas ranches and pours itself crisply into deep Canyon Lake and out the other side.

Every summer, throngs of people jump in the cool water somewhere along the riverbank to escape the oppressive heat. At dozens of designated put-in and take-out spots, entrepreneurs with specially outfitted jeeps and trucks hauled the tubers, inner tubes, and ice chests full of beer back to their cars. Tubers who discover the spot known as *the horseshoe*, can walk across a small bridge and put themselves back in to float the bend in the river repeatedly. On a busy day, small groups of tubers bump into and pass each other like free-floating molecules as they go down the river.

Kylee was tubing with a group of her friends. Stephen was there with a different group, including the nineteen-year-old daughter of a prominent socialite who was a friend of his mother. His mother had always disliked Kylee because she came from no means, and so she ardently tried to play matchmaker between Stephen and the rich sorority girl.

When Stephen's group bumped into Kylee's group, instead of letting her pass by, Stephen used his long arms to connect the tubes. He had grown bored of trying to put on a false face for the sorority girl. Apparently Kylee had grown tired of trying to make it on her own and seemed willing to forgive the cellphone full of other girls that she'd discovered.

At the next exit landing, he and Kylee jumped out of the river together, leaving the stunned, young beauty queen to float to the next landing with Stephen's drunk buddies. He knew it would cause quite a scandal with his mother, but he didn't care.

When they got back to Austin, Stephen called his grandparents and persuaded them that he was going to enroll in college, a ruse that had more than once landed him enough money to lease an apartment, buy furniture, and register for classes. Somehow, he always missed the registration deadline or dropped his classes when he could still get a refund. Instead of tuition, he spent the money at bars, partying with Kylee and her friends.

When the money ran out, and he could produce no grades, he moved in with Kylee and her two roommates and began keeping Ian, so that Kylee could work as a waitress. She was once again working at the gentlemen's club. Her taut body, skimpy clothes and sultry good looks always resulted in great tips from the men who frequented the club.

Kylee was earning an honest living, and Stephen enjoyed being a stay-at-home "dad." Her two roommates, a hairdresser and a retail salesclerk, seemed pleased with his contribution to the household. Stephen bought the groceries, mowed the yard, and kept Ian bathed and out of trouble. Since Kylee was never home at bedtime, Stephen even found himself implementing the same routine with Ian that his dad had compelled upon him.

At dinner time, he started setting the expectation that bedtime was around the corner. He made the boy help with dinner preparation, then after dinner, he would draw Ian a bath and set him in it with some toys and go clear up the kitchen. After bath, no more videogames, only books. Ian was starting to read well, but it would inevitably make him sleepy. Stephen thought it was possible his dad might have been right about all that routine because Ian was blossoming.

At the swimming pool that beautiful, hot day in Austin, Stephen began to believe his past was behind him and domestic tranquility—or the modern version of it—was his calling. It had been a little over two years since he had last seen Marco or sold anyone marijuana. He felt like he could finally stop looking over his shoulder.

Two days later, he rose early and shuffled into the kitchen for coffee. He noticed some movement outside the kitchen window and leaned closer to look outside. A black Cadillac Escalade sat parked across the street. Before he had time to digest who might be driving an Escalade in their working-class neighborhood, a deafening thud hammered the front door. The DEA agent waited only a split second before pounding the door again. Stephen could see dark figures filing past the windows and back door and knew the house was surrounded.

There was no place to run.

He opened the door and was swept down the river and over the plunging waterfall.

CHAPTER 6

Stephen – September 2005

The DEA agents handcuffed Stephen and placed him in the back of the black Escalade, in a special restraint that left him unable to move his arms or legs. It looked like a cruel version of an amusement park ride. He was bare-chested and wearing pajama pants. Even though it was early morning—about the time that ordinary Austinites head off to work—it was quite warm already. With the windows rolled up, sweat soaked his pants and Stephen found it hard to breathe.

Stephen watched helplessly as agents swarmed in through the front door wearing what looked like black combat gear. Several agents wearing full body armor, shoulder radios, and rubber gloves, meticulously inspected the yard and his and Kylee's vehicles.

Rivers of salty perspiration poured into Stephen's eyes and his head began to pound. By the scorching, sticky feel of the leather seat and the weight of the air, he guessed it was pushing 100 degrees in the black vehicle. One agent stood guard outside the Escalade with his arms resting in front of him, thumbs tucked into his belt. Stephen began knocking on the side of his "cage" with his forehead. The agent was talking with another agent near the front of the vehicle and didn't seem to hear him.

Stephen kept knocking, and one of the agents opened the door and told him to stop hitting his head. Beginning to hyperventilate, he pleaded for the agent to open a window so that he could breathe. The agent paused for a moment and slammed the door back in his face. Before the door shut, he noticed that neighbors had gathered in concerned little circles across the street.

Finally, after what he believed to be about an hour based on the change in the angle of the sun, an agent opened the door and began to interrogate him. He felt delirious and later remembered telling someone that he didn't have any drugs. He knew they weren't going to find any—he was telling the truth—but he began to have paranoid imaginings that the agents were planting drugs around the house.

The agent handed him a pair of jeans, a T-shirt, some tennis shoes, and told him to get out of the vehicle and get dressed. The ensemble wasn't one he would have chosen. He wondered if they went through everything he owned. Stephen didn't know it at the time, but he would never enter that house again. After he changed in the car, the agents transported him to the Travis County Jail, in south Austin.

The Travis County jail did not ordinarily house federal prisoners, but there was no federal prison in Austin, so Travis County served as a temporary holding arrangement. The jail, teeming with a variety of offenders, was dirty and smelled like a mixture of body odor, mildew, and bleach. As Stephen listened to conversations around his holding cell, he noted that much of the talk had some connection to drugs. The guy next door had apparently stabbed his friend in the arm while high on drugs. Another guy apparently ended up in jail because he had an ancient, unpaid traffic fine when he got pulled over for speeding. Mr. Forgot-About-My-Old-Traffic-Ticket sounded like a regular-Joe businessman who was going to be in serious trouble with his wife. Except for the businessman, most of his fellow occupants acted like they'd been there before.

Stephen had himself spent a night there. He had been picked up for "theft of services" when he tried to take a taxi home from a bar and was too drunk to operate the automatic teller machine at a gas station to pay the cab driver. Kylee had bailed him out. The place had not improved any in the intervening years.

Two days after he arrived, Stephen was moved to another cell. He heard a familiar voice as he was being escorted down the hallway and turned to look. He saw his good friend Jackson being escorted to another cell, looking anxious and ashen. When their eyes met, Stephen's head hung down and he let his arms go limp. They felt like iron weights. A gut-wrenching pang of guilt for his friend shot through Stephen. Jackson had trusted him.

Jackson had some skills and could have had a nice life as a general contractor or maintenance technician at a manufacturing plant somewhere. Stephen had co-opted Jackson into working with him for a short while. Jackson followed instructions well and never slept late like Tom.

Stephen knew how to make driving a van full of marijuana across the country sound normal, and Jackson had believed him. The same persuasive techniques had been used on Stephen. Now here they both stood, in a cold reality which was not at all normal.

A sheriff's deputy returned an hour later and notified him it was time for his one phone call. Who should he call? Kylee, Mom, or Dad? Dad might not want him out. Kylee might not be able to answer the phone. He decided to call his mom because she would have more access to resources to get him out.

He dialed her number not knowing exactly what he would say.

"Hello?" she said tentatively.

"Mom, it's me, I'm in jail. I need an att—"

"I almost didn't accept the call."

"Thank God you answered. I need help." There was a very long pause.

After several soft expletives, she asked, "What for?"

"I need your help because—"

"I'm not asking why you need my help. I'm asking what are you in jail for?"

"I don't know what the charges are. But they searched the house for drugs. They didn't find any."

"Thank goodness. What do you want me to do?"

"I need you to call one of your lawyer friends and ask for a referral to someone who can handle this." There was another long pause.

"Mom, I'm sorry."

"I'm sorry too," she said softly and hung up.

Stephen wasn't entirely sure what she'd meant when she said she was sorry. Sorry he was in trouble? Sorry he was being wronged by the criminal justice system? Sorry he'd ever been born? The deputy deposited him in a new cell. It was occupied by an older Hispanic man who stared at him sullenly and would not return polite conversation. Three days later Stephen was given another phone call. He tried his mother again. He was so grateful when she answered.

"Hey, it's me. Can you tell me what's going on? I have no news on this end. Am I going to stay in here? Or—"

"We found an attorney in El Paso who handles these matters. His name is Sid Addleston. We understand he is the best. He should be contacting you soon. He's working on how to get you out on bond."

Eight days later Stephen was taken to the federal courthouse to be arraigned. He had not notified any family member, or even Kylee, about the arraignment. He did not want anyone to hear the charges against him. The guards drove him and Jackson, handcuffed and shackled, to the federal courthouse. They were told not to speak to one another. No words were necessary. Jackson's eyes spoke volumes of regret.

As he shuffled into the court room in shackles, Stephen was shocked to see his father sitting in the back row. He had assumed that since he'd only spoken to his mother, that she was the only one who knew what was happening. He also recognized his father's good friend Ken, whom Skip must have brought along for support. Most of his dad's straight, conservative friends made Stephen a little uncomfortable, but Ken was different. He didn't mind having a beer now and then, and he could make you bust a gut with his quick wit. Stephen also liked to make people laugh. It was a great way to hang out with other people, without ever opening up. The two older men looked out of place in the courtroom gallery, like walking advertisements for the Nordstrom's menswear department.

Stephen's face felt hot. He broke eye contact with his father's entreating gaze and stared at the front of the court room. He froze when he heard Jackson's soft sobs beside him. Apparently, Jackson had seen Stephen's dad, too. Jackson had always been fond of him. When they were younger, Jackson enjoyed having Skip around and tried to win his approval with skateboarding tricks, basketball shots, whatever. Stephen had never understood this. Stephen considered his father about the most unexciting, unglamorous person in the whole world. Jackson's father had left their family when Jackson was young, so he had understandably low standards in that category.

Jackson's crying was weakening Stephen's emotional force field.

Oh God, please shut up, Jackson.

He held his tongue, not to spare Jackson's feelings, but because he was afraid of being noticed by the judge.

After the judge dispatched numerous other cases, the bailiff called Stephen to the bench.

"Please state your name for the record," he instructed.

Stephen's eyes were fixed on the judge, a handsome, fit man of about 45. A large plaque with a seal above the judge's head read "Hon. Judge Earl Leroy Yarbrough, presiding."

"Stephen Taylor," he replied.

"State your address."

He gave Kylee's—his most recent.

Then Stephen heard the most horrible words imaginable. He was being charged with seven counts of trafficking thousands of pounds of marijuana, one count of cocaine trafficking, and conspiracy to do both. There may have been other charges. Stephen wasn't sure because a roaring sound had filled his ears. He felt queasy and had a bitter, metallic taste in his mouth. He needed a cigarette and a drink badly. Stephen's emotions churned inside him as he heard the DEA agent testify why he should not be allowed to post bail.

Then something worse happened. The judge pointed to Stephen's father and asked him to identify himself. Stephen had hoped to escape without speaking to or hearing from his father. He probably was feeling smug now that all the things he had warned Stephen about were coming true.

The judge asked if Skip had any personal or retirement savings.

"Yes, Your Honor, I do." Skip replied. His voice sounded overly loud and awkward.

The judge then astonished everyone in the room, including the federal prosecutor, by opting to allow Stephen's father to post bond and obtain Stephen's supervised release. Nevertheless, he warned Skip that if Stephen did not return for trial, he could lose his entire life savings.

Stephen was both horrified and grateful at the same time. The idea of being under house arrest at his dad's house was awful, but the prospect of returning to Travis County Jail was slightly worse.

Stephen sat back down on the worn wooden bench. He tried to focus on the scratches and carvings in the wood. Jackson stood, and the federal prosecutor read similar, but not as many, charges against him. Stephen did not look at his friend as he stood before the judge. With no one to support him, Jackson was going back to jail to await trial. Stephen felt a wave of compassion and sympathy he could not remember feeling before. Perhaps a puritanical, out-of-touch dad was still better than no dad.

CHAPTER 7

Stephen – April 2006

Sid Addleston sat behind his big oak desk reviewing evidence related to several ongoing criminal cases. He had a ten o'clock appointment with a prospective new client, so he set the other files aside and began to study the complaint filed against Stephen Mayfield Taylor. Some firms used young attorneys to conduct the initial client intake meeting, but Sid did not. He never decided whether to represent a client until he had interviewed them personally. The air conditioning hummed quietly, cooling his comfortable office. He glanced out the large window at the view of the mountains that divided the modern city of El Paso where he stood from the drug-infested city of Juarez, across the border.

It was common for him to be hired by wealthy parents to represent their adult children. The file in front of him contained some very serious charges against a young man who apparently had no previous criminal record at all. Sid felt certain that the people about to enter his office had no idea how serious the charges were, and that prison was likely in this young man's future.

Sid's legal assistant, Sylvia, knocked on the door and announced that his ten o'clock appointment had arrived.

"Offer him something to drink and seat him in the conference room," said Sid. "And tell him I'll be with him in a moment."

Sid answered a few urgent email messages, and then picked up the file and a notepad and headed to the conference room. The door was slightly ajar and Sid stopped to study the young man for a moment.

The clean-cut young man in the conference room looked to be in his early-to-mid-twenties. One knee bounced up and down nervously as he looked at something on his smartphone. He wore high-end, well-fitting clothes and looked comfortable in them.

When Sid entered the room, the handsome young man stood up and introduced himself with a firm handshake. He was very tall, with broad shoulders and a nice smile.

Those good looks and good manners are not going to help you much at all in front of a federal judge if any of these charges are true.

After a round of polite introductions, Sid began the real conversation. "Did you bring the arrest warrant?"

His prospective client, Stephen Taylor, slid the paperwork across the table.

"So, why don't you tell me the short version of how you got yourself charged with this offense?" Sid could tell that Stephen was trying to put a good spin on his story, so he added, "If you want me to be able to do my best for you, I will need you to be truthful."

"Is this conversation privileged?"

"It is, because you are seeking legal services. But that does not mean that I am your attorney. I only take cases I feel good about, and I'm sure that you want to feel like you've chosen the right attorney as well. Who else do you plan to speak to?"

Stephen explained that he was researching one other attorney who was also well known in El Paso. Sid nodded professionally and was not displeased. The other attorney that Stephen was considering, Andy Haywood, was an excellent attorney who had earned some measure of success and was a personal friend.

"Tell me about your work history before the activity that got you in trouble and in the three years since you left El Paso," Sid pressed on.

For the next forty-five minutes, Sid laid bare Stephen's life, and he wasn't entirely pleased with what he had to work with. His potential client was a child of privilege who had never held a real job. But despite the thin defense material, he liked Stephen anyway. That's why he did what he did so well. He could always find humanity, even in a person who had done something bad. The fact that Stephen had gotten away and started a new life made a positive impression on Sid, and he made up his mind to take Stephen's case.

Unfortunately, once he had made the client feel comfortable, he couldn't shut him up. For another thirty minutes, Stephen insisted on sharing all sorts of facts that he thought were helpful or mitigated his guilt, most of which were irrelevant or inadmissible under the criminal law. In a break in the conversation, Sid agreed to represent Stephen. Handshakes and a retainer of $25,000 from Stephen's mother were all that were left to solidify the relationship.

CHAPTER 8

Stephen – September 2006

"Y ou want a sandwich, Babe? I just bought some cold cuts," Kylee asked as she dropped the plastic grocery bags on the counter.

"What kind of bread does Dad have?" answered Stephen.

"Some kind of healthy oat nutty stuff. You won't like it. So, I bought you some French bread."

"You're the best." He smiled and returned to his laptop and stack of documents on the table. His pretrial officer had given him strict instructions. To remain free while awaiting trial, he had to work and be drug tested regularly. These two tasks didn't go well together. How was he going to find an employer that would permit him to take off at random times and drive the twenty-mile trip to the pretrial officer's location to pee in a cup?

He sat at a long, polished oak table. His dad was ridiculous about keeping it clean and unscratched. It was almost like he didn't want anyone to use it. So, they ate lunch at the granite kitchen countertop on barstools, instead of at the table.

"You want to go look at venues around town later?" Kylee asked.

"Babe, you know I need to find a job. There doesn't seem to be a lot of opportunities for someone with very little work history, so this isn't going to be easy. But

I can't stay out on supervised release unless I get a job."

"Can't your dad just get you a job with his company or with one of his friends?"

"I hinted at that already. But you know how he is. He thinks you have to earn everything you have. He keeps telling me that if I go get something on my own and work hard at it for a bit, then he will help me get something better. He doesn't seem to realize that it's the first door that is the hardest to open."

"He has so much. I don't understand why he doesn't help you more."

"I think he's doing quite a bit, but yeah, it would be nice if he would use his influence to open some doors."

***

In the months before the trial, it was almost possible sometimes for Stephen to forget that he might lose his freedom. Surprisingly, Kylee had come right to his side. He had expected that she would not ever want to see him again. How many girls would want to be with a man who caused their home to be raided and them interrogated by the DEA for hours? Yet, somehow, she always saw the tiny fragment of good in him. Of course, lots of women were attracted to him. There had been dozens of women in and out of his still-young life. They all thought he was a real estate agent or a boat broker or one of his other believable lies. But Kylee knew exactly who he was, and she still loved him.

They moved into his father's large, comfortable house and Kylee's mother kept Ian for a while. Skip required them to sleep in separate rooms, which they found both ridiculous and a little bit romantic. They slept well, talked for hours, bought groceries, and cooked in the expansive kitchen. Stephen still drank beer, but he had cut out the hard liquor, which had been quite difficult at first. He felt healthier than he had in a long time. One day, as they chatted over a real breakfast—one that did not include any beer or pizza—Stephen decided to ask Kylee to marry him. They had been through good times and terrible times together and still loved each other.

Even though he was facing trial and possible prison time, Stephen convinced Kylee and their families it was safe to get married. The judge would show leniency. After all, Stephen had stopped dealing, had not been caught with any drugs, and it was his first criminal offense. He almost believed it himself. Somewhat surprisingly, Kylee said yes.

The next few weeks, they threw all their efforts into planning a sweet, small ceremony, officiated by his father's pastor, on the banks of the creek in the quaint Hill

Country town where his dad lived, about an hour from Austin. Along with Kylee's mother, his dad's many friends from church pulled out all the stops, organizing a cake, flowers, invitations, and food. It was a most amazing distraction from his upcoming trial.

The big day, September 10, dawned crisp, clear, and beautiful. Stephen's best childhood friend, Arnie, had arrived from out of town, and they drove around town laughing and drinking. As a condition of a pretrial release, he was not allowed to have any alcohol. But it was his wedding day. He didn't tell Arnie how many rules he was breaking. And Arnie certainly didn't know the details of what Stephen had been up to. Stephen had lied to Arnie, like he had lied to everyone else.

When they arrived at the river venue, he and Arnie had a good talk on the lawn. *How lucky am I to have a real friend like this?*

Later, they were in a cabin alone putting on their wedding attire when Arnie asked, "Are you sure you're doing the right thing?"

"Well, it's a little late now if I'm not, isn't it?"

"You're facing some type of trouble. You make it sound like it's going to blow over. And with your family's resources, that's probably true. But what if it doesn't? What if Kylee is marrying someone who isn't going to be there for her?"

"Arnie, Kylee knows what's going on here. And we're gonna be OK."

Arnie put his hand on his friend's shoulder and nodded and smiled.

Stephen's dad poked his head in the door. "Could I say a few words to Stephen before the service starts?" he asked.

After Arnie stepped out onto the porch, Skip gave him a fatherly lecture about being a good provider to Kylee and Ian. It seemed rather old fashioned, but Stephen had to endure it since his father was paying for all the festivities.

The three of them walked out onto the lawn. Stephen's longtime friend David was playing soft acoustic guitar as the guests were all seated. And then, there she was, at the top of the stairs.

Kylee had never looked more beautiful. She wore a flowing white, strapless dress that complemented her figure. Her copper shoulders seemed to be dusted with a little bit of glitter, because her skin shone golden in the late-afternoon sun. She had highlighted her soft brown hair with some lighter, honey-colored strands and straightened her curls. Stephen loved her curls, and he had never seen her with this smooth, sleek bun before, but it suited her. She looked elegant, and he felt lucky to have her. Even knowing what he had done in the past and what potentially lay ahead, she still pledged her heart to him. As he put the ring on her slim finger, he thought with satisfaction that this grown-up decision to settle down would unleash an avalanche of wisdom and good karma.

They had to spend that night at his dad's because he was still under house arrest. After they were married, Stephen's pretrial officer permitted him to move out of his father's house, and into a nearby apartment with Kylee. They had a few good weeks of honeymoon. He made a valiant attempt to live in the present, but the future often consumed his thoughts.

His mother had hired one of the best criminal defense attorneys in the state, a specialist in drug cases, to represent him. The government's primary evidence was the testimony of other accused drug traffickers. He tried to convince himself that a modern jury, well fed on a TV diet of crime-solving shows, would expect to see more hard evidence. So, Stephen was convinced that with his pricey and talented attorney by his side, along with his pretty new bride, he would somehow beat the rap.

CHAPTER 9

Stephen – November 2006, T-minus 176 Days

Sid still wasn't sure that Stephen fully understood the federal sentencing guidelines and what was likely to happen in this case. Since his first meeting with Stephen, Sid learned that the young man who replaced Stephen in the drug organization had been caught transporting drugs. That man had agreed to trade names, including Stephen's, in exchange for a reduction in his own sentence. Sid knew that defendants facing a federal drug charge are almost always convicted. Federal prosecutors do not ordinarily bring a criminal charge unless they have compelling evidence. Because of their successful track record in front of juries, the prosecutors rarely offer plea deals unless they can get information that leads to more arrests.

It's all about the number of arrests and convictions, thought Sid. *That's what they're after. That's how they measure success. Once a person is in their sights, he's no longer a person with a life about to be ruined; he's just a performance measure on their scorecard.*

Sid had also learned that, in addition to the testimony of five other defendants, the federal prosecutor had obtained, using subpoenas and warrants, a paper trail that showed Stephen had rented storage units and rental trucks under his own name on multiple occasions. Unless Stephen could convince a jury that he had moved his own household goods every eight weeks, his signature on this stack of rental agreements was going to look very suspicious.

Sid set up a meeting with Stephen and his parents to explain their limited options. He had his secretary make a carafe of coffee and place some muffins on a platter. His client and his divorced parents were all traveling on the same plane to meet with him this morning, which he also found interesting.

"Good morning. Nice to see you Stephen," Sid said as the young man politely introduced his mother Savanah and his father Skip. *Those two don't strike me as a pair who would ever have been a married couple,* thought Sid. But he could certainly see the combined gene pool in Stephen's face.

Sid sized up Stephen's parents for a moment. The mother was privileged. She had smooth, white skin; an expensive manicure; and stylish clothes. The father looked more middle class. He had a pleasant look: close-cropped gray hair, starched white shirt, tanned skin and big rough hands that didn't quite match the rest of him.

This was always an awkward and sad moment. He was about to tell these nice people that their son was probably going to go to prison. It never got any easier.

"I've been in contact with the federal prosecutor, and here's what we've got. As you are now aware, there are five other defendants listed in the charge against you. Four of those five defendants have agreed to testify against Stephen in exchange for a lesser sentence. This is important. These defendants know that their testimony has to please the prosecutor, or the prosecutor won't recommend the lighter sentence. If this case were to go to trial, I would have to somehow discredit each of these other witnesses and convince the jury that each witness was fabricating or exaggerating Stephen's involvement in the conspiracy. One or two witnesses could probably be discredited, but four or five…" He paused. "…that's going to be quite difficult."

"But I've never even met most of those guys," protested Stephen. "How can they testify against me?"

"I believe that they will likely testify to getting orders from you indirectly, that you were sending orders down the food chain and that they knew where you fell in the organizational chart. The other evidence the jury will hear will include the fact that you leased a home in El Paso for twenty months and paid rent without any apparent source of income, along with your signature on numerous rental units and on numerous rental cars and vans. Finally, even though you've been gone from the area for some time, early recorded calls obtained by the DEA and FBI listening to several of the defendants, included your name and instructions you supposedly gave to some of the members."

There was a palpable silence in the little conference room. Stephen's dad held a cup of coffee in his hand, but information was the only thing he was consuming. Sid let it sink in a bit. It was his normal practice to be honest up front and put the worst possible outcome on the table. That way, if anything less actually happened, the client would generally feel his services had been useful.

"And, because of the federal sentencing guidelines, if a jury finds Stephen guilty of all the charges, the minimum penalty will be twenty-five years in federal prison."

Stephen's mother gasped, and tears filled her eyes. "Even though he has no criminal history? Isn't there something about a first strike?"

"Even though it's his first arrest and first offense, yes, he could receive twenty-five years. And there are very few things—we call them mitigating circumstances—that can reduce the sentence."

"How can this be?" the father asked hesitantly, coughing to cover up the tremor in his voice. "Stephen was never caught with any drugs. How could he be given a twenty-five-year sentence for talking to other guys about selling drugs? Talking isn't illegal, is it?"

"It's called conspiracy, and, yes, it's illegal," answered Sid. "If an individual talks to another individual and agrees to commit a crime and then that individual takes any step or action toward the commission of the crime, a separate crime—the crime of conspiracy—has been committed. Conspiracy to commit a crime usually carries the same sentence as actually committing that same crime. It's actually one of the government's best tools for putting people in prison, especially those that might be involved with selling drugs but aren't caught with any.

"I'm talking to the prosecutor about what he might accept as a plea deal," offered Sid. "There's really no evidence linking Stephen to the cocaine charges. The key link is the man who was found transporting marijuana. The only conversations they have that included Stephen's name are discussions about moving some marijuana, not cocaine. This is important because the cocaine charges carry the longest sentence. Now, if Stephen is willing to give testimony against members of the distribution network higher than himself, we can get more years shaved off the plea offer." Sid paused, and then finished, "Right now, the prosecutor is offering a sentence of fifteen years, if Stephen pleads guilty."

"Could he get out sooner for good behavior?" asked Stephen's mom.

"Federal prison really does not have the option to reduce your sentence with good behavior."

"What about the fact that Stephen hasn't been involved in this lifestyle for three years and has begun to turn his life around. Doesn't that count for *anything?*" pressed Skip.

All pretenses of believing Stephen was innocent were evaporating. Sid could tell that Skip had deeply conflicted feelings. If it were anyone else being charged, Skip would probably have believed a long jail sentence appropriate. Sid surmised that the man had never done illegal drugs and considered it a serious crime. He felt sorry for him.

He noticed Skip searching Stephen's eyes, hoping for Stephen to deny everything. Sid could see that the mother was not as surprised as the father to learn the truth.

"No," Sid explained. "The federal prosecutor who recommends the sentence does not care about that at all. They work on a quota system. If they put bad guys away, they look good. If they don't get many convictions, they look bad. We're within the statute of limitations, and that's all that matters."

Sid knew the government's strategy brought him a lot of well-paying work, but it still made him sad when he saw how it affected families. Sometimes he could distance himself from their pain; other times it got under his skin. The saddest cases were the young ones, like Stephen, and the clients who had young children they would have to leave behind.

He didn't want to leave them without any hope at all, so he continued, "Stephen's years of distance from the crime without any further criminal activity *might* be persuasive to the judge who has to impose the sentence. We will certainly make every attempt to introduce it as a mitigating factor."

All the hopeful energy had left the room. What was left was something close to despair. Sid took charge again.

"If Stephen will plead guilty to the conspiracy charges related to the marijuana, I think I can get the prosecutor to drop the more serious of the charges."

Sid felt compelled to tell Stephen again, in front of his parents, that he could possibly get a further-reduced sentence if he was willing to provide the federal prosecutor with names and additional evidence against others involved in his activities higher up the ladder. "I will get you connected with a different attorney to represent you if you want to do that," Sid told them. "I really don't like the way they threaten you with a twenty-five-year sentence if you don't give up names. I think a lot of people who were very minor actors get long jail sentences that way—like your friend Jackson—and I don't think it's right. But I don't want to sway you. This is a serious decision."

All eyes were on Stephen, who had been very quiet.

"I don't have any information I can share," he said. Despite pleas from his parents, he refused to provide any names or information about the organization that he had been associated with.

Sid knew all about Jorge's murder. Stephen was afraid, and rightfully so. But Sid could not share any of the things that Stephen had told him in confidence in front of the young man's parents.

After Stephen and his family left the office, Sid called the prosecutor, Cooper Brandt. "Hey, how are you, Cooper?" Sid said. "On the Stephen Taylor matter, we'd like to explore that plea deal a bit more."

CHAPTER 10

Stephen – January 2007, T-minus 95 days

Sid had convinced the prosecutor that Stephen was going to be a better witness than those the prosecutor planned to call and he could place doubts in the jury's mind about the extent of Stephen's involvement. But a federal judge is not required to accept the recommendation of the prosecutor, even after the prosecutor has offered a defendant a plea deal. So, although the nine-year plea deal was far longer than Stephen and his family had hoped for, they were still nervous until the final moment of the sentencing hearing. And they were right to be nervous.

At the hearing, the federal judge was clearly not pleased with the prosecutor's decision. Stephen's clean record and the flood of letters written on Stephen's behalf to the court from his parents' and grandparents' many reputable friends and colleagues didn't seem to influence the judge's opinion that drug crimes should be punished harshly. When the judge slammed his hand down on the desk and berated the prosecutor for not insisting on giving Stephen fifteen years behind bars, Stephen felt his heart beating in his temples and something lurched in his stomach. The next thing he knew, the judge was pointing a finger at him and saying in an angry voice, "Well, Mr. Taylor, this is what your expensive attorney bought you—a cop-out from the federal government. All because the federal prosecutor doesn't want to face Sid

Addleston in front of a jury. I sentence you to nine-and-one-half years of confinement in prison to be followed by five years of probation." The judge then turned his attention to the paperwork in front of him and said to the bailiff in a terse voice, "Call the next case." Stephen was handed several papers to sign stating that he agreed with the sentence. His hands were shaking so badly, he could hardly hold the pen.

Including Stephen, the federal prosecutor brought charges against six men based on the testimony of the first man who was caught with drugs. Four of the men provided evidence against Stephen in exchange for shorter sentences, mostly in the range of five to seven years. Stephen's friend Jackson was the only one not willing to testify against him, and he received a four-year sentence. The prosecutors had almost no evidence against Jackson, except his name in one text message from another of the conspirators. But he pleaded guilty because of the threat of a twenty-five-year sentence, which would automatically apply if a jury didn't believe his story. When the full weight of the federal government presses down on you, you're not likely to win.

Stephen did not start serving his sentence immediately. Due in large part to the success of dragnet activities like the one that caught Stephen, all the federal prisons within a 500-mile radius of his home were full. So, he had three months under house arrest to get his affairs in order.

As his self-surrender date approached, Stephen drank heavily and sank into a deep depression. To make the final days more bearable, Stephen's dad paid for him and Kylee to have a last weekend together at a comfortable resort hidden in the lost pines of Bastrop. They made the most of it, sleeping late on the sumptuous beds, getting massages, and enjoying drinks by the enormous fire pit beside the wide and lazy Colorado River.

Early morning on Monday, April 14, they stood by the river, weeping. Stephen held Kylee close, her head on his chest, his chin on her curls.

Kylee whispered into his chest, not looking up, "Do you want me to go with you this morning? I'm a wreck. I think I'll make it worse."

He could feel her trembling.

Stephen's dad would be at the resort in an hour to pick him up and drive him to the federal prison in Bastrop, Texas, twenty minutes away. Stephen took a deep breath and savored the feeling of her in his arms and the sound of the wind on the water. Barring a miracle, he would not see a river for the next nine years. As for Kylee, they might be allowed a brief embrace when she came to visit, but there would be no more moments alone. Not for a very long time.

Finally, he spoke softly into her hair. "No. You don't have to go with us." He could feel some of the tension leave her shoulders. Her embrace was so close now, he felt not even an atom could squeeze between them.

The final minutes of his freedom evaporated, and they were forced to walk back to their room. Stephen gave Kylee the rest of his clothes, even his toiletries. He wasn't going to be allowed to bring anything inside the prison—not even a wallet. He wouldn't need his driver's license; he was about to get a new identity.

They checked out of the resort, barely able to make conversation with the pleasant young woman at the front desk. When they walked to the parking lot, Skip was waiting for them. He loaded their bags in the truck camper and they drove Kylee to her car, which was parked in a distant lot. Stephen let Skip transfer Kylee's bags to her car. When she was ready to leave, he stood to embrace her one last time, but his legs wouldn't hold him up. He sank back into his father's pickup truck.

Kylee wiped her eyes on the back of her hand, went back to her car, and quickly drove out of the lot.

Stephen thought Skip was acting a little unsteady as well. They sat in the truck for a long moment as Skip seemed to be trying to slow his breathing. They both noticed that Kylee's brake lights had come on and she had pulled on to the shoulder. They watched her car quietly, waiting, and didn't move until she drove off.

They said nothing on the way to the prison. Patches of colorful wildflowers dotted the sides of the highway as they drove along. Stephen tried to imprint these images on his mind as they flew by.

"Did you bring it?" He asked his dad as they pulled into the parking lot of the Federal Correctional Institution, Bastrop.

"Yes. I did." He handed Stephen a piece of paper.

There was something wrong with Stephen's eyes. Everything on the page looked fuzzy. But Stephen knew that his dad always did everything according to the rules, so he signed his name to the piece of paper that said *Power of Attorney* at the top of the page.

"Did you tell Kylee?" Skip asked.

"No. I didn't want to waste even one second with her being mad at me. I wanted to make the most of our last hours together."

"We may not need it. But if we do, you know she won't like it."

"I know. But she has very little experience managing business matters. She might need help with the tax return. Or if that old car breaks down and she has to buy a new one. You know. Stuff like that. This way, you can help her. I think I can explain over the phone and she will understand." By granting power of attorney to his dad, Stephen hoped that Kylee might stay connected to his family.

"I'd like to say a prayer," said Skip. It was really a question.

Stephen kept his gaze straight ahead and nodded his head imperceptibly. He didn't want to hear his father's prayer, but he also didn't want to leave the safety of the truck. His eyes stayed fixed on the front door and terror filled his heart as his dad laid his hand on Stephen's shoulder, praying fervently for God to put a hedge of protection around Stephen and show him favor.

I need more than a hedge. And if God was going to show me favor, I wouldn't be here.

When the prayer was finished, Stephen stepped out of the truck and walked across the asphalt toward the front door, his mouth dry and blood pounding in his temples.

On his way up the steps, he looked at the outside of the door, committing the image to memory. It would be a very long time before he saw it again. So many family members and friends had pledged their support and letters before he left. But with just a few steps between him and the razor wire, he wondered who would be standing there to receive him nine years from now, on his way out of this place.

Stephen, who had grown up with a silver spoon in his mouth, no longer had a single personal possession.

But he did have a new name: Federal Prisoner 8329-180.

PART II

RAZOR WIRE IN THE LOST PINES

CHAPTER 11

Skip - Day 1

Skip Taylor watched, transfixed, as his son Stephen walked across the parking lot and through the front door of the prison. He sat in his five-year-old, spotless Chevy pickup truck which was enhanced with a custom grill guard and rugged mud tires. What was the protocol for this sort of situation?

Skip always believed in being appropriate in every situation. An absurd old memory popped into his head. He remembered an unwritten rule from his college days. If the instructor was late, the class was expected to wait ten minutes before leaving. If the teacher was a full professor, the class was expected to sit there waiting for fifteen minutes.

What an odd thing to think of at this moment. No unwritten rules were keeping him there. Truthfully, he was half-expecting Stephen to come running out the side door, making his escape. Skip let out a long, shaky breath. It felt like an earthquake building inside of him and he tried to brace himself by squeezing the steering wheel.

When the federal prison system did not take Stephen into custody right after the sentencing, Skip had worried that Stephen would run away. Stephen had been running away from things all his life. As a small child, he had on numerous occasions jerked away from Skip as they walked in a crowded mall or a busy carnival. If his son saw something he wanted, the boy would leave the safety of dad's hand and follow the cotton candy, the music, the friend.

As a teenager, Stephen had stubbornly ignored every curfew. No matter how long he was grounded or what privilege Skip took away from him, he would sneak out in the middle of the night and hide at a friend's house. Skip even nailed Stephen's window shut, but Stephen found other ways to sneak off. Nothing ever worked. His son seemed to have come hardwired to desire whatever was just over the horizon.

Once, when Stephen was a boy, he begged Skip to buy him a gerbil and Skip relented. They bought a cage that looked like a McDonalds' jungle gym with tube slides and little add-on compartments. It looked like a mansion at the pet store, but apparently the gerbil didn't think it looked so spacious.

The little creature—*what was his name?*—spent every waking hour scratching and clawing at the little circular covers over the holes where more sky tubes could be added. The gerbil just wanted to be free. What it didn't know is that an abundance of cats, dogs, caracara eagles, and coyotes waited just outside the walls of the small house on the island. Freedom without knowledge would lead to instant calamity for the gerbil. And sometimes for handsome young men.

Skip had tried so hard to protect his son from the bad things waiting in the outside world. He remembered how he would wake Stephen up for school, feed him breakfast, drive him right up to the door of the school, and watch him walk in. Then, midmorning, he would get a call from the county sheriff's deputy indicating that Stephen had been picked up for truancy, apparently having continued walking right out the back door.

Now Skip knew exactly where Stephen was going to be for the next nine years. And for some reason, he had not allowed his always-prepared mind to consider how terrible it was going to feel. He tried to get his mind off what felt like a crushing weight on his chest, so he cranked the engine and started the long drive home.

A myriad of memories flooded his mind: hunting, fishing, watching Stephen play football. Stephen was a natural athlete and it had made Skip so proud. Tears came and regret ate at his stomach like cancer. Stephen had everything Skip had ever dreamed of having, including good looks and a wealthy family who gave him everything.

Why would a young man with so much blessing intentionally throw it all away?

Skip thought about his own father. Nate Taylor had been a good man, and a good provider, but an old-fashioned strict disciplinarian. Nate didn't believe in hugging or coddling his boys. He taught them to work hard and to be responsible. He never came to one of Skip's football games or baseball games, but he would give a total stranger the shirt off his back. Three months after Skip graduated high school, his father told him it was time to move out and be his own man. The conversation had come as a shock because Skip was working full time and pulling his weight around the house. But Skip had done what his father had asked, without looking back. He used every skill his dad had taught him, and he had become a very successful man, at least in economic terms. Nate was dead now and Skip would never know if his father was proud of his accomplishments. If Nate had been proud of his son, he never told him.

Skip had been determined to show more affection to his own son than his father had shown to him. He told Stephen that he was proud of him. He told Stephen that he loved him. And now, his son was in prison.

Skip tossed up an accusing prayer, "Lord, You know that I worked hard at showing my love. I tried to be there for Stephen. I quit a job I loved, so that I wouldn't have to travel and could spend more time with him. I went to his ballgames. I volunteered at his school." Skip let out a short, bitter laugh. "And the son I devoted my life to has rejected everything that I stand for and thrown away the bright future I tried so hard to give him. My sacrifice didn't benefit either one of us. I guess love just isn't enough."

CHAPTER 12

Stephen – Night 1 of 3,061

S tephen stayed awake most of his first night in prison. The unfamiliar sound of other men sleeping in the same room, accompanied by noises up and down the hall, was unsettling. Someone was having a nightmare; someone else was yelling at the dreamer to shut up. The strange noises in the dark reminded Stephen of a time when he went tent camping with his dad. He had found it difficult to sleep with just a thin piece of nylon separating them from a cacophony of crickets, croaking frogs, buzzing insects, and unseen wildlife in the woods outside.

As a young child, Stephen had always had a room to himself. Later, as a teenager who had gotten in trouble at school, he had been shipped off to an expensive boarding school. There he had learned to share a dorm room with another person. Those tiny dorm rooms, which had seemed so sparse at that time, now seemed like luxury accommodations. He was lying on a blanket on the cold concrete floor of a tiny cell which was home to three other men, one of whom was a Goliath.

She did this on purpose, thought Stephen, and he hated her in that moment.

He had hoped when he checked in, his quick wit and good looks would win him some favor with the powers that be, but it couldn't have gone worse. The female correctional officer whose duty it was to issue him prison-khaki, utilitarian clothes had ordered him to strip naked and had left him standing naked in front of her for a long and humiliating time while she slowly, painstakingly inventoried his clothes. He had stupidly not thought to wear less expensive clothes.

Her name badge read *Denise* and Stephen could tell that she had sized him up as a rich white kid who probably felt entitled to special treatment from her.

She left him standing naked as she wrote the inventory list, even though his prison-issue clothes lay neatly folded beside her. After she inventoried his clothes, she inspected the form to be sure it had copied onto the duplicate form below. Where her writing had not copied well, she—with all the speed of a glacier—recopied the words on the duplicate form.

Stephen's feet had begun to ache on the concrete floor.

After carefully inspecting every item of clothing, including each seam and pocket, she folded them carefully, placed them into a box, and sealed it. Then she asked another correctional officer to enter the room and witness as she looked in Stephen's throat and every crack and crevice of his body. Finally, she handed him his prison clothes and smiled as she informed him that there were no beds ready on his unit, and he would sleep on the floor in a cell already full of other men for a night or two until it was ready.

When he was delivered to the cell about 8 p.m. that first evening, he saw it was occupied by three African American men. One was shaving in a tiny sink and the other two were lying on the bunks, reading. The standing man was enormous and looked to be in his mid-to-late thirties. All of them stared at him as he approached the door with the correctional officer (CO).

"This is Stephen Taylor. He will be staying in this cell tonight," said the CO.

No one moved or spoke. They stared at Stephen like he had three heads.

"Why isn't he being put in the chicken coop, officer?" Said one of the older men.

"It's full. But it's not any of your business to ask." Answered the CO curtly. He pushed Stephen through the door and walked off.

Stephen nodded at the two men lying in bed. The one on the top bunk turned back to his book, but the man who had asked the CO a question gave him a slight smile and said, "Guess you'll have to sleep on the floor. You can have one of my blankets." The man handed him a small, thin blanket. Stephen looked around on the floor for a good spot to put it down and as he did, he brushed a box on the floor. The largest of the three men approached Stephen and put his face within inches of Stephen's and said, "You touch any of our stuff and you won't make it to breakfast."

The man stood as tall as Stephen, which was unusual, but must have outweighed him by seventy pounds. Stephen could smell the man's breath and feel the man's spit on his face, but he didn't back up. Instead, he stared straight ahead without making full eye contact and gave an almost imperceptible nod of his head. He couldn't fight three men.

Stephen understood that it was no accident that he had been placed in this cell and that no one was going to help him if anything happened. This was Denise's way of saying, "Outside of prison you may have had better breaks than me, but inside this place, I control what happens to you, and I can make your life miserable if I feel like it."

Stephen was 6'5" tall and the two blankets that he had been given seemed like towels. He lay on one just to quell the chill from the concrete; it provided no cushion from the rock-hard floor. He tried to cover himself with the other, but every time he moved slightly he uncovered an arm or a leg—or risked touching something. He forced himself to lay so still, his joints ached.

Sometime after daylight, he was finally dozing off when one of the men jumped up and started urinating in the small toilet in the corner. Stephen had a moment of panic about the restroom situation. Men are accustomed to urinating in front of one another, but not other toileting necessities. That was going to be very uncomfortable, especially given the fact that sitting might be perceived as touching something.

He felt the urge to pee also but decided to hold it. Maybe at least one of the men would leave. The largest man did, in fact, dress and leave. Stephen remembered being told the previous day that the metal door to their cell would lock at 11 p.m. and reopen at 5 a.m., so it must be after 5 a.m.

Stephen was so tired he thought about going back to sleep. But now he needed to pee badly. So, as quietly as he could, he got up from the floor and walked the three steps to the toilet. Because of his height, it was impossible to pee quietly in the tiny metal toilet, so he just tried to be quick. Fortunately, the men on the other two bunks didn't wake up. Rather than lie back down and attempt to sleep on the stamp-sized blanket, he peeked out the cell door.

The clock on the wall said 5:30 a.m. Here and there other men, dressed in khaki uniforms, were headed for the cafeteria. Stephen remembered that he had been told that breakfast was served very early and shut down quickly. He threw on his clothes, which he'd used as a pillow, and folded the blankets. He remembered he was not allowed to leave the bed, if you could call it that, unmade.

He followed the other men to the cafeteria, picked up a plastic tray, and stared down the line. Something was being slopped directly onto the pre-sectioned trays. It was too runny to be oatmeal. Grits? And toast. That was it. No eggs. No pancakes. No cereal. No fruit. He was going to starve to death in this place.

He paused to look at the grits as the tray was handed back, glanced side to side, and seeing no one, he asked the server, "Is there any butter or sugar?"

The man stared at him blankly for a moment and then barked, "Keep moving!"

Stephen ate the toast but couldn't stomach the grits. He spied a coffee urn at the end of another counter and made a beeline for it. The coffee was weak, and there was no creamer. An inmate standing behind a counter near the coffee, apparently in charge of condiments, gave Stephen one sugar packet. The coffee was bad, but the grits were awful. So, he dumped the sugar into the grits and was able to eat a few bites. Still quite hungry, he headed back to the serving line again to see if he could get another piece of toast.

When the man who had barked at him earlier saw him approach the line, he said, "No seconds!"

Stephen left the cafeteria.

Here and there a few expressionless correctional officers stood watching. The COs all sported a similar look. They were muscular and fit, with short-cropped hair or shaved heads. Most were Anglo, but many were Hispanic. They looked like they would be right at home in football shoulder pads or Army fatigues.

In another life, Stephen might have liked to have struck up a conversation with them about football or weapons, but he quickly learned that he was not someone they wanted to talk with. To the COs, Stephen was not a regular guy who liked football and fishing. He was a criminal, a number, a bad-seed, part of the problem with society today.

He walked into the TV room, hoping to find a place to rest his head. The sleepless night had left him exhausted. He pulled a folded chair from where it was stacked against the wall and tried to slide down in it and put his head back, but the chair was too small for his frame. If he tried to lean his head back on the back of the chair, his butt left the seat. So, he headed back to the cell where he was unwanted and lay back down on the floor.

It turned out that you can sleep almost anywhere when you're tired enough.

When he woke it was much later and he was much warmer. He opened his eyes and saw the dirty underside of the toilet and closed them again quickly. He snuggled the little, scratchy utility-type blanket up to his neck and realized that he had acquired another blanket. He opened his eyes again and saw one of the cellmates looking at him from the bunk. He lay sideways, with his head propped on his elbow reading a book in front of him.

"What's your name?" the man asked.

Stephen rolled onto his back to stretch it and said to the ugly ceiling, "Stephen. What's yours?"

"Dion." Dion appeared to be younger and less hostile than the other two men. Stephen lifted his head and stared down his chest in Dion's direction. He feared that he might be framed by Goliath for taking the extra blanket, so he thought he better address it. "Where did this extra blanket come from? I know I didn't touch anything in here."

"I had a friend to acquire it for you, because the sound of you shivering was disturbing my reading," said Dion.

"Thank you. What's Mr. Big gonna say when he sees me with it?"

Dion thought about it for a second and said, "You better fold it up now and put it under your other two. He probably won't notice, but if he does, I'll take care of it."

"OK," Stephen said again and left it at that.

Dion nodded and went back to reading his book. Then Dion added without looking up, "His name is Big Mike—the big guy. He's as bad as he looks. Don't get crossways with him."

"Thank you," Stephen said again. "Do you mind if I ask you another question?"

"Um hmm," said Dion.

Stephen wasn't sure if that meant the man did mind, or if he didn't, but he plowed ahead.

"What's the chicken coop?"

"It's where they house prisoners when they have no space. It's a TV room with ten bunks in it. They shoulda' put you on the floor in there last night. Not sure why that didn't happen."

Stephen folded the blankets and left them stacked under the bottom bunk. It was the only space in the tiny cell that didn't look like it was already claimed.

Stephen walked down the hall to the CO's office, as he had been instructed to do the previous day. There, he was placed on work detail with an older Hispanic man, named Manny. Stephen followed Manny to a utility closet, where the small, gray-headed man retrieved a broom and mop bucket. Stephen assumed that he was supposed to be observing and learning, so he made no offer to assist as Manny positioned a few plastic cups to cordon off a section of floor to keep traffic off it long enough to sweep it and mop it.

Wordlessly, Manny handed Stephen a broom. Stephen didn't like the look of the mop water, so he was glad to be sweeping. Unable to dispel Manny's look of disapproval with his sweeping efforts, Stephen tried to lighten the mood with a joke in Spanish. To Stephen's surprise Manny laughed and jumped in with another clever joke.

Stephen noticed that Manny did not look at him when he spoke, but instead seemed to glance up and down the hallway or directly at the floor. After they had been at it for about forty-five minutes and had gotten into a comfortable pattern, Manny suddenly tensed, but his eyes didn't leave the floor. He sloshed a little water on Stephen's pants as his mop strokes got shorter and faster. He said quietly under his breath, "Look mad and yell something at me."

Stephen wasn't following this instruction. He stared at Manny wordlessly.

Then, out of nowhere Manny shouted at Stephen: "*Pendejo!* You're stepping all over the clean part!"

Stephen, used to observing his surroundings, had noticed the two large men with shaved heads approaching out of the corner of his eye. The men were now staring at him and Manny. One had his arms crossed across his enormous chest.

Stephen didn't turn his head, but he knew they were inmates, not prison staff, and Manny was obviously afraid of them. What had Manny just said? *You need to look mad*—and what else?

Stephen reacted. "Why don't *you* move a little slower with that mop, Pay-dro? What's the hurry? Is it time for your siesta?"

The two men laugh approvingly and moved on.

Stephen didn't understand what just happened. When the two strangers appeared to be out of earshot, he said, in Spanish, "*What was that about?*"

Manny cut him off. "Speak English."

Stephen wanted to press for more information, but Manny had clammed up and put a little more distance between them. The jokes were over.

For the rest of the day, Stephen spent his time observing patterns. Who spoke to whom. Pecking orders. He couldn't quite figure out the relationships yet, but he could tell there was some sort of unofficial "order." At the dinner meal, he saw Manny in the cafeteria and wanted to talk to him more about the identity of the men who had watched them earlier. Manny was sitting with a group of other Hispanic inmates. Stephen sat down next to him at the table.

A man with a long, gray ponytail joked loudly, *"Quién es tu nuevo amigo?" Who is your new friend?*

"Cuidado. Este guero habla español," said Manny. *Be careful, this white guy speaks Spanish.*

"Guess he will have to choose for himself," said ponytail man, who also had a huge mustache. "But if he doesn't go sit with the skinheads, he's probably going to wake up dead."

They all laughed.

Glancing nervously around, Manny said to Stephen, "Those guys we saw earlier are Aryan Brotherhood. If they hear you speaking Spanish, you could be marked for trouble. We don't want any trouble."

Stephen got up from the bench and sat by himself. No one joined him at the table and he felt lonely and foolish for finding himself in this situation. He was grateful for Manny's warning and that Manny had protected him earlier in the hallway. Apparently, just talking to the wrong person could get him killed.

It was a surprise that federal prison was such a segregated and racist institution. In Stephen's hometown, the population was more than 50% Hispanic and many of his friends and the influential adults in his life had been Hispanic. Kylee was biracial, born to an Anglo mother and African American father. So was Stephen's friend, Arnie. His good friend Jackson was Hispanic. Racism was a new experience. He didn't really know if he could fake it.

The question in his mind was answered quickly, when some white inmates came and sat down, surrounding Stephen. He noticed that Manny and his crew got up quickly and left their table empty.

One of the inmates said, "So, you likin' your cellie situation?"

Stephen sized him up quickly. He wasn't one of the two who had scared Manny earlier in the day, but his head was shaved. He had a tattoo on his neck. Stephen answered, "No. I belong somewhere else."

The three men smiled and introduced themselves, as if he had passed an initiation.

Stephen felt ashamed. Dion had been good to him and had found him some shower shoes in addition to the extra blanket. He and Dion had had a few conversations when Big Mike was out of earshot.

Dion is much smarter and more interesting than any of these boneheads, he thought.

To preserve the peace, and his general welfare, he let the skinheads talk and made brief affirmative comments that made it seem like he agreed with them. He had already learned that the last thing an inmate wants in prison is to be noticed for being different.

CHAPTER 13

Stephen – Day 16

In the months leading up to his incarceration, Stephen had lain awake at night wondering what type of people he would meet in prison. He dreamed of gang members and perhaps swindlers, but in his worst nightmares he could not have imagined the individual who confronted him the day he moved to his new cell in the Austin Block.

The man was unshaven, with bad teeth and long stringy hair. He got in Stephen's face and said, "I am the speaker for the *Consejo Natal*. Who do you represent?"

Stephen had no idea how to answer. He said, "I represent myself."

"What are you in for?"

"Marijuana got me here. What are you here for?"

"Where are you from?" Mr. Bad Teeth probed, ignoring Stephen's question, and standing so close that Stephen had to once again fight the urge to take a step back.

"Spent the last three years in Austin. You?" Stephen relaxed his shoulders and lifted his chin slightly, trying to look calm and confident and intimidate the slender man with his size, but his heart was pounding out of his chest.

"There's someone you need to meet." Bad Teeth turned and began to march off.

Stephen didn't know what to do, so he stayed put.

The man turned back and barked, "Come here!"

Stephen followed a few paces behind, taking everything in. Inmates were watching them. He felt like a dead man walking. They turned the corner toward a TV room.

"And who do we have here, D.J.?" a huge, bald, tattooed man asked.

Stephen felt his insides go watery. His mouth felt like ash. He felt like he'd just come face to face with Satan.

D.J. said, "This here's a new guy. He's from your backyard. Marijuana."

Just moments ago, Stephen had wished D.J. would back out of his personal space; now he was dismayed when the old man stepped to the side, leaving a vacuous opening between himself and the bald man, who continued to stare.

"I know you," he finally said.

And he did. They had met before. When Stephen was just out of high school, he'd had had a brief fling with a pretty, redheaded girl who had the sad distinction of having also dated Happy Sampson. When Happy found out that the girl had been seen about town with Stephen, he ordered the rival beaten, kidnapped, and brought to him.

Stephen had been watching a football game at his apartment with some friends when the thugs had shown up at the door and asked for him. Thinking they wanted to buy marijuana, he stepped outside so as not to be awkward in front of his football buddies.

One of the two big men was wearing a long-sleeve flannel shirt over a white T-shirt. When he told Stephen to get in the car with them, he had one hand on his hip and slid the other down the front of his shirt stopping on the big bulge of the handgun tucked into his belt. Stephen left with the gang members without telling his buddies what was going on. He didn't want his friends to get hurt for being in the wrong place at the wrong time.

Prior to that day, Stephen had never heard of Happy Sampson, but it was certainly a face he would never forget. The way the man carried himself; the way he shaved his head so that you could see the tattoo on the back of his skull; the way he had held the gun sideways and pointed it right at Stephen's face. Those images were burned in his consciousness. Happy had instructed him never to contact the girl again. Stephen never did.

He never told his parents or his friends about the terrifying ordeal, because he knew if his parents found out they would want to call the police. If they did that,

Stephen had no doubt that Happy would find him and kill him. Stephen's parents thought the police had the power to make people play by the rules. But people like Happy didn't care enough about their lives to worry about rules.

Now, eight years later, Stephen wondered what Happy recalled about their encounter and what he might do now, surrounded by his gang members. Stephen didn't dare turn his head to look; he already knew there were no guards around. He didn't want to look afraid. He said nothing, and he tried not to look threatened or threatening.

After an eternity, Happy's glare turned into a smile and he said, "I sold you weed. A long time ago, right? Well, I'm a little short on supply right now. But maybe later." He snorted at his cleverness. "You can come under the protection of the *Consejo Natal*," announced Happy and walked off with his gang members in tow.

Stephen let out a ragged breath and felt the blood reenter his fingers. His temples throbbed. He remembered hearing about the *Consejo Natal* when he was growing up in South Texas. He understood it to be a Hispanic gang, but apparently ethnicity wasn't a strict requirement. He was being offered protection. Did they know about Stephen's ties to Mexico? Had they seen him speaking Spanish with Manny? His association with Marco had been nothing like this. Marco was an educated man. No one in Marco's employment had any tattoos or looked like a thug. Marco had been easy to follow because he was smart, articulate, and rich. These men were brutal, boorish, and unsophisticated. But Stephen also didn't want to be thought vulnerable or alone. He had no desire to join a gang, but he had to find an alliance somewhere.

He decided to try to become acquainted with his new cell mates, Kip and Crawley and determine where their allegiances lay. They were each quite different from the other, but they got along. Kip was from the Island of Samoa and Crawley was a Texan from Fort Worth. Neither man claimed to be affiliated with a gang, and both were serving long sentences for drug-related offenses.

Kip was serving twenty years for selling marijuana and cocaine. Crawley had fallen asleep in the getaway car while his buddies had gone to purchase methamphetamine. He got caught with the money and the drugs in the car and his buddies got away. He was charged with intent to distribute the drugs. The presence of a gun in the car significantly heightened the charges against him. Crawley had been 26 years old when he was arrested. He'd served fourteen years of a twenty-five-year sentence. Both men would probably have gotten half that time if they committed an armed robbery or killed someone while driving drunk. That was one of the big differences between state and federal prison. Federal prisoners generally received longer sentences for less-violent crimes.

Kip told him to find Ross, the speaker for the independents. Using Kip's description, Stephen located Ross the next day. Ross was a thin, handsome man with close-cropped hair and a receding hair line. His hair was so short that it merely added a little color to his skull, but he sported an impressive red-brown beard. It had that days-old casual look.

That must be a difficult look to maintain. Does he have access to trimmers?" Stephen made a mental note to ask about that later.

Stephen wasn't sure how the affiliations worked or what to say. So, he stated simply, "I hear you're the spokesperson for the independents."

Ross tilted his head slightly and studied Stephen.

Stephen continued, "I've never been in a gang. I don't want to associate with any gangs. Is it possible to stay independent?"

"It's possible," answered Ross in a measured tone, "but it's not automatic that you can become independent, either. You have to earn that right. And the established gangs have a right to recruit you if they want you." He paused. "Or confirm that they don't have orders to kill you. I don't think you understand the meaning of the word 'independent' in here. The guys that have earned the right to call themselves independents are essentially in a gang, similar to the other established gangs. You get protection if you need it, but you also have to step up and defend your independent brother if he needs protection from one of the other gangs."

Stephen walked back to his cell with low spirits. The fact that all these gang alliances existed told him that the need for protection was a real concern. But he didn't identify with any of them and he didn't want to commit without understanding what was really required. He was crowded together like cattle with almost 1,400 other men, but at that moment he also felt terribly and totally alone.

CHAPTER 14

Stephen – Day 160

Stephen stared at his breakfast tray. Bran cereal was on the menu today, as it was three days a week. He looked at the expiration date on the baggie of milk. Expired. By two weeks.

It must still be fit for human consumption, or surely they would not serve it. We are human beings, after all.

Unpleasant as the thought was, he had to use the expired milk. The cereal was full of weevils and pouring milk on it was the best way to get rid of the bugs. He poured the expired milk into the bowl and waited for the small brown insects to float to the top. Then, he scooped them out with his spoon, and put them on the thin, brown napkin.

He stirred for a while, to find as many bugs as possible. Finally, when he was confident the weevils were extracted, he sampled the cereal. It tasted like cardboard, but it was better than nothing. Even down to the last bite he had to watch carefully because a few of the tiny bugs always somehow clung to the final flake.

He wondered what to do for the next hour. It often helped quiet his mind to be outside, but he was concerned about going out today. Happy had run into him several times yesterday and made a point to tell him to be in the exercise yard after breakfast. He said he had someone he wanted Stephen to meet.

Stephen was suspicious and didn't really want to have anything to do with Happy or meet anyone in his gang. But he was also fearful of getting on Happy's bad side. He'd heard what happened to people Happy didn't like. He decided that it wouldn't hurt to just go exercise and meet whoever it was that Happy wanted to introduce him to. Then, he would head back to his cell to finish up a few letters and get them in today's mail. Letters going out meant letters coming in, which was often the highlight of his day.

He tossed his tray on the conveyor belt and hurried down the hall because the ten-minute *move* time was almost up. On the hour, the doors to each zone were locked. But ten minutes before every hour, inmates could move to different locations. As he reached the doors at the end of the hallway leading out to the exercise yard, he saw Crawley moving toward him at a good clip.

"Where are you going?" Stephen asked.

"I'm headed back to the cell. I just got word the CO is doing a random check of our space right now," said Crawley as he hurried past.

The doors were about to lock and Stephen made a split-second decision. It sounded like the perfect excuse to skip out on a meeting with Happy. He turned and ran after his cellie.

They arrived as the CO was locking the door. He held it open a moment longer, hurling threats at them, but let them pass.

When they got to their cell they found Jose Gutierrez, the orderly, standing in the hallway with his cleaning cart. Jose was part of a crew of inmates who were paid five dollars a month by the Bureau of Prisons to sweep and mop the hallways and clean the showers. And five dollars' worth of labor is about what they provided. Stephen, Kip and Crawley had agreed to pay Jose a book of stamps every month to clean their cell weekly, outside of his regular work hours.

Jose said, "I was cleaning, but the CO, he told me to wait out here."

Herman Espinoza, the correctional officer who managed the Austin unit, was inspecting their cell. Espinoza was a short, thin Hispanic man with bulging biceps. He wore latex gloves and inspected the underside of the bottom bunk; behind and underneath each locker; and even their clothes, dropping them back into the locker unfolded. They were required to keep their clothes folded, so the CO was creating busywork for all of them.

Officer Espinoza flipped through some of Stephen's books. As he set the books aside he paused and stared into Stephen's locker. Then, he reached in and pulled out a grapefruit.

Stephen panicked when he saw the pale, pink-orange orb. They weren't allowed to have any perishable food in their cell. Stephen's throat went dry. Would he get a shot[2] for this?

CO Espinoza turned toward Stephen, cocked his head and said, "You know the rules. You cannot have this in here." He took a knife from a scabbard snapped to his belt and cut the fruit almost in half. Then, he held it over Stephen's pillow and with one hand he simultaneously twisted the fruit open, squeezed it and smashed it onto the bed. Pulp and sticky juice left a dark stain on the pillow and the thin sheet. "Don't let me catch you with fruit in this cell again. If I do—"

Before he could continue, static-punctuated words blasted out of his shoulder radio.

Stephen couldn't understand what was being said because the COs were using code. But judging from Espinoza's grim expression, it clearly wasn't good. The officer rushed out and locked the unit doors behind him, leaving the inmates in the Austin unit alone and unsupervised.

Crawley sat down on his bunk.

Stephen used one of the paper napkins they kept on the windowsill to start cleaning up the grapefruit.

Jose stuck his head in. "You want me to finish?"

Jose had put some pine-scented cleaner in the toilet, which Stephen was happy to see. That seemed like a good start. He was about to try to enlist Jose's help with the grapefruit mess, when Jose shoved his mop into the toilet, and started using the toilet water as his mop bucket to mop the floor. Stephen wanted to gag. He was about to stop Jose when more coded announcements came over the intercom.

They all grew quiet.

Disembodied voices whispered up and down the hallway.

Stephen and Crawley wandered into the hallway to look around. Other inmates stood outside their cell doors, staring at the large, metal unit doors. Several inmates were peering out the unit doors' tiny windows, but no one said anything.

---

2   A shot is a disciplinary consequence for an infraction of the rules. A written report will go
     in the inmate's record and punishment will be applied which might include a loss of certain
     privileges, a period of solitary confinement or even a move to a higher-level prison.

Then, the inmates at the door sprang back and their CO re-entered. His short hair was wet, and his cheeks mottled and flushed. The crackling voices coming out of his shoulder radio were loud and confusing. The CO yelled to everyone standing near the door, "Get back and move to your cells! Now!"

Everyone was walking toward their cells, but no one wanted to get there quickly. Stephen turned from the door and angry CO and found Crawley hovering near their cell.

More announcements blared over the loudspeaker.

They stood near the cell door, hoping to hear more.

"What's happening?" whispered Stephen.

Crawley said, "I don't know what happened, but I know who's going to get punished. Us."

"What do you mean?" asked Stephen.

"How do you think they enforce the rules so well with so few correctional officers around here, son?" Crawley drawled.

Stephen ordinarily didn't like to be called *son*. But he didn't really mind it when Crawley called him that, because Crawley considered it a compliment. As if being related to him would have been an honor. Crawley continued, "You're about to discover collective punishment."

Espinoza was now locking each door with a key and the whispers were getting harder to hear. The CO looked at Stephen and Crawley and yelled, "In your cell!"

They quickly stepped inside and soon heard the door lock behind them. They both stood staring helplessly at the door.

Crawley wondered out loud, "Where was Kip when they announced lockdown? I wonder why he was not able to make it back?"

"You don't think that Kip was involved, do you?" ask Stephen.

"I hope not. He's a good cellie. Keeps his stuff picked up. Doesn't get written up. Doesn't keep grapefruit in his locker. Doesn't talk too much," said Crawley. His mouth was pursed tight and thin, but small crinkles around his eyes told Stephen that Crawley wasn't angry at him.

"You know you love shootin' the breeze with me, old man." Stephen smiled.

This passed for levity between them, but it didn't last long. Stephen was still processing and rewinding the radio crackle and the voices that had echoed up and down the hall before the doors locked.

Was it a fight?

He stood right at the door, looking through the little glass window and then turning his ear toward it so he could hear what was going on. The CO's office was right across the hall and Espinoza was still standing in the hallway, looking toward the unit doors and talking into his shoulder. Stephen thought he heard names of the inmates involved in whatever this was. A group of inmates that belonged on the Austin unit, but who had apparently been trapped elsewhere when the units were locked, were let into the locked unit from outside. They streamed past Stephen's door lighting rumor-fires up and down the hallway with their whispering about *the fight*.

***

They were locked down all afternoon and evening, the time they ordinarily would have been allowed to watch television. Fortunately, Stephen had one book in his locker that he hadn't read. At dinner time, Espinoza brought them baloney sandwiches on white bread with a short bottle of water and a small plastic fruit cup. Stephen and Crawley asked about Kip the next morning, when the CO brought them granola bars and bottled water for breakfast, but he didn't answer their questions.

Stephen never thought he would miss eating weevils in the chow hall, but right now he did. "Do you think they will let us out to walk or shower?" Stephen asked.

Crawley snorted. "What do you think? They don't call it a lockdown fer nothin'?"

Stephen was beginning to get worried. The daily routine of getting out of the cell, having a meal, and walking around the track, helped lift the despair. Outside the cell, when his body was moving, he could daydream about how his life would rocket to success when he finally got out. He could make a phone call and hear something about the outside. He watched television and, through it, saw scenes that depicted real life. A life he hoped to live again one day.

But inside the cell, staring at gray walls, Stephen could not escape the harsh reality of confinement. It was impossible to dream or even think about something happy in a ten-by-ten room that seemed to be growing smaller and smaller. He felt indescribably, undeniably confined. Not being able to leave the cell was going to impact his mental stability.

Surely, it won't last more than a day or two.

Another day and night passed. They heard a voice outside the door and were almost joyful when the door opened and Kip stepped inside, although that meant the cell would be even more crowded. At least Kip might know what was going on. Not having any information had caused their imaginations to run wild.

Kip looked like he had not slept at all. He crashed into the bunk bed on his back, shutting his swollen eyes. His long kinky hair splayed every direction. He looked like someone being electrocuted.

"Where have you been?" Stephen asked.

"What did they do to you?" Crawley asked at the same time.

Stephen and Crawley glanced at each other. Stephen was surprised at Crawley's odd choice of first question.

"I saw it, man," said Kip. "It was bad."

Stephen and Crawley looked on while Kip took long deep breaths with an arm draped over his eyes, as if he were seeing it again from behind his eyelids.

"Harley is dead. Maybe some of his guys too. We were walking around the track, so we saw everything. Harley and all his *Tejas Familia* gang were talking on one side of the yard, by the fence. Happy marched up to them lookin' real angry. I never seen him look like that. The conversation was real heated. Then, Happy put his hands on his hips and turned his back on Harley for a minute. We thought it was over. But that must have been a signal.

"The *Consejo Natal* came from everywhere and laid into the *Tejas Familia* dudes. Happy is a lot stronger and faster than you might have guessed. He hit Harley in the head with a rake handle so hard. It was just like a piñata, with his brains spillin' out all over the ground."

Crawley and Stephen stood frozen, staring at their cellmate, imagining the scene he described. Kip was a large, stoic guy who loved horror films and dark, violent rock music. If he was this traumatized, it must have been bad.

"There was blood everywhere. And brains," Kip repeated.

Stephen and Crawley waited anxiously for more information, but apparently Kip was done sharing.

"So, they've been interrogating you?" offered Crawley. "Trying to see what you saw? What you know?"

"Exactly."

"And what did you tell them?"

"Only what I saw."

"But you didn't tell them the reason for the fight?"

"I didn't tell them. But I think they know. It's the trash."

"Hot trash," agreed Crawley, nodding his head.

After a long spell of silence, Stephen asked, "So, what is *hot* trash?"

Not for the first time, they both looked at him like he was an idiot.

"Haven't you noticed how Happy always has the ability to procure things? Useful things?"

Stephen thought about the most recent conversation that he'd had with Happy. Happy called him down to his cell after the morning count last week and quizzed him on how he was getting along. He'd seemed unusually friendly. Stephen had been guarded but had loosened up a little after Happy had offered him a cup of instant coffee with creamer. It was a real treat.

Stephen assumed that those items were purchased at the commissary. But now as he thought about it, no one in prison would offer anyone else something they had purchased at the commissary. Commissary goods were too expensive and too hard to get. Nothing was offered in here unless something was exchanged in return. Every interaction was a transaction.

Stephen started to wonder and worry. What did Happy think that he had to exchange? Had he said anything that Happy could use against him now? He would be more careful in the future. And why had Happy insisted that he come out to the yard today after breakfast, "…to meet someone?" He stood silently, considering how lucky he was that CO Espinosa picked that exact time to inspect his cell.

He wanted to ask Kip and Crawley about the significance of the conversation with Happy. But they had both told him to steer clear of Happy. Stephen had not told them about his history with Happy prior to prison. Kip and Crawley were a little too talkative. He didn't want to do anything that might make waves with a powerful prison gang like the *Consejo Natal*. Nor did he want to be "invited" to join. Stephen nodded thoughtfully, hoping one of the guys would continue.

Crawley lowered his voice, as if someone else could hear them. "Happy and his guys take all the trash from all the offices, cafeteria, whatever, to the big dumpsters outside the gate. They sift through it to get all the useful stuff BOP[3] workers throw out, especially used ink cartridges, electrical cords, whatever. Also, some really useful and important things get accidentally dropped into the trash. Accidentally on purpose, if you know what I mean. The trash haul is when Happy and his gang get their

---

3   BOP is short for Bureau of Prisons.

hands on it. Apparently, something that Happy was waiting on made its way out of the trash and into someone else's hands."

"That's not all of it," said Kip, his eyes still closed. His breathing was getting more even, and he looked like he was almost asleep. "Harley and the *Tejas Familia* guys had made a *vice*—an *accord*—with the *Consejo Natal*. They were supposed to share the income from selling the hot trash in exchange for various protections for each other's guys in units where they are outnumbered. But Happy and his *Consejo Natal* guys weren't sharing the loot. They were keeping all the proceeds for themselves and cutting the *Tejas Familia* guys out of their hustle."

So, it's true then, thought Stephen. Harley and one of his lieutenants were dead. Happy had done it. The head of the *Tejas Familia* gang in Central Texas was dead, and the reason lay somewhere in the trash.

The sandwiches through the door continued for five more days. Stephen could not stand himself after the third day. His hair was greasy, so he attempted to run water over it in the microscopically small sink in their cell. He was sad he had not done laundry just before the lockdown, because his towel smelled as sour as his body. But he continued to wet-wipe himself down with water from the little sink every day in a vain attempt to feel less grubby.

Finally, on the seventh day, a CO came to the door and escorted them to the showers. Stephen had never appreciated a shower so much in his life, even though it was only lukewarm water. What he wouldn't give for a long, hot, steamy shower.

After fourteen days and nights the lockdown was lifted. After that experience, Stephen was more grateful for the privilege of exercise and a visit from his dad or his mom. He also decided that he would do laundry more faithfully and store some reading material and commissary food, in the event it happened again.

But no grapefruit.

CHAPTER 15

Skip – Day 190

Skip was standing at a cash register paying for his groceries when his phone rang. *No Caller ID* on the screen meant the call was likely from Stephen. He knew if he didn't answer Stephen couldn't call back for a while. And he could not call Stephen back, because the prison did not accept any incoming calls to inmates.

Skip apologized to the cashier. "I'm sorry I've got to take this call," he said as he swiped to accept the incoming call.

He put the phone to his ear hoping no one else could hear the familiar recorded message, "You have a call from an inmate at a federal prison. Press one to accept. Press two to decline." He pressed one quickly.

"Hey, Dad," said Stephen, "Glad to hear your voice. Is this a good time?"

"Yeah, I'm grocery shopping. But it's fine," he lied.

"I bet you wondered why I haven't called."

"I sure did. You always call and make sure I'm coming on my weekend, which is coming up. What's been going on?"

"Well, I experienced my first lockdown. We were not allowed to leave our cells for fourteen days."

"Wow. I'm sorry. That must have been awful."

"Worse than awful."

Skip was pushing his cart out to the car with one hand, trying to keep the phone to his ear listening to Stephen share the traumatic events of the previous weeks. Stephen was only allowed to purchase 300 minutes of phone time per month and wanted to save some minutes to call Kylee. So, they didn't have long to talk. Each call felt like a race to exchange information in the short time allotted.

When they ended the call, Skip stared at the phone for a second. He could hardly believe an inmate in Stephen's prison had been brutally murdered in broad daylight by a rival prison gang, and it hadn't even made the evening news in his town ninety miles away. He opened the internet on his phone and tried to search for newspaper headlines or other media stories and found nothing.

I guess if an inmate gets murdered in prison, no one cares. Oh, Lord, how did my son end up in such a place?

It made Skip both angry and afraid. He realized suddenly that, after Stephen went to prison, he had stopped praying "Lord, protect him one more day," as he had for so many years. He had mistakenly thought that Stephen's life was now safe, under the watchful eye of the federal government.

How wrong that idea had been.

Skip slowly walked the cart back to the cart corral. Many shoppers abandoned their carts in the lot, but Skip liked to follow the rules.

As he walked, he prayed.

"Lord, thank you for revealing to me how to pray for Stephen. Please, keep him safe one more day. And, Lord, will you please use this terrible experience to open his eyes to the fact that he needs You?"

CHAPTER 16

Stephen – Day 193

The commissary was busy the first day after the lockdown, and almost everything useful, like shampoo, sold out quickly. Stephen had filled out his list and handed it to the BOP employee at the window. He sat down on the bench to wait for his order to be filled. Often he would wait up to three hours. Today, it looked like it would take longer than that. He liked sitting outside the commissary. The space seemed less institutional than the rest of the compound.

It was quite small, smaller than a convenience store and with fewer items. But in Stephen's opinion, the small amount of food available in the commissary was necessary to survival. When he turned in his list he was told that some of the food items on his list were out of stock. He replaced those out of stock items with writing supplies, so that he could write some letters. The commissary had plenty of writing supplies in stock this day because the other inmates were focused on food after eating *Johnny sacks*[4] for fourteen days.

Stephen thought back to how he had loved purchasing school supplies in elementary school. Back then, he had enjoyed school. He liked the smell of new markers and erasers and the feel of crisp, fresh paper. In those days, he played

---

4 A *Johnny sack* is a meager sack lunch, provided to inmates on lockdown or in administrative segregation (solitary).

little league baseball and Pop Warner football. He had good grades in his subjects and citizenship. His mom was already drifting out of his life around that time, and so his dad had been the *room-mom* for his first-grade class. Skip was always there offering to help him with things. Stephen recalled being a little embarrassed about his dad coming to school functions, and people asking him why he didn't have a mother. Why had school become daunting and incomprehensible around age twelve?

He visited with other inmates who were waiting and even closed his eyes and rested for a while. Eventually, someone barked at him to come get his order. He headed back to his cell and surveyed his large haul:

Two packages of tuna. (He wanted three, but they were only allowed two).

One cheap razor.

Hair conditioner (It could double as shaving cream).

New lock for his locker (A CO searching for contraband cut his off one day when he was away from his cell. The COs knew that a new lock would cost a fortune to an inmate, but that didn't stop them from cutting off locks to be sure the lock didn't hide contraband).

Batteries. (He didn't have any need for them yet, but he hoped to buy a radio soon and had heard that batteries were hard to come by.)

One spiral notebook.

One writing pen.

He put all but the pen and notebook in his locker. He let out a sad chuckle at his change of fortune. He had once thought nothing of dropping $300 on dinner. Now, he could barely afford a three-dollar notebook. With nowhere to go and nothing to do, he sat down on the bench looking out at the exercise yard. There was no evidence of the bloodshed that had occurred here a few weeks ago, except that the COs removed all the weights and exercise equipment. Now there was just a walking track and benches.

Stephen ranted into his notebook about the removal of the weights that he had enjoyed. He questioned how the lockdown could be legal. He wrote notes about unofficial rules and jargon he had learned in prison. Having never written more than two pages in his life, even for a book report, Stephen found himself surprised at the volume of material he generated. As thoughts, ideas and experiences spilled out; he wondered if someone else in the wide universe might benefit from his insight? After a few pages, he stopped and went back to the first page. At the top of the first page, Stephen wrote:

How to Survive in Federal Prison.

Here are some things to expect if you are sentenced to federal prison.

If you are Anglo, you will be in the minority. Around 30% of federal prisoners are Anglo. The rest are Black, Hispanic or another race.

Many, if not most of the inmates are in gangs. Be careful to learn the gang signs and symbols and avoid them at all costs. The gangs are very powerful, and they will hurt or kill you with little provocation.

Prison is not like what you see on TV. It's much worse. Especially the food. When I was assigned to work in the kitchen, I read the following on the side of a box that contained meat being used in hamburgers and served to inmates: "Hearts/Parts. Not for human consumption." Yes. It's that bad.

"Escape by Death" is a slang term for when an inmate dies in prison. Once you get here, you will understand.

Inmates were not ordinarily permitted to bring anything with them from their cell to any area outside the unit. However, Stephen had noticed inmates reading magazines outside. Some of the guys on the track wore headphones and carried radios, so he assumed it must be loosely enforced if you weren't making trouble. Still, when he heard someone approaching, he flipped the notebook shut and tried not to look guilty. Stephen relaxed when he saw Sean. Sean was a smart, intense bookworm covered with tattoos. They lived in the same unit, but Sean worked for Unicor, which limited the amount of time they saw each other.

"It's nice to be out of lockdown finally, eh? Gonna be more quiet around here without Happy," Sean said as he sat down next to Stephen. "I heard he's on his way to Beaumont USP," he added.

Stephen felt a chill on the back of his neck at the mention of the US Federal Penitentiary in Beaumont, Texas. It had an awful reputation.

"Hey, Sean," Stephen said, as he tried to push USP Beaumont out of his thoughts, "You're a tattoo artist, right?"

"I'm not a tattoo artist; I'm an artist. In here, my canvas sometimes has to be the human body, because we don't have much else to draw on," Sean said, eyeing the notebook jealously.

Stephen smiled. Sean's answers were always so interesting. Sean didn't smile much, but his eyes were curious and expressive, like he was cataloging everything and drawing it in his head. Stephen had seen several tattoos done by Sean and they were beautiful works of art. Stephen didn't have any tattoos and didn't ordinarily like that sort of thing, but Sean's work made him think that if he were ever going to have a tattoo, he would ask Sean to design it.

"What on Earth do you use to tattoo someone, by the way?"

"An ink cartridge and some sharp wire."

"And where would you get an ink cartridge? Or a wire?"

"Well, one of the *Tejas Familia* guys saw me drawing on a tablet. He brought me a photograph of his girl and asked me to draw it on the tablet. I did, and he liked it. He asked me if I could tattoo the drawing on his back. I told him I didn't have the right equipment. He came back the next day with the ink and wire. He's been supplying me ever since, along with the clients."

Stephen sat amazed and appalled.

"So, this man let a perfect stranger tattoo something permanently on his back using a piece of wire and a stolen ink cartridge from an office he had probably been responsible for cleaning. How do you know that printer ink isn't poisonous?"

"I don't. But he paid me forty dollars in commissary. So, it was pretty lucrative."

"Hey, speaking of commissary, what would you charge me to sketch some little drawings in my journal here? I thought perhaps it would be a way of chronicling my journey."

Sean didn't reply immediately. It was his quiet way to think through an answer. When he did answer, it sometimes seemed like he was reading Stephen's mind.

"Like this?" Sean took the pen out of Stephen's hand and doodled a picture of a broken heart, pierced and bleeding.

"Yes. Exactly like that."

CHAPTER 17

Stephen – Day 250

Visitors were permitted at Bastrop FCI Saturdays and Sundays only, during limited hours. This was subject to change. Visitation might be cancelled at any moment as punishment to the inmates. Families eventually learn to expect the unexpected. Prior to visiting Stephen, his family and friends were required to apply, a process which included a background investigation.

Stephen sent applications to his mom, dad, Kylee, his grandparents, and several friends. He hoped they would all want to visit, but he was embarrassed about how invasive it was. It required a prospective visitor to provide extensive personal information before approval. And it took several weeks to process.

His mother passed the test, and today was one of her rare visits. Stephen shaved and bathed early. He wanted to look as normal as possible. He dropped by early to see Joe Rodriguez. Joe and another inmate ran a business ironing clothes for other inmates. Stephen paid Joe with the currency of FCI Bastrop: stamps. Stephen had not yet come up with a hustle, like ironing, and he wasn't sure how to find one. Thus far, his family had been willing to place enough money in his account to cover his payphone calls and other limited supplies. Inmates like Joe, whose family either couldn't—or wouldn't—send money to his account had to find services they could provide to other prisoners, such as ironing. They received their payment in postage stamps, which they then traded for other goods and services.

An announcement notified him that his visitors had arrived, so he headed for the communal meeting room. It was off limits unless you had a visitor. There were probably about 200 people in the room. The inmates stood out, clad in khaki uniforms and each surrounded by two or three people in civilian clothes. Stephen spied his mom and stepdad, Jack, across the room, sitting near the entrance door and looking out of place. No other family members in the room were dressed quite as nicely as his mother or wearing as much jewelry. He wondered why she didn't dress down a little bit, but then decided she might not own anything ordinary or old.

They spotted him quickly and stood to wave. Stephen winced and wished they would be a little less conspicuous. Instead of heading directly over to them, he had to walk to the front and place his ID card with the CO who sat on the big podium overlooking the cavernous room.

His mother embraced him. Limited displays of affection were permitted. His mom was trying to put on an encouraging face. She appeared to be sober and edgy.

They settled into one of the molded plastic chairs which were all bolted together facing forward toward the watch CO.

"You're so skinny! Are you eating OK?" she asked.

Stephen told them that the sleeping and eating conditions were terrible. It was so loud in the crowded room that he had to repeat every answer twice, first to his left and then to his right, like a tennis match. He wanted to complain a little more about how tired and hungry he was, but his mom launched into news of things going on in her life. She was trying to be helpful, but it hurt him to think of life moving on without him.

At some point in the conversation his mother shared with him that she had called Kylee.

"You reached her? How did she sound?" Stephen was elated, assuming that his mother had called Kylee to encourage her, or possibly offer financial help.

"I asked her not to come today. We have to travel so much farther to see you and it would be so much less enjoyable with another visitor here competing for your time and attention. Especially since it's so impossibly loud in here."

Stephen felt a mixture of emotions. He was flattered his mother didn't want to share him with Kylee. But he was sorely disappointed that she cared so little for

Kylee. He didn't mention that Kylee had only visited one time and was now barely answering his calls.

After a short catch-up, Stephen looked longingly at the big stack of one-dollar bills in his mother's little clear plastic bag. One end of the room contained vending machines and Stephen could see that dozens of family members were queued up, buying junk food from the machines. Stephen's mother was oblivious, but Jack picked up on the situation.

"Savanah, go get the boy some food, or there won't be any left."

"Oh," she stood and started, then turned and said, "What can I bring you?"

"A hamburger, two Dr. Peppers, chips and a honeybun. And anything you want to eat, of course," Stephen added.

She scrunched up her nose, took the little plastic bag and marched over to the line. The inmates were not permitted near the vending machines or allowed to touch the money the visitors brought in. Stephen didn't know everything that was in the machines, but he had heard from others what the best items were. It was a big source of conversation after visitation day. The vending machine food was not good, but it was better than prison food, so everywhere around him inmates were gobbling it hungrily.

Stephen and Jack talked about college football until his mother came back with the nectar of the gods. He greedily enjoyed the Dr. Peppers, a treat not available anywhere in the prison, not even the commissary. There were no plates, so he had to eat the microwaved hamburger off a napkin. His mother had also brought him packets of mustard, ketchup, and mayonnaise. He put all three on the sandwich to make it more palatable. It was the best thing he'd eaten since the day before entering prison.

His mother had to jump up and run to the restroom several times, because her allergies were acting up and visitors were not allowed to bring in tissues. Visitors could bring nothing into the prison except their car keys, identification, and one-dollar bills in a clear plastic bag. Everything else had to be left behind in the car. For most visitors, leaving their cellphone behind was the hardest part. Visitors with infants could bring a larger, clear plastic bag containing diapers. Why anyone would bring an infant into this terrible place, Stephen could not fathom. But toddlers were running everywhere, so clearly, he was in the minority in his opinion.

When visiting hours were over, Stephen's mother and stepfather got up to leave. They walked together to the front of the room where the CO had kept all their identification cards. After receiving their driver's licenses and another quick round of hugs, they were gone.

Stephen turned to head back to his cell, when the CO called after him and ordered him to start cleaning up the now-empty room. Stephen looked around and saw how disgusting it was. Food, napkins, wrappers, and empty containers littered the floor. After picking up trash for a while, he tried to leave again, but was ordered to clean the ladies' restroom. He walked through the doorway and got quite a shock. Someone had left a used sanitary napkin on the floor next to the overflowing trash can. Dirty diapers lay nearby.

He asked the CO, "Can I have some rubber gloves? There's blood and body fluids in the trash that needs to be picked up in there."

"Shut up and do what you were asked to do," said CO Espinoza. "Or you will get a shot right now."

Stephen took a deep breath and headed back into the room. The paper towel dispenser was empty. Stephen used wads of toilet paper to pick up the disgusting refuse and squeezed it all into a large trash bag.

As he cleaned the filthy debris, he thought about Gracie, his mother's longtime housekeeper and felt a twinge of guilt.

Did I ever leave her anything this gross to pick up?

When he was allowed to leave the visiting room, he went straight to the communal restroom on his cell block and took a shower. He decided that he would not stay until visiting hours were over ever again, even if it was rude, not to mention heartbreaking, to ask his loved ones to leave.

CHAPTER 18

Stephen – Day 290

In the world outside of prison, *snail mail* has largely been replaced with e-mail or instant messaging. But in federal prison, where there is no access to the internet, mail is still a big deal. It is an inmate's lifeline to family and the outside world.

At Bastrop FCI, the mail came every weekday at around 4 p.m. A CO came down each cell block for mail call, and most prisoners waited anxiously for something to come in that magical mail bag.

Stephen received a surprising amount of mail, especially cards and letters from his dad and his dad's family. Even his dad's friend Ken and his wife sent cards and letters of encouragement, though they didn't know Stephen well. He had no idea why they felt compelled to write to him, but it was very encouraging to receive their letters. It was also a source of pride for him in front of other inmates.

Every letter arrived already opened. Stephen's mail was inspected and read by a prison employee prior to being delivered. And someone listened to every phone call. Stephen imagined that there was a bespectacled employee somewhere creating a spreadsheet of the people he communicated with and the topics of their conversations, cross referencing for clues as to further criminal behavior.

In addition to letters, the only items that inmates could receive through the mail were books and magazines. Prior to coming to prison, Stephen had never read a book cover to cover.

Stephen grew up surrounded by books, especially at his grandparents' house. Henry Mayfield had a small library including encyclopedias, classic literature, and modern works of fiction and nonfiction. Stephen never opened or desired to read a single novel in that library. But on this side of the razor wire, where time moved slowly and information was scarce, books suddenly became important.

One of the first books he had received from his grandmother was a leather-bound Bible. Like all the other books in the world, for Stephen the mysteries of the Bible remained unplumbed up to this point. When he was a boy, his father took him to church, where the pastor read from the Bible, but Stephen kept the little one his dad had given him pristine by not opening it or bending any of its pages. By the time he was a teenager, the church started putting song lyrics and Bible verses on a projection screen behind the pastor. Stephen assumed it was because so many people forgot to bring a Bible. As an adult, he had long since quit going to church, and the only Bible stories he could recall involved fish or fishing.

Cards from his dad and grandmother often included a scripture reference at the bottom of the letter or card. One of the references he noted quite often was Jeremiah 29:11. He was curious what that scripture said, but not curious enough to open the Bible and find out. One day though, he came back from a jog around the track to find his Bible lying open on his bunk, open to the page which contained that verse.

Stephen was very surprised to see it laying there. He generally did not leave anything on his bed but locked everything in his locker. The cell doors were unlocked during the day and any inmate could sneak in and steal something. Even the most mundane item could be a target for theft, a possible item of barter.

At first, he was angry because either Kip or Crawley had obviously touched his book. But when he noticed it was open to the verse he had seen on so many cards; he scanned his finger down the page and read it. "'I know the plans I have for you,' says the Lord. 'Plans to prosper you and not to harm you. Plans to give you hope and a future.'"[5]

He thought about it, and then questioned why anyone would choose that verse. It seemed like a naïve sentiment to send to someone in prison. If they had

---

5   Jeremiah 29:11 (NIV)

ever been here, they would know prison was a hope-stealing place, and his future was a distant dream.

Stephen decided that he would trade the Bible to another inmate in exchange for something more useful. Until he could learn what it might be worth in a barter, he stuffed it in the bottom of the locker. Later, he called out Kip and Crawley for touching his stuff, but they both denied having touched the Bible, so he had to let it go.

The following day, Stephen's father visited. To Stephen's surprise, his dad's visits were very encouraging, even though Stephen knew that his dad was devastated by this state of affairs. They discussed fishing, football and ideas for a cool restaurant concept Stephen might start when he got out. During their visit, Stephen brought up the idea that he would like to sign up for college correspondence courses. His dad would have to do much of the registration paperwork, and, of course, someone needed to pay for it. His dad seemed to support the idea, but Stephen could tell he was also a little skeptical. Stephen remembered his previous starts and stops in the education arena and understood that skepticism was warranted.

CHAPTER 19

Skip – Day 375

Skip eased into the hotel pool slowly to adjust to the temperature. The air was hot and muggy, but the pool was colder than he expected. A pleasant ocean breeze filled the air around him with some of his favorite aromas: a scent cocktail of hamburgers on the poolside grill, mixed with suntan oil. Calypso music drifting from speakers hidden in a nearby palm tree added to the relaxing atmosphere. His ballcap, flip-flops, folded towel and e-reader lay on a chaise lounge a few feet away.

He was attending the annual conference of his professional CPA society. This year he would introduce some of the speakers and serve as a conference committee member. Skip knew many of the other attendees and committee members well. Today, as so often happened, polite acquaintances had asked, "So, how's your son? Does he live in Austin?"

It was always so hard to know what to say. And it was harder not to be jealous of their kid stories. Jason's daughter was an international business student at UT. John's was a recent graduate of nursing school. Susan's twins were high school seniors, looking to pick a college where they could continue competitive horseback riding and jumping. Never once had he ever heard anyone say, "My son's serving a sentence in federal prison."

Skip was not one to lie. But he found himself saying things like, "Well, Stephen's going through a bit of a rough patch right now. He's not quite where I want him to be, but I know God's got a plan for him."

Skip's muscles loosened as he did some long, lazy breast strokes. He was a strong swimmer. Memories of teaching Stephen to swim came flooding back. Stephen was a natural, and fearless in the water. By the time he was in kindergarten, Stephen was a skilled swimmer. He could even paddle on a surfboard and stay balanced on a wave. His son's surfing ability had prompted Skip to get a surfboard, too. He didn't take to it quite as easily as Stephen had, but it created some father-son bonding opportunities for a few short years. By the time Stephen was twelve, he was spending hours at the beach, unsupervised. Skip never worried about him.

Skip felt deep sadness sink into his consciousness. It felt like lead in his chest. He could keep it at bay most of the day, but when he allowed his mind to wander, the black ache would sometimes catch him up short, like a boat reaching the end of its anchor line. He missed Stephen. Not the alcohol-addicted, adult Stephen who lied about who he was and what he did. He missed the boy, the golden-haired Stephen who had freckles all over his tan shoulders and loved to swim.

It broke Skip's heart that Stephen would not get to swim for a very long time. It also broke his heart that Stephen would never go hunting with him again. As a convicted felon, Stephen could never again own or handle a gun. Never.

Skip swam more laps to shake off the sadness, and then lay in the sun for a while. He loved the sun. And the sound of the ocean comforted him. Through his sunglasses, he squinted up through the palm fronds which seemed to pay homage to the Creator. Now alone at the pool, he quoted Psalm 19.

"Lord, the Heavens declare your glory, and the sky above proclaims your handiwork."

Skip liked to talk to God by repeating God's own words back to Him.

He closed his eyes but could still see the shadow of palm fronds waving over his head. The mesmerizing sound of the ocean and the breeze through the trees made him feel drowsy. Soon, it was time to go. He forced his eyes open, located his Teva flip-flops and made his way back to his room.

He had a few minutes before anyone was expecting him, so he sat down in the comfortable chair in the corner of the room and got out his Bible. He grabbed a legal pad from his briefcase, took his favorite pen and started journaling.

What can I do to honor God while I'm waiting?

The tears had not come for a long time. But now, at this inconvenient moment, they did. Skip put his head in his hands and wept.

"God, I wanted to be a good dad. I thought I was raising my son in a way that honored you. What did I do wrong? I took him to church. I worked hard. Why is this happening to me? Where are you in this?"

He allowed himself to give in to some anger. His voice rose an octave as he talked to the ceiling. "If my son had an illness, I'd be surrounded by love and encouragement. But my son is in prison and so I have to go through this alone. Your word says that 'All things work together for good.' How can this mess possibly be used for anything good?"

When he could focus again, he read the Bible for a while to the sound of the ocean, coming in through the sliding glass door that opened onto the balcony. Whenever he was really hurting, Skip read the Psalms. It was such a beautiful book of poetry, written by King David, one of the best and most faithful kings of Israel. King David endured serious injustice, and even had a wayward son. His pain often poured into his poetry. Yet, most of the King's poems ended with praise to God for His goodness, mercy, and love. Skip highlighted some parts of Psalm 112 that he liked. He tried to read them like a promise.

"How blessed are those who revere the Eternal, who turn from evil and take great pleasure in His commandments. Their children will be a powerful force upon the earth… When life is dark, a light will shine for those who live rightly, those who are merciful, compassionate, and strive for justice. Good comes to all who are gracious and share freely… They will not be afraid when the news is bad, because they have resolved to trust in the Eternal."[6]

After highlighting the verses, Skip wrote them out on his tablet. He said out loud, "God, I believe that somehow you will bring light in this darkness. I believe

---

6   Psalm 112, (The Voice)

that Stephen will become all that You destined him to be. And I trust you with this circumstance. Teach me what you want me to learn from it. I am in great pain over it, and I don't think you allow pain without a good purpose."

As he headed out to join his friends, he hoped that the conversation tonight wouldn't turn to talk of children. He didn't like to lie, and the truth was very ugly.

CHAPTER 20

Stephen – Day 440

Stephen was looking for Hussain, "The Marketing Muslim." Hussain ordinarily set up a little store outside of his cell, selling his wares. Somehow, Hussain obtained things that people needed and then made up little jingles to entice inmates over to hear his sales pitches.

The entrepreneurial inmate earned his nickname by somehow being in the right place at the right time to barter almost anything. Technically, he was not supposed to have so many personal items in his possession outside of his cell and, technically, the inmates were not allowed to trade or sell *anything*. But the CO left his office to walk the unit infrequently and no one was complaining, so the marketing continued. When Stephen found Hussain, he was carrying on an intense negotiation with another inmate. A few others appeared to be waiting for their turn. Stephen also waited, listening to who needed what. When it was his turn, Stephen looked at Hussain's pile.

"Hussain, I need shower shoes. Not for me. For a new guy."

"I can get you some."

"His name is Gavin. Ross has asked me to show him around. He seems like a real nice kid. Very young."

"Watch the store. I think I know where I can get some right now." Hussain took off down the hall.

Stephen waited impatiently. A few inmates walked by slowly, and Stephen waved and joked with them, trying to set their minds at ease. Hussain owned this little piece of real estate and Stephen didn't want anyone to think he was infringing on Hussain's territory. He also didn't want the CO to walk by at this moment and give him a shot for being caught with all these items.

Miraculously, Hussain returned with shower shoes within a relatively short period of time.

"How much?"

"For you, only twenty stamps. I know you do this thing for good purpose."

"It'll come back to you, Hussain."

"Yes. I believe it will."

"I think more good will come to you if you give them to me for fifteen stamps."

They bargained for a while, and eventually Stephen handed Hussein seventeen postage stamps in exchange for the shoes.

Earlier that day, Ross had approached Stephen at breakfast and introduced him to Gavin. Stephen was impressed with Gavin right away. The young, black man had been a star football player at a top-tier school and had an amazing physique. He was only twenty-one years old.

Stephen knew from experience that on your first day in prison, the BOP provides you only with a toothbrush, a packet of baking soda and a tiny bar of soap. So, when an inmate first arrives, he has no toiletries—no shaving cream, shampoo, or laundry detergent.

Gang members take care of their own, providing them with basic toiletries from their own stores. Inmates with no gang affiliations must fend for themselves, and it could be three weeks before an inmate is permitted to go to the commissary. That is why Ross, spokesperson for the independent inmates, wanted Stephen to help Gavin. Stephen thought the best way to start was to acquire shower shoes. No one wanted to step into the communal showers barefoot.

After acquiring the shoes from Hussain, Stephen proudly took the shoes down to Gavin's cell. The door was cracked. Stephen knocked politely. He could make out the large, young man lying in the top bunk. Gavin didn't get up. Instead he told Stephen to leave the shoes by his locker. He sounded choked up and his eyes looked like he had been crying, Stephen noticed with some surprise. It didn't match the young man's strapping, beefcake exterior.

"Now that we have had the count, we are allowed in the exercise yard. Would you like to join me?"

"No." Gavin shook his head and turned his face to the wall.

"Well don't leave the shower shoes outside of your locker. And get a lock as quickly as you can. They are a hot commodity, and someone will steal them."

Gavin was not talking, so Stephen headed out to the exercise yard, a little frustrated.

He didn't even thank me. Those shower shoes just cost me a fortune. He certainly has a lot to learn.

Stephen spied Dion walking by himself, which was unusual, and caught up with him.

The inmates associated with the Aryan Brotherhood frowned upon mixed race conversation but, they didn't seem to have much of a presence in the exercise yard at the moment. To avoid making trouble for himself, Stephen looked straight ahead and didn't smile, so it would not appear that he and Dion were friendly.

"Have you met the new guy, Gavin?" Stephen asked.

"Yes. I met him last night."

"Ross asked me to show him around, but Gavin acted like he couldn't stand the sight of me right now when I brought him some shower shoes. I look pretty non-threatening, right? Why didn't he speak to me?"

"I think I know what Ross was trying to do. But it appears like Gavin's going to have to find his own way."

"What do you mean?"

"Big Mike already found out that our boy Gavin had an upbringing like yours. Silver spoon and all that. So, Big Mike knows he's gonna have some real adjustment problems. He already promised Gavin protection and a group to belong with, if you know what I mean?"

"Well, I wish I'd known that before I spent seventeen stamps on him."

They walked in silence for a lap.

"Dion?"

"Yeah?"

"What did you mean Gavin's upbringing was similar to my own? How do you know anything about my background?"

"People talk."

"What is it they say?"

"That you grew up in a nice family. Big houses, nice cars, educated. All that." They were working up a decent sweat now, walking at a brisk pace. Dion was much smaller, but he was fast.

"I don't believe I've talked about that to anyone. Who could possibly know where I grew up?"

"Some of the guys in Happy's gang grew up right down the road from you. They saw your dad dropping you off at school in his nice truck. The type of clothes you wore. The type of girls who liked you. People see stuff."

Stephen recalled now that some of those guys had looked familiar. He guessed there wasn't much he could do about their talk. But it bothered him. He had worked hard at blending in. "So, what's Gavin's story?"

"His mom's some sort of medical professional. Psychiatrist maybe? And his dad is a successful business guy. Gavin was a good athlete, and a good student. Got caught with a couple of gallon-size Ziploc bags full of marijuana he had scored for a big party. 'Nuff for the whole football team. He got five years."

"A real shame."

"Yep, a real shame."

They looked at each other and chuckled at how it was easy to see when someone else was throwing their life away.

"I've been working on a little guidebook to help inmates like Gavin, someone who might not have a clue what to do when they get here. I'd really like to get some of my stamps back. Think you can help me sell it to him? He needs it."

"He might not listen; he seems to be under Big Mike's spell already. But I don't mind mentioning it to him. How much you want for your sage wisdom?"

"It's worth at least ten stamps, but I'll sell it to him for eight."

Dion laughed. It was a very gentle, honest sound. Stephen liked it.

"Forget the stamps. I'll give him the guidebook if he wants it. You gave me a blanket when I first got here.

"Nice of you to remember." Dion laughed again.

"But he has to buy me a new notebook on commissary day."

"Fair enough."

Stephen started to say something else, but Dion had placed a hand on Stephen's forearm, as if to interrupt him. "Listen, I never told you this," he said. "Don't trust Big Mike. Seriously, don't trust him. He communicates with Happy somehow up the chain, and I think Happy still has plans for you."

"What is 'up the chain' and what kind of plans?"

"You know. *Up the chain.* We're in medium and Happy's in max now. Listen to me. Look over your shoulder and listen to your gut. Don't make alliances with anyone you don't know."

"How could Big Mike and Happy possibly communicate? What vendetta does Happy have against me?"

Stephen wanted to know more, but Dion was walking swiftly back into the building. Stephen saw Dion glance quickly over each shoulder, checking his surroundings, something Stephen had apparently neglected.

CHAPTER 21

Stephen – Day 480

Gavin was the perfect candidate for his guidebook. Stephen felt he had been rather worldly before he was incarcerated, and he was still shocked by a lot of what went on inside the fence. Surely, others would find a first-hand account helpful. He started carrying his notebook with him at mealtimes and writing in it after he finished eating. Until recently there had been a little wooden shelf in each cell that, if he sat on his locker, he could use as a desk. But an inmate in another part of the compound had ripped his shelf off the wall and assaulted his cellmate with it. So, as usual, they took it away from everyone.

There wasn't enough room to sit up between the bunkbeds, only enough room the lay down. So, Stephen lay on his side propped on an elbow, writing. He jotted down another prison fact that people like Gavin might not know.

Prison has its' own economy. The entire prison is operated, for the most part, by inmates. Every inmate works. Serving food in the cafeteria, washing dishes, mowing grass, sweeping sidewalks, cleaning toilets, all these tasks are assigned to inmates, who are compensated at approximately $5 per month by the Federal Bureau of Prisons. It does not matter if you are the CEO of Enron or the lowest member of a drug gang, you will work. Unfortunately, $5 does not go very far at the prison commissary where everything costs twice as much as it does in the outside world.

Trying to write in the bunk was very uncomfortable, but he liked to keep the notebook handy and jot things down as he experienced them. He jumped down and headed for the chow hall, taking the notebook with him. He now enjoyed margarine and jelly on his breakfast biscuit, a treat not every prisoner received. His fortunes in the chow hall had greatly improved after Stephen had asked his grandmother for a monthly stipend on his prison account. Now, he could buy stamps to pay the required bribe to the prisoners who served the food.

He had learned the drill one day as he walked down the tray line at dinner. He watched as the two inmates ahead of him were served four chicken strips with their tray. When his turn arrived, he was served only two. He followed them and struck up a conversation. That was when he discovered that a ten-dollar monthly bribe paid to one of the inmates assigned to work in the kitchen would purchase a full serving of whatever unappetizing item passed for food each day. So, at least now he was in less danger of starving. He had lost about thirty pounds, which he didn't really mind, except it was not easy to get issued new pants.

He looked up and surveyed the room, brushing his fingertips over his lips. What were some other things that a new inmate would not yet know? As he considered what he'd learned thus far, Stephen flipped to the next page in his notebook and wrote:

The small amount you are paid cannot sustain you. If you want to be able to buy phone minutes to call your family, your family will have to put money on your account, or you can develop a hustle. This is when you barter services or prison currency from other inmates. Prices of various services which can be purchased in Federal Prison from another inmate:

shoeshine – 15 stamps

haircut – 20 stamps

tattoo – 20 books of stamps

laundry – 2 books of stamps/month

Stephen left some harder-to-describe examples off the list of ways that inmates made *money*, but he had to give them credit for their ingenuity. One inmate regularly purchased a large bag of lollipops at the commissary and resold them in smaller quantities by hawking them in *Fancy Fo-Packs* or *Sassy Six-Packs*. He drew attention to his wares with a freestyle dance. It was very popular.

Stephen hated depending on his parents for commissary money, but he had not yet come up with a hustle. There were plenty of unmet needs, but it took real ingenuity to meet them. For example, the commissary sold popular items like ramen noodles and instant coffee, both of which required hot water to prepare. Unfortunately, there was no hot water. So, some enterprising inmate had created the *stinger*. Those sold at a premium and could also be rented for a cooking project. Stephen added to his handbook:

> **Food Prep with a Stinger:** A stinger is a small handmade electrical device made from a stolen electrical cord which uses a dead short to boil water quickly if placed in a plastic container. It is a highly-sought-after contraband item in prison for preparing food from the commissary because inmates in a federal prison classified as low security or above do not have access to any way to heat up food. It's important to use a *plastic* vessel, such as a trash can, when using a stinger, and not material that conducts electricity. Also, be very careful not to touch the liquid or food to test it for temperature while the stinger is plugged in, as you could be electrocuted. You will forget how to cook in a conventional way while you're in prison. But you will be hungry, and you will find yourself eating things you never thought you would ever eat. The stinger is considered contraband. Don't get caught with it. You will get a shot and possibly go to the hole.

There was one big problem with Stephen's idea to sell his *How to Survive* guidebook. The brand-new inmates—the ones who might want to read the document—needed it immediately upon arrival but could not access any money. Even if their families put money on their account, the BOP wouldn't let them have access to it or go to the commissary to buy stamps for several weeks. Stephen had sold one to a guy who had promised to pay him back but thus far had failed to do so.

As he considered his options, he thought again about how tattoos were a popular hustle for those inmates with artistic talent, like Sean. Stephen wasn't artistic. Even if he was, he would avoid an enterprise that involved exposure to blood because quite a few inmates had hepatitis. Stephen had, however, recently taken special notice that many inmates got religious tattoos even though they swore like sailors and stole ink cartridges. If religious images and references were popular, Stephen certainly knew where to get more information on that subject, his dad. Perhaps he could create some type of hustle of his own by advising Sean on tattoo-worthy sayings? He wrote to his dad and his grandmother for help.

> Dear Dad,
> Please send books. I can have five in my possession at a time. I found a newspaper with some book reviews, and I think I would like to read *The Purpose Driven Life* by Rick Warren, and perhaps something by Max Lucado (someone else told me those were good). I seriously need some books to read quickly, if possible. I know this request will surprise you because I was never much of a reader before. I feel like my brain is turning to mush already. There is some type of process for requesting books from the Austin public library (not sure why Bastrop Library does not offer), but I understand that the process is very slow. Magazines about fishing would also be appreciated. Thanks for visiting last week. It really means a lot.
> Stephen

As he passed by a television room and observed an inmate saving seats for some friends. That prompted yet another pause to write down an observation. New inmates should know that watching television in prison wasn't just a mindless activity; it had more significance. He wrote in his future guidebook:

> There are several television rooms in a federal medium prison. Like the cafeteria, they are segregated by race and for the most part you will be wise to stay in your designated room, unless and until you earn some special dispensation from the inmates who operate the other rooms. In the White television room, they primarily air news programs, talk shows, and NASCAR. In the Hispanic

television room, they watch a lot of *novellas*—melodramatic soap operas—and a lot of baseball. In the Black television room, inmates are watching NBA basketball and reality TV programs. By making friends and doing favors, you can arrange a system of saving seats for certain shows. If one prisoner sits in another prisoner's saved seat, or the space where he likes to place his folding chair, he can and will be expected to move when the owner arrives. And *everyone* gambles. If you like to gamble, you will have the opportunity to bet on everything from the NBA finals to American Idol.

He started to walk away. Then, remembered to add:

It is so loud in prison that it is almost impossible to hear the television. So, inmates who want to watch television must pay about $40 for a basic AM/FM radio (bet you haven't used one of those in a while). The radio can be used to listen to whatever local radio stations might be near enough to the prison to catch a signal, and the radio serves as the all-important audio device for the television. It's one of the few personal items you are permitted to carry around with you. Inmates tune into a dial number and hear the audio of the program on the television through headphones. So, a radio is an important commodity that you will need.

He looked down at his messy handwriting and realized that he was going to need to buy a new notebook and recopy his material in more orderly fashion if he was going to sell it to someone. He didn't have any money on his account right now to buy a new notebook; he'd spent it all on food. Contemplating the process involved in buying a new notebook made him realize he's left out another important topic. He flipped to the Table of Contents page and added at the bottom "How to get money on your account – page 20." Then he flipped back to the next free page and wrote:

There are two ways for your loved ones to put money on your account so that you can make phone calls and buy toiletries and food from the commissary. They can:

1) wire funds using Western Union, or

2) mail a money order to BOP post office box in Iowa.

Obviously, Western Union will get on your account faster, but it will cost the sender more.

Stephen had to stop writing because it was time for the CO to come by for count. He trotted quickly back to his cell where he found his grumpy cellies, who appeared to have slept through breakfast. They seemed to be dealing with incarceration by going into suspended animation, as if they were on a journey through space instead of dealing with life behind bars.

"Hey, guys, get up," he said. "It's time to show yourself present."

CHAPTER 22

Stephen – Day 521

They were running. Dutch was running ahead of him. At first, they were playing Frisbee in the park. Many smiling people stopped and admired the beautiful, chocolate-colored lab. But something shifted. The playful running turned into panicked flight. Dutch was leading him away from danger. They were being followed, but Stephen was losing ground. He could hear footsteps getting closer and see Dutch getting farther away. Dutch turned and looked at him with a sad, almost human, look in his eyes.

Stephen's eyes jerked open, and he remembered where he was.

He wiped the cold sweat from his brow and let out a long shaky breath. He hoped he hadn't disturbed his cellies' sleep. He listened for their snoring and didn't hear anything, which wasn't a good sign. Kip could be quite cranky if he didn't sleep well. Stephen knew this from experience because he had woken Kip several times when having a nightmare, and Kip would sulk the better part of the next day.

A wave of sadness swept over Stephen as he thought about Dutch. Dutch was a good dog. Dogs don't care if you're a bad human being. They only care if you love them. If you do, they will love you unconditionally. Stephen had loved Dutch very much. That dog went everywhere with him. Even if he got up from the couch to go to the kitchen for a beer, Dutch followed. Dutch never complained, never judged, never told him to get a real job. Dutch was loyal.

Stephen had tried to find a good home for his dog when he received his prison sentence. He and Kylee had had a huge fight about the dog. She said that Dutch would never answer to or take commands from anyone but Stephen, and she refused to take him and care for him. Stephen had thought this a shockingly cruel thing to do to a guy heading off to prison. But, in hindsight, she had been right.

Stephen tried leaving Dutch with some good friends, but the dog's separation anxiety caused him to damage property and other animals. Dutch seemed to sense that he and Stephen would never see each other again, and he grew more and more anxious and out of control. Dutch was one of many precious things Stephen lost by crossing that invisible line with those marijuana plants.

Two weeks before he had to surrender, Stephen found himself sitting in front of the veterinarian's office with his best buddy's head in his lap. The veterinarian had been very kind, and obviously had seen a grown man cry over a dog before. He allowed Stephen to stay in the room whispering to Dutch as first a sedative and then a euthanasia drug dripped into the big, handsome dog's vein. Stephen received a heavy wooden box in the mail a week later containing Dutch's ashes. It hurt him still.

The dream had been dark and disturbing. As he lay there, his heart still racing, Stephen recalled how much fear had been associated with transporting marijuana. At the time, he had tried to convince himself that the fear was an adrenaline rush, like riding a roller coaster. He also told himself that it helped him stay keen and alert. Some element of that was true.

Once, he had a colleague in a car ahead of him who was going through the border checkpoint to look for the presence of the drug dogs. The front man phoned and tipped him off that the dogs were on duty. Stephen turned the truck around and headed back toward a predetermined location to wait until the next day. A sheriff's deputy vehicle appeared out of nowhere and pulled up behind him. That moment had been so terrifying he had had to remind himself to breathe. He'd gotten so light-headed that he'd pulled into a gas station parking lot, and when he did, the sheriff drove on by. Perhaps his panic attack and inability to keep driving had made the turn-around look less suspicious.

Lying in the darkness, Stephen wondered if he would ever be free of the deep-seated fear that his past, or people from his past, would always follow him. That fear lived inside of him like a parasite, a nagging, painful thorn in his flesh that never quite went away, even when the danger was not close.

In the dream, Dutch was always running just ahead of him, pointing him to safety. Even though it was just a dream, Stephen wondered what or who would point him to safety now? In his quiet cell, he put his hands under his head, staring at the ceiling. The room was so small he could easily touch walls at both ends of the bed with his feet and his hands. From his top bunk, he could stretch out his arm and touch the ceiling as well. A faint sliver of light shone through the four-by-twelve-inch window in the locked, metal door. Stephen could hear the two men snoring below him. Apparently, he had not disturbed their sleep. Or if he had, the disturbance was short lived.

His dad had always found so much comfort and solace in his faith. Stephen wondered why he had never really developed a spirituality of his own. In the dark, his mind replayed the times that his mother had called his dad a Bible-thumper. He had heard his granddad, Henry Mayfield, call some Christians hypocrites. Stephen thought that the faithful people in his family seemed nicer and less selfish than most of the others. But the God-rejecters in his circle seemed smarter, edgier, and much more fun. For a moment, he tried to picture God. Stephen imagined a Zeus-like character on a big throne throwing down thunderbolts at Earth, punishing people for misdeeds.

Stephen was sure he was being punished, possibly by God or possibly by fate. Maybe karma. If only he could still talk to Kylee. She understood him. What was she doing now? He shuddered to think about that and tried to push out the thoughts that crowded into his mind.

He put his hands behind his head and felt the little notebook under his pillow. He groped around and found the pen he'd hid there also. He rolled onto his side, centered a page in the slender beam of light from the tiny window, and wrote:

> You will lose more than your freedom and dignity when you become incarcerated. You will lose the ability to talk to and touch the people you love. I miss my wife. I miss my dog. I miss my grandmothers, who will likely die while I'm in here. I wish I had invested a little bit more in the people that loved me while I had the chance. Instead of only taking from them, I wish I had left a

little bit more of myself with them, stored up a few more positive memories before I deserted them.

Stephen heard footsteps outside in the hallway and shoved the little notebook back under the pillow because he was not permitted to have it in bed. Moments later a flashlight shined in his face, as it would every night for the next 2,540 nights.

CHAPTER 23

Stephen – Day 615

Stephen headed out to the track to walk. A terrible drought was plaguing the entire state and the heat was oppressive. A lavender haze hung in the air, caused by smoke and ash from dozens of wildfires. Stephen wondered what on earth they would do to evacuate a federal prison if the fire drew too close? They were trapped behind tall fences topped with razor wire. Could the few federal employees who worked here get 1,300 men transported out of the prison in an emergency? Or would they drive off and let them burn? No one would probably blame them if they did.

He was looking at the ground in front of him but glanced up from his troubled thoughts and noticed a clean-cut, tall inmate on the track. Stephen noticed hygiene. Because of the mandatory sentencing guidelines, many if not most of the prisoners in Bastrop FCI Medium were serving fifteen to twenty years. Perhaps they had kept themselves groomed at first, but after a few years many lost interest in their appearance. Compounding the situation, any poor habits an individual had prior to incarceration were exacerbated by the poor nutrition of the prison diet and the scant availability of dental care. Many inmates had teeth missing. Others had scraggly, long hair. The BOP didn't provide haircuts. Like everything else, prisoners who wanted haircuts had to earn enough money from their prison assignment, their hustle, or by begging family members and friends for money.

Stephen was determined not to go to seed. He found an inmate skilled at cutting hair. He used stamps purchased with money from his family to pay Joe Rodriguez for haircuts, and he also paid Joe to iron his prison uniform too, sometimes even when he didn't expect visitors.

The other inmate on the track looked like he was working hard at taking care of himself. Out on the track, they were permitted to wear a white T-shirt and gym shorts purchased at the prison commissary. This was much more comfortable than the prison uniform. Stephen wore his workout clothes, paired with too-tight athletic shoes. The prison commissary had not yet thought it necessary to offer shoes in size thirteen. He had written several requests to the prison administration, but so far without result.

He caught up to the other man and introduced himself.

"Nice to get outside," said Stephen. "Even though it's hot out here, it's still cooler outside than it is inside."

"Hey. I'm Paul," said the other man in a strong, pleasant voice. "I'm trying to get in a walk early, so that I can spend the afternoon watching college football playoffs."

Stephen's hopes began to rise. He rubbed his hands together. "My team is out, but we made it to the national championship last year and I'll have to live on memories for another year."

"I'm still riding high from when they won the Rose Bowl," Paul's voice became more animated. It turned out that Paul had attended the University of Texas. Upon learning that, Stephen's opinion of Paul went up even more, and so did his insecurity level. He had never attended college.

Paul was moderate in his political leaning, which was also extremely unusual in the prison community. Of course, politics didn't matter much. As convicted felons, they had lost the right to vote. Stephen walked much farther than he was used to, but he didn't want the intellectually stimulating discourse to end. The opportunity to talk to someone who had informed, reasoned opinions about things energized him.

"Talking to you reminds me of what it was like to talk with my granddad, Henry," said Stephen. "I'm glad he died before I was arrested."

Henry Mayfield had died still believing that Stephen was working at a cell-phone store.

Stephen was embarrassed at having just shared this private thought with a stranger. After all, a lot of posturing and bravado went on in prison, to establish pecking orders and privileges. Being vulnerable wasn't consistent with building a tough image.

Paul softened the awkward moment. "I know what you mean. I'm glad my mother died before I was arrested. Seeing me in this place would have broken her heart. She died when I was a teenager."

Paul was incarcerated for the same crime that had landed Stephen in prison: conspiracy to sell marijuana. He received a sentence of twenty-two years even though, like Stephen, it was his first offense. Also, like Stephen, Paul had left behind a young wife and child. Stephen was surprised and encouraged to hear that Paul's wife had been standing by him for five years. Paul was housed in the Bowie Unit, a separate building, which explained why Stephen had not seen him before. The buildings were something like dorms that shared a common cafeteria, commissary, and visitation room.

Over the next few weeks, Stephen walked at the same time every day, hoping he might run into Paul. Paul stayed current with the national news, giving them a generous supply of discussion topics.

One morning, Stephen woke a little earlier than usual when he heard Crawley say, "Hey man, I'm sorry, but I'm sick. You guys need to exit." Thankfully, it was 6:05 in the morning and the door to their cell was now unlocked. Stephen and Kip threw on their clothes and bailed out of the room. Stephen headed down to the cafeteria and was surprised to see Paul sitting on one of the benches with his food in front of him and his head bowed slightly.

Not quite ready to face the tray line, he slid in next to Paul. Paul finished his quiet prayer and looked toward Stephen, who smiled and said, "You prayin' that that food won't kill you?!"

"Yep, it's workin' so far. Want me to put in a good word for you, heathen?"

"Sure, I need all the help I can get," laughed Stephen.

Stephen noticed a newspaper in front of Paul from Galveston, Texas. "No way! You're from Galveston? Do you like to fish?" he asked.

"*Love* to fish."

"Gulf or bay?

"Bay. For redfish, trout, and drum. You?

"Well, my favorite daytime activity used to be surfing. I was pretty good. I had a sponsor. Won some divisions. But I do like to fish. Used to go with my dad. He's a lifelong angler."

Manny Escobar, whom Stephen had met his first day in prison, walked in for breakfast.

Stephen had helped to broker a deal between the Aryan Brotherhood and Manny's gang that involved staying out of each other's territory at various times of the day. The agreement had eased some tensions and enabled Stephen to practice his Spanish with Manny.

Simultaneously, Stephen and Paul greeted Manny in Spanish.

They exchanged shocked looks.

"How do you speak Spanish so well? You look even whiter than me," said Stephen.

"I'm actually Hispanic, you dork. My full name is Paul Gonzales."

"Hm. So, explain the red hair and freckles."

"My grandmother was Irish."

They continued sharing stories about fishing, growing up in a small town, and argued about what made the best marinade for grilling seafood. Paul told him a story with great flourish and hand motions, about hooking a big stingray while fishing in the Laguna Madre.

It was the first time Stephen had laughed a real laugh since the day he arrived.

For a fleeting moment, he forgot where he was.

CHAPTER 24

Stephen – Day 639

Finally, it arrived. A smooth, heavy packet with Ohio University on the return address. Ohio University offered a curriculum designed especially for incarcerated individuals. The semester could start whenever the student was ready and could last longer than a regular college semester if the student needed additional time. Stephen's dad, his Gram and his uncle Sam split the cost of the tuition. Finally, he could use all this wasted time more constructively. After only twenty-one months behind bars, Stephen was weary of being confined. Every morning when he opened his eyes he felt the bitterness and regret seep in. He hoped taking college courses would provide a distraction from the pain.

The thick envelope felt substantial and looked official. Inside were letters from his English and math instructors, course syllabi, and his first assignments. The math assignment looked doable. It contained lots of illustrations and simple business math situations. The English assignment looked rudimentary as well. His instructions were to write several short essays. These brief essays, it explained would assist the instructor in getting to know him better and in evaluating his current skill level.

After dinner, Stephen headed to the library, instructions in hand. The library was a classroom-size room with a few hundred books, many of them quite old.

There were no helpful employees, no computers, and very few tables or chairs. It seemed that almost everything owned by the federal prison system was old and broken and not likely to ever be repaired.

He realized that in his excitement he had forgotten to bring paper and a pen. He wouldn't be allowed to change locations for another hour so he approached the inmate in charge of the library and asked if he could borrow a blank piece of paper. The other inmate lent him a pen and gave him a sheet of paper in exchange for one stamp but told him to return the pen before he left the library.

The first question of the English assignment asked him to describe his favorite holiday and state what traditions and activities made the holiday special. He thought about Christmas. His first Christmas in prison had been so hard. There were no decorations, no presents, no special food. It was just another dreary day.

But he had some fond memories of Christmas as a child. Because his parents were divorced, he experienced two different holidays in one. On Christmas Eve, he and his dad would go to a candlelight church service, then on Christmas morning they would exchange small gifts and have a big homemade breakfast. Later that day he would head over to his mother's where her side of the family would be enjoying luxurious foods, like duck, oyster dressing, and shrimp cocktail. Cigars and brandy would come out during the much-anticipated football games on TV.

While Stephen was with his mother, his dad would go visit Gram and Papa Taylor, where they would be eating honey-glazed ham and Gram's delicious homemade buttermilk pie. When he was younger, Stephen usually stopped by there after the football games to get some of that pie. But as he got older he had to skip the visit to Gram and Papa's, because he would be drunk by the early afternoon. He left that part out of his essay.

The next question instructed him to discuss an article or short story that he had read which contained a conflict and describe the primary conflict between the characters and how it was resolved. He still hadn't read many books. He thought about various magazine articles that he had read on sports and men's fitness; they didn't seem very relevant. Then he had an idea. Why not use a story from the Bible as fodder for this answer? The Bible was a book, after all, and it seemed like a way to potentially score points with the professor to outline something deep and profound from the Bible, as opposed to an article from Sports Illustrated. Stephen was not very familiar with the stories in the Bible, but he knew someone who was.

When permitted, Stephen stepped out of the library to call his dad for help with the answer. He stood in line to use the payphone and when it was his turn, he entered the information of his prison account so his account could be charged for the call. After what always seemed like forever, Skip's voice finally came on the line.

"Hey, big guy!"

"Hi, Dad, what's up?"

"I just got in from a business trip to Nebraska. The weather was so bad, my flight was cancelled. So, I had to rent a car and drive to Denver to get a flight home. I'm sure I made those Midwesterners crazy on the highway, because I was driving like an old man. I don't know how to drive in snow and ice. I'm from Texas!"

"Hey, listen, Dad," Stephen interrupted, "I only put a few minutes on the phone, so I can't talk long. I got my first assignment from Ohio University.

"Awesome!"

"Yeah, I'm excited about it. And I'm working on an English project. Can you think of a Bible story that involves conflict?"

"The whole Bible is the story of conflict, son. The conflict between good and evil, remember?"

"I just need one specific story. Hurry, I'm almost out of minutes."

"Well, since I have to give it to you in a split second, I will go with the story of Jacob somewhere around Genesis 28. It was in my Bible study this morning. Quite a bit of conflict in Jacob's story. He has a conflict with his brother and his father-in-law. And some with his two wives."

"This guy you want me to read about had two wives? That sounds like a recipe for conflict."

Skip obviously wanted to say more about the story, but the recorded mechanical voice informed them both that there was only one minute left on the call, so Stephen just said his thank yous and goodbyes.

Stephen had to pack up his things and return the pen for a few minutes to go get the Bible from his locker. It wasn't smart to leave anything lying around even for five minutes. Anything not tied down was likely to get stolen. He didn't want to forget the scripture references, so he wrote *Jacob-Genesis 28…* on his hand.

Stephen rummaged around in his locker and found the Bible. To his surprise, he enjoyed the story. It wasn't too long, and it was full of interesting twists and turns. After reading it, Stephen put down the pen and stared at the bookshelves for minutes. He thought about the line in the story that said that the seven years Jacob worked for Laban in order to marry Laban's daughter, Rachel, had seemed like only a few days because Jacob loved her so much. Then, when Laban double-crossed him and substituted Rachel's sister Leah, Jacob had worked another seven years to accomplish his goal of marrying this woman.

Stephen couldn't begin to imagine what it might be like to wait for something for fourteen years. He was pretty sure he had never waited for anything. He had taken the easy route at every turn, until now. Drugs and alcohol had for a long time been his only coping mechanisms. Because he had always been given everything he ever needed with little or no effort on his part, he had no idea how to wait through a difficulty or demonstrate self-discipline. Now, he had to wait nine years to be a free man again.

Stephen had hoped that the correspondence course might distract him from such defeated thoughts. But here he sat, face-to-face with his reality. If only he had something to work for, or wish for, that would make the time seem like a few days.

He thought about quitting for the day, but pushed through and read the last question: "What techniques have you found helpful in dealing with a family conflict?"

Had the instructor somehow forgotten the audience of this correspondence course? Every man in prison probably came from a dysfunctional family. His only coping technique for dealing with his mother when she was angry was to try to convince his grandmother to intercede on his behalf. Of course, there was no helpful strategy for dealing with a conflict when she was drinking. Anger and drama ordinarily accompanied his mother's drinking. Come to think of it, he usually dealt with conflict by having a few beers. When it came to Kylee, conflicts usually devolved into screaming, then slamming of doors, and leaving. When it came to a disagreement with his parents or friends, he usually just disappeared into silence and denial until the other person sought reconciliation. In hindsight, these may not have been the best strategies.

As he considered the question, he decided that he would have to give some credit to faith. Those families in his circle of influence who genuinely believed that there was a higher purpose outside of their own self-fulfillment seemed to care more about other people's feelings. He decided to write something about how the other person's feelings and perspective should be considered to work out a conflict. This was the first time he had ever genuinely thought about this.

After penning his answers, he folded the sheets, slipped them into the envelope provided by his professor and affixed a postage stamp. He hoped he wouldn't have to wait too long to get a response and, hopefully, a good grade on the assignment.

He dutifully returned the Very Important Pen.

CHAPTER 25

Skip – Day 662

S kip stood in the shower, letting the hot water stream over his broad shoulders. It was early, and he was getting ready to attend his 6:30 a.m. men's Bible study group. They met at a little coffee shop called Blue Moon. The coffee was good and the camaraderie was better.

Skip liked each guy in the group very much. They laughed a lot and had great conversations about the scriptures they studied, working hard to understand the application to their daily lives. But Skip hadn't shared his dark secret. He looked like one of them on the outside. He drove a nice truck and wore a Rolex watch. He went on hunting and fishing trips, like the rest of the guys. He was a successful businessman. But Skip's only son—his handsome son who should have graduated from college a year or two ago—was in federal prison for trafficking marijuana.

The Bible says to bear one another's burdens. Skip understood that to mean that Christians should share their sorrows with each other, pray with and encourage one another through the trials of life. He was always happy to pray for these other men and thought of them truly as brothers. It felt like such a deception that he had withheld from them such a heavy burden. He wanted to tell them, but he just could not find the courage to admit his life was so broken. Surely they would think less of him. And why not? He judged himself harshly. God must be punishing him for being divorced.

He turned off the water, wrapped a towel around his waist, and sat on the bed. He reflected on some of his biggest mistakes. In retrospect, it must have been unwise to marry Savanah. She was beautiful. Everyone said so. And he had been so proud that she had chosen him. But early in the marriage, it became painfully clear that he was more committed, more in love, than she was.

Her parents, Henry and Lila, loved him. They loved that he worked so hard to support their daughter and they lavished material things on the young couple. Skip and Savanah prospered outwardly. The Mayfields admired his skill with horses and the successful horse training and boarding business he built with their daughter.

Savannah was good on a horse but treated it more like a hobby. She didn't like the long hours of training and didn't deign to groom or feed her horses. Still, she had a regal way of riding that brought the best out of an animal. Skip was a good horseman too. They both had championship buckles to their name, which attracted customers.

Skip had been certain that when they had children, he would secure the place in her heart that he longed for. But when Stephen came along, she grew even less interested in their marriage. Savanah enjoyed motherhood at first. Stephen was a splendid child, and as beautiful as his mother. The boy had her auburn hair and delicate features. But he also had Skip's athleticism. He was the best of both of them. And Savanah's parents adored Stephen, their only grandchild. The Mayfields loved Stephen so much that they bought a small horse ranch close to Skip and Savanah, just to be closer to the boy.

Skip had been proud of producing such a fitting heir-apparent for the Mayfield family. But rather than feeling the same affection and pride, Savanah seemed to resent the attention her parents gave her son. Skip suspected she viewed Stephen as competition for her parent's affection—and money.

The more distant Savanah became, the more Skip tried to please her. He worked fifty hours a week at the refinery. Then, every evening he fed and walked the horses and took care of everything around the house, including his dinner. The more he did, the more passive she became.

Savanah bought expensive clothes and flew to Dallas for appointments with an exclusive hair stylist, easily spending a week's worth of Skip's income in one day.

They would not have been able to pay their bills, but for Skip's very long hours and frequent help from the Mayfields. By the time she told Skip she was leaving him, it shouldn't have been a surprise. They hadn't spent any real time as a couple in quite a while. But it still hurt. He gave everything he had to give, and it still wasn't enough.

Sitting on the bed, Skip thought of the great guys in his study group. Many of them had terrific sons that Skip admired. Boys who hunted and fished and had good jobs and made their fathers proud. Skip tried to put on his shoes, but his heart filled with pain and his eyes with clouds. Suddenly the pain was just too much.

What did I do to deserve this? He sprung up off the bed and slammed his fist into the wall. He was strong and the blow left a grapefruit-size hole in the sheetrock. Almost instantly, he felt foolish. All he had done was transfer the pain in his soul to his fist. Now he would have to spend money and time repairing the wall. He had Sheetrocked his garage before, so he could do this repair. But how was he going to fix the hole in his heart?

On top of his anguish over Stephen, he now added guilt over his hypocrisy. How could he go to the Bible study and expect to enjoy the study and the fellowship, and not share this heavy load? He'd had opportunities, but fear of the other men's rejection prevented him from speaking when the leader asked for prayer requests.

But one friend did know. They didn't talk about it much. But Ken knew the depths of Skip's brokenness and didn't reject him, and that was enough. Somehow that small kindness helped him bear the load. So, Skip conquered the thoughts that told him not to go to the study today, and he got in his truck.

The sun was rising over the rolling hills on the way to the coffee shop. Skip talked to God as he drove.

"Father, I know that you are still good, despite my pain. Right now, I can only talk to You about how much it hurts for my son to be in prison. I can't call him, and I cannot rescue him, and I don't even have the comfort of knowing that he has You to talk to. Please forgive me for not sharing this private pain with anyone at church. I'm so ashamed that I cannot speak it out loud."

Skip tried to reinforce faithful thoughts to combat the negative ones trying to enter his mind.

Surely, there is a creator. Look at this beautiful sunrise. It can't be an accidental convergence of mass and energy. There is a design to this beauty. And the only thing I know that describes the One who made it is scripture.

As a comfort to his soul, Skip quoted part of Psalm 121. It was one of several beautiful scriptures that he had memorized to help him in dark times.

"I look up toward the hills.
From where does my help come?
My help comes from the Lord,
the Creator of these hills, along with the heavens and the earth!
The Lord God will keep me from all harm;
He will watch over my life."[7]

"Lord," prayed Skip as he drove up to the coffee shop, "can I transfer some of my protection that you promise in Psalm 121, to my son? Is my faith big enough for both of us?"

---

7   Psalm 121: 1-2,7

CHAPTER 26

Stephen – Day 736

"How are your college courses going?" asked Paul as he and Stephen walked around the track early in the morning.

"Great," answered Stephen. He liked discussing his assignments with Paul, who was very well read and always had ideas that Stephen could use in his homework assignments.

"I made A's in both my English classes and a B in math. I'm really disappointed that I don't get any credit with the BOP for going to school. I want to get out of here and get placed at a camp, so I had to sign up for trade mechanics class because they wouldn't accept my college classes as proof that I'm trying to better myself. It seems pretty stupid to me that college courses don't count, and a mechanical class that they teach does count, when the college classes seem more likely to benefit me."

Stephen was working up a sweat to keep up with Paul and continue talking. "So, I went to the first BOP trade class, and right away something didn't seem right. The instructor was working on some sort of project at a table in one corner. A group of guys were talking in the other. Most of the inmates were from other cell blocks, so I didn't recognize anyone. I felt awkward and didn't know what to do and no one told me anything. Turns out the 'teacher' has been doing this for like, twenty years. He gets the guys in the class to work on barbeque pits and stuff he can sell to his friends, and he does his own stuff in there too, using the tools and equipment. The inmates aren't learning much of anything. A total waste of time."

"Well, you're in rare form today," Paul said with a smirk.

"I didn't sleep very well last night."

"Is one of your cellies a snorer?"

"Yeah, but I've learned to tune it out," said Stephen. "I keep having the same dream over and over, and it's pretty intense."

They walked about 50 feet farther, then Paul asked, "Is it one of those dreams where you need to run from danger and can't move?"

"Not exactly," Stephen answered. "I'm definitely running from something dangerous. I seem to know what it is in the dream, but when I wake I can't remember the pursuer, just being pursued. I can move in the dream. I'm running as fast as I can, just not moving fast enough. It's catching up to me. And my dog is always in the dream. I had this great dog, and I had to put him down when I came in here. I'm always sad in the dream because right before I wake up, I realize that Dutch is going to get away but I'm not. I'm more worried for him to be alone in that moment than I am for myself."

Paul slowed and then stopped walking. He looked right at Stephen. "Do you believe in God?"

Stephen did not answer, because he wasn't sure what he believed. He did not want to believe in the God of judgment, but a small piece of him wanted to believe in the God of mercy. Was it possible to have one without the other?

"I do," Paul said, interrupting Stephen's thoughts. I know you think it's not intellectual to believe in God, but the truth is, God is real and you can know Him." After a long silence Paul offered, "Perhaps God's trying to get your attention through the dream?"

Stephen remained silent. Paul turned to continue walking.

Stephen felt disappointed in Paul's response. He thought he had found one normal, honest person in this dreadful place, maybe even a friend. Now, he felt foolish and a little betrayed. Was Paul just pretending to care about him, so that he could preach to him?

Paul walked off the track without looking back. Stephen continued a few more laps alone, to clear his head. As he made his laps, he always moved slower on the end of the track where he could see a little neighborhood just across a field and a street.

How odd that the federal prison is this close to a residential neighborhood. Who would want to see this place from their front porch?

Stephen could see people mowing their yards and bringing groceries in from the car. He thought about how the most mundane chore around the house was so much better than being in prison. Why had he never taken much pleasure in life's simple tasks? Did even one of the wood-framed house dwellers have any idea how good their life really was? Because of his family's wealth, he would have once felt superior to them; now he envied them.

CHAPTER 27

Skip – Day 752

The redfish on Skip's hook took an unexpected turn back toward the boat, releasing the tension on his line for split second.

Smart fish!

This fish was a monster. Skip jerked the rod tip up and back over his shoulder, simultaneously walking backward on the bobbing boat and reeling the line in smoothly and swiftly.

The twenty-pound fish bent the fiberglass rod like a reed and line zipped off the reel in short bursts as the muscular creature jerked to the left and tried to shake off the hook.

Sweat dripped from Skip's face. His polarized sunglasses helped him see the shiny scales of the fish in the shallow water of the Laguna Madre.

Reel, pull, reel.

Skip drew the fish in to the boat with a practiced motion, trying not to tangle his line with his younger brother Sam's. When he finally landed the fish, he reached down and grabbed it by the mouth, holding his rod tip up with the other hand. The big-daddy redfish measured thirty-seven-inches long. After Sam used his smart phone to capture some photos Skip put the lustrous, silver-red fish back into the water. It gave him a flip of its tail, darted away from the boat and headed South.

"Maybe I can send that picture to Stephen," said Sam. "I never know whether to tell him about fun things that we do without him. Or just talk about the weather and football scores."

Skip sat on an ice chest for a moment, catching his breath. "Yeah, I've had that same thought. I wonder how he feels when I tell him we're planning a hunting trip, or bought a new gadget for the boat or something? Will he think that we've forgotten him because he's not here to enjoy it with us? I guess I'll just ask him."

They had been fishing the Laguna all day. Now that all the bait was gone, it was time to head back. After he caught his breath, Skip piloted the boat back through the shallow water they knew so well and through the canals to the boat ramp. After loading the boat onto the trailer, they drove back to Skip's small, neat weekend home.

"How 'bout a burger before you go?" Skip asked.

"Ok. I'll go start the grill," Sam said as he went up the stairs to the upper deck.

Sam had the patties on the grill when Skip came out the sliding glass door with two beers. When the sizzling smell of beef on the barbeque reached him, Skip realized how hungry he was from a day on the water.

"I think I'll send Stephen those fish pictures," Sam said, shuffling the hamburger patties with a spatula. "I'm glad they let him have pictures. But it would be even easier if we could just attach it to an email."

"I doubt that will happen. Email has certainly improved communication, though."

Stephen now had the ability to use email through a government-sponsored email system called Corrlinks. It was so much easier now to send a message instead of having to write an old-fashioned letter as he'd done for the last two years.

"I just want to tell you how much I appreciate what you do for Stephen," said Skip. "I know how much work it is to write to him, to mail him books and letters, and to go visit him. I know it is helping to keep him sane in that place."

Sam nodded. It really wasn't their way to talk about deep or painful things.

Even though Sam looked a little pained and uncomfortable at his brother's gratitude, Skip continued, "You could have just written Stephen off. Instead, you have never said one judgmental word to him, or about all that's happened. You'll never know how much that means to me."

Sam quit pushing the hamburger patties and their eyes met.

Sam's eyes were red. It might have been the sun, but Skip didn't think so. Sam, who had no children of his own, was very fond of Stephen.

They washed down their burgers with one more beer before Sam left. It was still early, so Skip decided to go to the Saturday night service at the outdoor Catholic church. Skip was not Catholic, but he appreciated the reverence and beauty of their service. And he always felt closer to God outdoors. What could be more pleasant than going to a church with no walls—on an island?

Later that evening, Skip sat at the bar in his kitchen and opened his laptop to catch up on the news. Whenever he was getting ready to visit Stephen, he tried to familiarize himself with what was happening in entertainment, sports, and world events. Before prison, he and Stephen never spent three hours talking to each other in one day. But now, since there was nothing to do but talk on visitation day, Skip had to plan ahead if he wanted to carry on a long conversation.

Skip jotted a football score on his legal pad in his neat, left-handed script. When he laid his pen down he knocked an envelope off the counter. As he leaned to retrieve it, something red caught his eye. A little, red-leather Bible sat squeezed in between other books on a low shelf of the bookcase. He hadn't opened the little Bible in many years, but tonight it called to him, as if it might hold an answer. He took it from its place on the shelf.

He had owned the Bible since junior high school and the leather was peeling off the binding. One corner was tattered, and the gold lettering had worn off the spine in the place where his hand used to hold it. He didn't use it anymore; it was a King James and he preferred a more modern translation. It was also fragile, and he wanted to preserve it. It held a special memory.

Skip was thirteen years old and didn't want to go to church. But something— probably his dad—compelled him to go that Saturday night. He rode the bus home from baseball practice, took a shower, and wolfed down a sandwich. On his way out, he grabbed the little red Bible from his desk. He didn't read it much, but probably took the Bible because he thought it looked appropriate to carry one to a church meeting.

Despite not wanting to go to church, Skip was curious about the guest speaker. Jack Brown was an ex-convict. Skip wondered if he would share some stories about what it was like to do hard time in prison.

Jack had a powerful voice and a sad face. He told the small congregation how his drug addiction led him to sell drugs and how he had to leave his young wife and children behind when he was sent to the United States Penitentiary in Leavenworth, Kansas.

Jack spent eighteen years in prison but his wife was still waiting for him when he got out. Days after his release, she asked him to go to church. Already entertaining thoughts of getting high, Jack Brown went with her, hoping to find a new channel for his desires. He heard the story of Jesus' redemptive love that night and realized that he needed a higher power in his life to overcome addiction. Jack Brown's decision to surrender his life to the Lord saved his life and his marriage, he'd told the crowd.

Jack Brown invited everyone in the audience who wanted to accept God's free gift of salvation to give their heart to Jesus. Skip said yes, and from that day forward, his life was changed. There *was* more to life than what the world had told him.

Skip touched the soft, leather surface of the Bible, remembering that when he was a boy of thirteen, he met a man who had spent a good part of his life in prison, and meeting that man had sent Skip's life in a new direction. Now his son Stephen was in prison and in dire need of a touch from God.

God, you sent someone all the way from Leavenworth prison to share your love with me. Please send someone to Bastrop Federal Prison to meet Stephen there.

CHAPTER 28

Stephen - Day 784

Stephen wondered whether he should wait to take his walk. He hadn't talked to Paul in a while and tried to act like the God talk had never happened. Stephen did not want to talk to Paul or anyone else about God. First, Christians hated everything fun. Second, they acted self-righteous and judgmental. And what about all the crazy stuff in the Bible? Ridiculous stories from his childhood swam in his head. The virgin birth. Jonah swallowed by a whale for three days and then spit out alive. Noah and the ark.

Stephen went to the chow hall and walked through the line grabbing whatever food was left. He sat alone, comparing his mom's lifestyle with his dad's.

His mother was ethereal. A ghost who floated in and out of his life. Carefree and prosperous, she mostly only invited him into her life for vacations. A few times he had even gotten to miss school to go on a vacation with his mom. Days with her were filled with fun because there wasn't any work to do. The housekeeper washed his clothes and picked up his messes. And his mother never talked about God or wasted any time going to church.

He grew up hearing about God and going to church with his dad. His dad was present for the day-to-day pains of growing up. Skip bandaged him up when he fell off his bike and applied meat tenderizer when he was stung by a jellyfish. Skip went to parent-teacher meetings. Skip made him do chores. His dad was a hard worker; Stephen had to give him that. But there was nothing exciting or exotic about the man, and Stephen had always been drawn to the exotic, exciting and dangerous.

He didn't want to dwell on these thoughts. He saw his new cellie sitting nearby. Like Stephen, Andrew was eating alone. Stephen considered whether to strike up a conversation with him. Andrew had been placed in Stephen's cell about three weeks ago and was sleeping on a pallet on the floor. FCI Bastrop was completely full and overflowing and there was no bunk available for Andrew. Stephen hoped that Andrew's presence in their cell had a deeper meaning. Perhaps it meant he would soon be transferred to FCI Three Rivers Camp? Perhaps someone knew the transfer was in the works and had placed Andrew in their cell, knowing a bunk would soon be available?

Andrew Parker was about forty years old and had been convicted of defrauding the Export-Import Bank of the United States, to the tune of $107 million. Like Stephen, Andrew received a nine-year sentence for his crime. And, like most people Stephen had met in federal prison, Andrew maintained his innocence.

Andrew spent quite a bit of time brooding, but Stephen remembered how miserable it was to be sleeping on the floor. Stephen decided to try making conversation again.

"Hey, Andrew. How's it going?" Stephen said, as he sat down next to his new cellmate.

Andrew looked at him suspiciously, "I'm stiff, bruised and exhausted. I think it is against the law for them to make me sleep on the floor. Do you know how to make a complaint?"

"I know what it's like to sleep on the floor. They made me do it too, for about three weeks. About the moment I thought I could not stand it any longer, I was moved to a regular cell. You can file a grievance, but it will take weeks to get a response and by then, you'll probably have a bunk. Since you came here straight from sleeping in a big mansion, I'm sure this is quite a shock."

Stephen regretted opening the door for Andrew to talk about his material losses. A lot of inmates bragged about what they had on the outside. Sometimes they exaggerated, but in Andrew's case it apparently was true. Stephen found a newspaper article in the library about Andrew's trial. It described how the government had confiscated his large mansion, along with many expensive cars, and a lavishly stocked wine cellar.

Stephen grew uncomfortable with their chatter very quickly. When Andrew talked about his boats and trips, it made Stephen want to engage with similar stories and memories, which could reveal his family's wealth and whereabouts. He did not think that he wanted anyone he had met so far to know too much personal information about himself, so Stephen bit his tongue.

After answering Andrew's many questions about how the prison system worked, Stephen explained that he had written down a guidebook on *How to Survive Prison* and offered to sell Andrew a copy. Andrew grew instantly suspicious again. He bristled and insinuated that Stephen was only visiting with him to get money from him. As soon as the hour marker buzzed, Stephen left Andrew to his misery and went to look for Paul.

Despite Paul's willingness to bring God into ordinary conversation, he was one of the most sincere and interesting people Stephen had met in prison thus far. As Stephen walked to the track, he pondered how ironic it was that when he was free and unconfined, he had chosen to hang out with gangsters and unsavory characters. Here in prison, he gravitated to the normal people.

When he arrived at the track he did not see Paul, and for a moment he was disappointed. Then, he spied the tall man with the stately gait round the south end of the track. Paul smiled when he saw Stephen. Stephen replayed a memory in his mind: he had been in the visiting room with his dad on visiting day when he noticed Paul having a visit from his wife. From across the crowded room, Stephen had seen the way the couple had looked at each other, the way they smiled and laughed. Stephen wanted to know how it was possible that they were making this long separation work.

Lately, when Stephen talked to Kylee she was angry and distant. Stephen had always made most of the decisions in their relationship, and now he felt powerless to help her. Kylee would tell him that her finances were desperate, and she resented him not being there to take care of her. Angry over the poor choices she seemed to be making with what money she did have, Stephen would try to give advice. Kylee never took this advice well, which deepened the chasm between them with every conversation. She hadn't written to him even once, and had only visited a handful of times, claiming that she had no money for gas. When he had money in his account, he would call her and if she didn't answer, thus wasting his turn in the phone line, he would fume.

Paul passed Stephen. Stephen tried to fall in step. If he weren't so tall, he would not have been able to keep up with Paul, who had a long stride and a quick step. Before Stephen said a word, Paul asked, "Have you thought more about our last conversation?"

"Nah," he replied. "After witnessing some of the things I've seen in this world, I have a hard time believing in this good God preachers are always talking about." Stephen was a little shocked at his own answer. Sometimes he had to take stock of whether he believed the words coming out of his mouth. He decided after a moment's reflection that his answer was true.

Paul asked, "What is it that you really would like to know from God?"

Stephen thought for a moment and said, "If I were having a conversation with God, I guess I would like to know why this is happening to me. I'm a good person and I don't feel like I've done anything bad enough to deserve nine years in prison. If I had run over and killed someone on one of those nights when I was drinking, I would have gotten about six or seven years in state prison and probably been out in four. But I talked to five other guys about selling marijuana and I get nine years? I didn't hurt anybody. I didn't force anyone to buy marijuana. Everyone who bought marijuana from me was happy to get it. How is this fair?" Stephen could feel the bitterness and emotion rising inside and he was struggling to modulate his voice. Too late, he remembered that Paul had gotten a sentence of twenty-two years for doing the exact same thing, which was clearly even less fair.

"Well that's what I'd ask Him, then—God, that is." Paul gave him room to process, but Stephen didn't know how to answer. "He knows the answer to that question and all your other questions."

They walked in silence for a bit. That was another thing that Stephen liked about Paul, the comfortable silence between them.

Stephen attempted to redirect the conversation. "Hey, you're married right?"

"Yes." Paul said nodding slightly.

"You seem to be holding up better than most to the stress of this separation. I miss my wife. But I'm also angry at her for not writing to me. And for not answering when I call. I even resent her for just being outside and free and not appreciating what she has."

Stephen was striding more rapidly now, with his words and his feet in sync, "Even though I know money's tight, I still expect her to drive all the way out here to see me. And when she doesn't, I get angry and jealous wondering what she's doing. Do you ever feel that way?"

Paul's answer surprised Stephen, when he said, "I feel the same way *inside*, but I don't let it show because I know it's twice as hard for her. I write to her even when she doesn't write back, and I tell her how much her prayers and encouragement mean to me."

"How could it possibly be twice as hard for her? She's free to go anywhere and do anything." He was sweating and breathing heavily trying to keep up with Paul, who didn't seem to be working hard at all.

Paul responded, "She has half the help and twice the work now. Not only am I not contributing to the household bills, but I need her to send me money just so that I can call her. It's a burden to her, but she has stayed with me. Supported me through all this. She does it because she believes it's what God would want her to do. It's her faith that convinced me, man. I just don't think anyone has that kind of strength on their own." Paul's calm voice suddenly became uncharacteristically loud. "So, one day I just said, 'God if I'm going to survive this, I need help. If you are real, please make yourself real to me, because I confess that I'm not sure you're out there.'"

They had reached the end of the track where the crushed granite path led back to the austere concrete building. Stephen wanted to hear more, but Paul said, "I won't bore you with the rest of the story right now. Better save that for another day." And he trotted back toward his building.

Stephen didn't know why, but Paul's last sentence hung in the air like an invitation and he was drawn to it. It didn't seem too committal. He liked the idea of putting the responsibility on God to do the work. So, he whispered under his breath, "God, if you are real, it's your move. Show me something I can believe in. Something tangible. Not just words in an old book."

CHAPTER 29

Stephen – Day 819

Stephen sat on an old, rusty bench by the track, sweating. It was 10 a.m. and it was hot. He considered walking more, but a stifling heat had settled in and there was no breeze at all. He had decided to stay outside one more hour, hoping Paul would show up. Now, he had to wait the entire hour to go back inside. He had watched for Paul the last few days, but his friend had never been back. Outside the fence, people were all connected, following each other on social media and smart phones. None of that existed in prison. Inmates who could afford to pay by the minute could call out, but no incoming phone calls were accepted. And of course, no one had internet access. So, Stephen had no way to get in touch with Paul.

The soft breeze from the pine trees brought with it a pleasant aroma. The smell of 1,300 sweaty men inside was bad. The heat sapped his strength but seemed to energize the flies and gnats. When Stephen thought he could stand the bugs no longer, the buzzer signaled time for a move and he headed back in and showered in one of the communal showers in the Austin cell block.

There was no hot water and no privacy. Stephen disliked showering with strangers and tried to find a time of day when it was less crowded. He showered quickly, dressed in the damp heat and headed back to his cell. Only a few hours into the day and already it was time for lunch. Prison meals are served at times that don't quite match the rest of the world's biological clock. Spaghetti was on the menu today. Inmates shuffled down a serving line pushing a plastic tray, like middle school cafeteria. The inmate responsible for serving the gelatinous-looking, limp noodles and the thin, reddish liquid next to it was absent from his post. Stephen could see that the ladle for the sauce had slipped into the tray.

The server probably went to find another utensil to retrieve it.

Suddenly, the inmate in line in front of him plunged his hand into the sauce, retrieved the ladle, and served himself.

Stephen stopped short and reversed a step, disrupting the march of the food line.

Randy, the inmate with his hand in the spaghetti sauce, had dirty fingernails and dingy looking clothes. Hygiene was not a strong suit for a bunch of men in a situation like this. There was a good chance that Randy had not washed that same hand in all the necessary circumstances.

Stephen debated whether to eat. Although he was hungry, he couldn't make himself touch the sauce Randy had just tainted. He opted for some of the sticky noodles with a little pat of waxy margarine—a special treat today—and some croutons and saltine crackers.

What I wouldn't give to have a steak and baked potato. Or a Whataburger with jalapenos and toasted buns. Why is there no fruit? Or vegetables? Or protein? School lunch programs are required to serve a balanced meal plan. Why not a prison?

He saw Will, a former political speech writer and book editor, sitting at a table nibbling and reading a newspaper and sat down next to him. "Hey, those crackers look delicious." They both laughed. "Man, I sure miss being able to buy an orange in the commissary. Do you think they quit selling fresh fruit because it was too perishable?"

Until recently, Stephen had been able to purchase a few fresh fruits and vegetables in the commissary. He craved them so much, he made the choice to spend less money on phone calls and stamps so he could spend some of his allowance on the occasional high-priced, dried-out orange or a tomato, even an onion. In recent weeks, though, all the fresh fruit and vegetables had disappeared from the commissary.

"No, sir," Will replied. "I think they quit selling produce, to punish us."

"What do you mean?"

"You know precisely what I mean. You were at the little *soiree* at Manny's house two nights ago.

Only Will would call a drunk fest with a bunch of Mexican drug cartel members, a *soiree*.

"I may have heard something about it," said Stephen.

Manny's cellmate Jose brewed moonshine in a plastic trash can he had hidden in a broom closet. Inmates performed the janitorial services for the prison and most of Manny's crew worked in that department, giving them access to the broom closet, a place less likely to be searched. They bought fruit juice and fruit in the commissary and then soaked stolen pieces of bread in the juice to release yeast. After straining out the bread, they put the mixture in empty shampoo bottles and Jose hid them under a dirty towel in the trash can. Every day when he retrieved the mop from the closet, he would burp the shampoo bottles, as the fermentation produced gas. On the day of the party, Jose smuggled the bottles into Manny's cell inside the mop bucket.

Stephen had heard about the availability of alcohol and the lure was too great. He wanted in. Ordinarily Stephen would not be able to visit Manny's cell because inmates were not allowed to go into a cell that was not theirs. But Jimenez, the evening CO, usually stayed in his office for long periods of time looking at his computer. They posted a sentry who was supposed to look like he was on the way the shower. The sentry would drop a shampoo bottle if he saw the CO leave his office.

Stephen paid his six stamps and was let in. Jose handed him a paper cup, filled with what he called *white lightning*.

"Bottoms up!" Stephen saluted and slammed a shot of it down his throat, as all the other men laughed. It was so caustic that he couldn't speak for at least two minutes. He could barely breathe. Stephen thought he had burned a hole in his esophagus. It tasted like drinking gasoline out of the pump or ingesting molten lava. Part of his brain knew that drinking the white lightning was a horrible idea, but the part that made terrible decisions asserted itself.

After so much time has passed, don't you want to see what it's like to feel a good buzz again?

So, he drank more. He woke up the next day with his head throbbing and his vision impaired. He saw double for the rest of the day and ached like he had the worst flu in history.

"All of Manny's guys got pretty sick," said Will, interrupting the fuzzy memory. "And Jose couldn't see to do any work for two days. He had to go to medical. When he did, the nurse must have figured something out. They all got interrogated and somebody squealed. They all got a shot. You're lucky that you didn't get one too."

"What exactly does this have to do with there being no more fresh fruit in the commissary?" Stephen asked.

"It's obvious, isn't it? The moonshine was made from fermented fruit. No fruit. No moonshine. So, now none of us can have any fruit."

Stephen shook his head and felt sad for the loss. Since he didn't have access to a computer, Stephen made a mental note to ask his dad to research how long it takes a body deprived of vitamin C to contract scurvy.

Something Will said bothered him. "A minute ago, you said I'm lucky I didn't get a shot. How did you know I was there?"

"I heard there was good food, so I connived a way to come over and join the party. I visited with you for a minute and you didn't look like you could pass inspection. I coaxed you into leaving and walked you back to your cell. That's why you didn't get a shot."

"Wow. Man, I owe you one. I don't remember any of that. That's kinda scary. I guess I blacked out. What was in that stuff?"

"Alcohol is poison, after all," said Will. "It can kill you all at once, or it can kill you by degrees. Your choice."

Stephen's stomach grumbled a little and he looked back at the spaghetti thinking perhaps he should have tried it, but all the noodles were gone.

"What do you miss more?" Stephen asked. "Eating real food? Or sleeping in a real bed?"

"Hm. That's a tough one. Now that you've posed the question, I miss real food more than sleeping in a real bed. Wouldn't it be wonderful to have a delicious shrimp taco from Torchy's? Or smell barbeque smoking on the pit at Franklins? It's the smells and flavors of well-made food that make it awesome. And sharing it with someone you like. Sleep is quite important and who can sleep well on the plastic mat? But, food, my friend, seems even more essential. And that is one thing I dearly miss."

They nodded in commiseration.

"Hey, speaking of good food, we know the food in here is beyond terrible," Stephen said. "But some people in here have the ability to make magic out of commissary items. Manny had some quesadillas at the party. I remember now they were pretty good. How did they do it?"

"They borrowed my George Foreman grill. I bought it from Big Mike for100 commissary," said Will.

Stephen whistled and said, "Ouch, that set you back. That grill was yours? And you let Manny borrow it for the party?"

"Yep, in exchange for hiding it for me. I can't keep it in my cell."

"Where did they get the ingredients?"

"Jose has a friend in the kitchen that got them an onion and tortillas in exchange for getting his cell cleaned. And Manny and I contributed string cheese and Slim Jims from the commissary."

"Those ingredients don't sound like they would make quesadillas as good as those tasted. The George Forman grill was a coup. I'm sorry you contributed food and didn't get to eat, because you were saving me from myself. Where do you think they hide the grill?"

"I have no idea. But if Jose can hide a vat of moonshine, I guess he can keep my grill hidden until I need it. Now, if you'll excuse me, I've got to go teach some drug lords to read," said Will with a grin.

He taught a GED class on Thursday afternoons. Will loved to read. He had probably read more books than any fifty random people on the street combined. So, he took great umbrage that so many men were behind bars for decades with nothing but time, and yet never learned to read. He thought improving their reading skills would open new worlds for some of them. It was the perfect volunteer activity for Will. Stephen hoped it would earn Will some points toward getting transferred.

"Keep up the good work." Stephen said to his new friend as Will was leaving. "We're gonna get there. We will. It's going to be so much better over there. I've heard that the Camps let inmates use a microwave oven, and you're not locked down all day long. You can just get up from the cafeteria and walk right over to the library anytime you want."

"You heard that from me, dimwit," Will laughed his funny laugh that sounded like he was choking and someone was pounding him on the back at the same time.

Stephen smiled. "Well, it must be right, then."

Stephen lingered for a few minutes. His mind wandered back to the fresh sounds and tastes of Padre Island.

As good as Austin is in the food department, it doesn't have the monopoly on delicious food, he thought.

He remembered his dad frying fresh-caught redfish and shrimp and serving the seafood with chopped red onions, avocados, and tomatoes. Sweet summer melons—watermelon and cantaloupe—grown in the Rio Grande Valley would be sliced and chilling in the refrigerator.

Growing up on a barrier island, Stephen learned to operate a boat long before he could drive a car. The feeling of balancing on a thin piece of fiberglass as it bounced up and down in the water, whether a boat or surfboard, was second nature to him. He longed at that moment to feel the hot sting of the sun on his tanned back, smell sunscreen and salt air, and hear the incessant cry of the seagulls. He even missed the funny smell of ozone and decomposing seaweed that would assault his senses as he left the mainland and approached the start of the JFK Causeway leading to the Island.

Two men sat down beside him and proceeded to slurp, bang, and chug, jerking Stephen back into his nasty reality. One of the men asked him if he planned to finish his milk. Stephen tossed him the unopened and unappetizing clear plastic baggie of lukewarm milk.

CHAPTER 30

Stephen – Day 920

Stephen received another badge of honor in the mail: his homework packet from the university. They came regularly now. He'd earned another A on his math assignment, with Will's help, and a B on his English assignment. He couldn't wait to tell someone about his little victory. Dad would enjoy knowing that his investment was paying off, but it was so expensive to call him. Will would be genuinely supportive. But he really wanted to share it with Paul.

Where has that guy been anyway?

Stephen suited up early and headed to the track. Paul was not there. So, at lunch he found a way to slip his accomplishment into his conversation with Will, his regular lunch companion now.

"B is for Baloney," Will said. "Why didn't you get an A?" But his smile conveyed delight. "Are you still using all the dysfunctional families of the Bible as material for your essays?"

"I've read quite a few other books. But when I started college, the Bible was the only book I had access to at that moment. What do you know about the Bible anyway?"

"I've read the Bible, Mr. I'm-a-college-student-and-I-know-everything-now. It's one of the greatest pieces of literature in human history. And if you happen to be in

132

a season of waiting, it's probably one of the most encouraging things you can read. Think of the story you read about Jacob. His twenty years of indentured servitude were something like a prison sentence. But he probably would not have become the man God intended him to be without that waiting period. And even though he had made some serious mistakes in his life, he overcame those bad choices to become a very successful guy. I like those kinds of stories. Don't you?"

Stephen wasn't sure what to say. Will had gotten more out of the story than he had.

Will didn't press him to answer his question. Instead he changed the subject: "I want to write a blog when I get out, about the psychology of waiting. I think this experience qualifies me as an expert."

Stephen had never read a blog, but he had read about them in a magazine someone had sent him. He assumed that's where Will had learned about it also, since technology was passing them by in prison.

"I found an article in a journal in the library," continued Will. "It was rather eye opening. I think there is something in our DNA or our chemical makeup that make some people better able to wait than others. And those individuals who cannot delay gratification often end up in prison. I have been told all my life that I can develop self-discipline, but I never knew how to make my mind work that way. I think I've discovered the secret, though, and I want to share it."

"That sounds like a blog I should read. I'll be your first customer," said Stephen.

"You don't become a customer of a blog, you Luddite. You follow, sir, follow."

Stephen made a mental note to look up the word Luddite later. He had acquired a dictionary. It had become a necessary companion tool to all the books he was reading. He was shocked at how much he was enjoying reading, but his vocabulary was somewhat lacking. Apparently, that was one of the things being taught in all those high school English courses he had skipped.

Will had a second job working in the library a few days a week, and it was time for him to go. Stephen decided to follow him and see if he could find the article Will had mentioned. Not only did it sound interesting, it would give him something to debate with Will, which would be fun. Will was much better educated and well read, so Stephen was often at a loss to carry his end of the conversation. Plus, the article might help him with a future English assignment.

Through Will, Stephen had learned the word *ambivalent*, which was how he felt about the library. In one way he enjoyed it, because it was quieter than any other place in the prison. With 1,300 men crowded into a concrete building, there were very few quiet spots. The library was one place where he could find a measure of solitude. But some odd characters hung out here. Because most inmates preferred to avoid the library, anyone who did not fit in with any group of prisoners or didn't have gang protection—like the *Chomos*—spent long hours there. Chomos were inmates convicted of possessing child pornography.

Child pornography was another one of those crimes, like drugs, where just possessing it can get you sent to prison. But Stephen thought their crime was much worse than his own. Children were hurt to satisfy their addiction, whereas his customers had been willing, adult participants. Stephen worried a little about his prison reputation being damaged by the time he spent in the library, but it was so hard to read anywhere else. And it was difficult to do the college homework in his prison cell.

They arrived at the small library. Will signed in and relieved the other inmate serving as the library attendant. Then he helped Stephen locate the magazine.

There was one small table and a few ancient plastic chairs in the library, but the Chomos were sitting in them and Stephen refused to sit near any of them. Even inmates have a pecking order. Instead, he sat down on the floor in the corner to read. He was grateful for the small dirty throw rug on the floor, presumably to help with sound absorption. It was the only floor covering he had seen anywhere, except the visitation room and the commissary, which had linoleum. The remainder of the building was bare concrete, floor to ceiling.

He recognized Fat Phil sitting with the group at the table. Fat Phil was morbidly obese. Stephen couldn't figure out how he maintained his weight on the sparse diet available in prison. He had to be supplementing his diet with junk food somehow.

Phil told everyone he was in prison for cocaine, but everyone knew he had been convicted of possessing a laptop containing more than 3,000 images of child pornography. Stephen was surprised to see him in the library; Phil spent most of his day in the TV room watching TV. Apparently, he made good money saving seats for other inmates.

Phil nodded in Stephen's direction and started a greeting, but Stephen cut him off and spoke to him harshly.

Stephen looked away and stared at the article for a few minutes without reading it. He hated to have to be cruel to Phil in front of others, but if someone saw him speaking to Phil, he could become a target himself. Chomos were universally hated *inside* and *outside* of prison.

The magazine article described the results of a study which began in the 1960s, conducted by psychology researchers at Stanford University. To study how important self-discipline was to lifelong success, the researchers offered hungry four-year-olds a marshmallow but told each child that if they could wait for the experimenter to return after running an errand, they could have two marshmallows.

According to the article, about one-third of the children grabbed the single marshmallow right away while some waited a little longer, and about one-third were able to wait fifteen or twenty minutes for the researcher to return. Years later, after the children graduated from high school, the differences between the two groups were dramatic: the marshmallow resisters were more positive, self-motivated, persistent in the face of difficulties, and able to delay gratification in pursuit of their goals. They had the habits of successful people which resulted in more successful marriages, higher incomes, greater career satisfaction, better health, and more fulfilling lives than most of the population.

Those who took the marshmallow were more troubled, stubborn, indecisive, mistrustful, and had less self-confidence. Stephen thought about how in high school, when it was time to study for a big test, he tended to be distracted, engaging in other activities such as video games. He would study only at the last minute, if at all. Sadly, according to the article, this character flaw followed the marshmallow grabbers throughout their lives and resulted in unsuccessful marriages, low job satisfaction and lower income.

Stephen put the magazine down on the floor beside him and looked around. He looked at Fat Phil and the other men he was sitting with. He felt disgusted to be in the same place as these men.

I bet every single one of us in this place, would have been a marshmallow grabber. We all probably knew that there was a better choice than the thing we grabbed.

He felt guilty but wasn't exactly sure what he was supposed to do with this knowledge. Apparently, some people were born with a propensity to wait, and others were not. He would need to read Will's blog when they got out. He wondered what secret Will had uncovered. Will always had a way of leaving you with something to think about.

Shortly before the hour marker buzzed, Will came over and handed him a book.

Stephen looked at the cover and read the title: *Blue Like Jazz: Nonreligious Thoughts on Christian Spirituality*, by Donald Miller.

"What's this about? Is this like a self-help kinda thing?" Stephen asked.

"Just read the first chapter and see if it doesn't capture your attention, make you laugh, and give you some new perspectives."

"Well, promise me it's more positive than that article you gave me to read. Because that was totally depressing."

"It's entirely more positive," said Will.

On the way back to his tiny cell, Stephen saw that Officer Ornales was handing out mail. Stephen had another fat, white packet containing a new homework assignment. He was always excited to get anything from the University, so he put the new book in his locker for a time and got out his ballpoint pen so he could work on his homework. As he took out his notebook and pen, he noticed the little journal/guide he'd been keeping. He hadn't added anything for a while. He flipped open to the next clean page and added to his survival guide:

> When you first lay down on the tiny bunk bed with the plastic, inch-thick mattress and small plastic pillow, you will be certain that you will never sleep again. But eventually, you will. Don't despair about the small, close bunks and plastic mat. Some people have to sleep on the floor.

He flipped through what he'd written so far and thought, *I wonder if this would make a good blog?* Then he laughed out loud.

CHAPTER 31

Stephen – Day 1019

Stephen awoke from a dead sleep with an electric jolt of fear. His heart was racing, but why? Then something crawled up his arm. He jerked violently and swatted it away, letting out a loud curse. Because he couldn't sit up in his cramped bed, he pressed himself against the wall pushing and kicking all over the mattress to make sure it—whatever *it* was—was no longer in bed with him.

His cellies shouted obscenities for waking them. Stephen knew that both Kip and Crawley had been in fights before and he did not want to anger them. So, he said in the calmest voice possible, "Some big bug was on me. It's still in here somewhere."

Seconds later, Kip slapped at something loudly and shouted another, more vulgar, obscenity. By this time, Crawley sat up from the bottom bunk and flipped on a tiny flashlight.

Stephen caught sight of a cockroach in the tiny flashlight beam and hollered to Crawley, "Over by the lockers! Stomp it with your shoe!" When Crawley aimed the light at the locker unit, all three men caught sight of what was crawling on them: Texas-size cockroaches.

Stephen felt a chill go down his spine at the sight of so many roaches, spreading bacteria to every surface with their swift, spiny legs. His skin prickled. Somehow, he had managed to conquer his fear of gang members with guns but not his fear of crawling insects. Apparently, Crawley wasn't a fan of roaches either. Stephen could hear him stomping and swearing as he kept dropping the light.

After the excitement died down, it took a long time for Stephen to go back to sleep. Now that he was fully awake and hyper alert, he could hear the bugs scurrying in the dark, or thought he could. Several times he woke up swatting at the sheet. Maybe the sheet brushed his skin? Or was it a filthy, disease-spreading cockroach crawling up his arm? In the morning, he was despondent, both from lack of sleep and the realization of all he had lost, including a clean place to sleep in peace. As catharsis, he sat down after breakfast and wrote a letter to his dad.

> Dear Dad,
> You're always saying that you pray for me all the time. Well one thing I don't understand, If God is real and listens to your prayers, then why am I here?? Why didn't he keep me out of this horrible, godforsaken place?
> Love,
> Stephen

Stephen regretted it the minute he put the letter in the mail slot. His conversations with his father had been encouraging. And Dad was paying for his Ohio U. courses. Stephen was sure he already knew how his father felt about his being incarcerated. Skip was old school. He had spanked Stephen as a child for infractions of the household rules and supported corporal punishment.

He surely thinks I deserve this fate and my letter will give him a good reason to say so.

***

Stephen did not call his dad for about ten days, hoping Skip would forget about the childish, self-centered letter he wrote. And it was the first time that Stephen was glad that no one could call him. When he received a letter from his dad, he didn't open it for a few days, thinking that it might be further condemnation, something he didn't need. But when he finally tore it open and read it quickly, it didn't contain anything he expected.

Dear Stephen,

I've thought hard about your question and I was glad you asked. I've asked myself that same question many times since you went to prison. I don't have all the answers. But this is what I do know:

God is eternal and amazing beyond what we can imagine. He is an artist. He created the Earth—and everything in it is a work of art—with mankind being his most favorite creation. He loves us very much. He created you for a good purpose and gave you gifts and talents that he wants you to use. He also gives us free will in how to go about using and enjoying the things he gave us.

You are free to go down any path. You may love him back, or you may reject him. You may use the things he gave you to better yourself and the world, or you can squander them. If you weren't free to choose, you could not love, because love is a choice. God even loves us enough to put obstacles in your path, to encourage us to change course and return to relationship with him. If you're choosing unwisely, God will do anything to make you change your mind, except control your mind.

Perhaps you are in prison because God is giving you a second chance, or a third, or 200th chance to hear from Him and choose the type of life he designed for you.

I think about all the times you have cheated death, like your many car accidents and all the dangerous things you did while using drugs, and I believe God did hear me and answer my prayers to protect you. And He will answer yours if you ask Him.

Love,

Dad

The letter was obviously meant to be encouraging and contained only subtle references to Stephen's responsibility for his own mistakes, but it still stung. Was his dad insinuating that God may have orchestrated the situations that allowed him to go to prison to give him a second chance? Stephen stared at the letter and questioned whether it would have been better to have died in one of those car accidents, instead of surviving to spend nine years in federal prison.

"If your prayers did this to me," Stephen said, "then I don't want to have anything to do with you or your God. Don't 'save' me anymore."

CHAPTER 32

Stephen – Day 1026

Stephen refused to call his dad for a few weeks. It cost money to make phone calls and he did not want to waste it on a theological debate. Instead, he focused on trying to call Kylee. She usually did not answer. When she did, she seemed guarded and they had little to talk about. They quarreled when he asked her what she'd been doing. It was a perfectly legitimate question for a man to ask his wife, but he supposed that it probably sounded like an accusation.

"Stephen, if you're just going to grill me about where I've been every day, I'm not going to answer the phone," she said coldly.

But he really wished he could know what she was doing and who she was doing it with. He longed for something tender to say, but the things that they had experienced together seemed to have happened in another lifetime.

Phone conversations and getting letters really helped to pass the time and his dad was the most consistent phone answerer and letter writer. Kylee never wrote. Ever. And Stephen's mom was almost as bad. After receiving nothing at all in the mail for three weeks, not even from the university, Stephen broke down and wrote his dad. Perhaps he could stay away from topics likely to elicit a response from the Bible. He couldn't imagine what the ancient text said that was relevant to life today.

The problem was that his dad seemed to think the answer to every situation in life was found in the Bible.

He was a bit surprised with what spilled out on the page.

Dear Dad,

I would like to believe what you said in your letter. Many times throughout my life you've told me that the only way to be truly happy is to trust Christ. There are people all over the place who claim to be religious and don't sound very happy. Half the people in here have a cross tattooed on their chest, and some of those guys have done some pretty terrible stuff. And they certainly don't seem happy. So, I am not persuaded. I have never been more miserable in my life, and I don't think that prayer or church or the bible is going to fix this.

Stephen

CHAPTER 33

Skip – Day 1,052

The highway to Bastrop was narrow, with only one lane in each direction. Today, it was foggy and Skip could only see about ten yards in front of him, so he had to go much slower than planned. He was on his way to visit Stephen, which was only allowed on Saturdays, Sundays, and occasional holidays. It meant getting up at the crack of dawn to be there before 9:30 a.m. The fog was threatening to make him miss the 9:30 cutoff, and he could feel his pulse pounding in his temples.

Finally, he pulled into the parking lot, distressed that the lot appeared quite full. He locked his cell phone and wallet in the glove compartment and grabbed the only items allowed inside: his car keys, driver's license, and dollar bills for the vending machines. He punched the door-lock button and dashed for the door. He was happy that he had made it to the door by 9:25 a.m. As he grabbed the handle on the door and began to open it, a female correctional officer pushed it back, closing it in his face and locked it securely.

Not processing this action, Skip assumed she somehow didn't see him. He pounded loudly on the door, held up his watch and yelled, "Hey, it's not 9:30!"

She gave him a disgusted look and turned on her heel.

He took a step back, and his breath left his lungs like a balloon deflating.

He stared at the locked door, wondering how long it would be before the count would be over and they would let more families in. He was brought back to his senses when another family walked past him and tried the door and was equally disappointed about being locked out. Skip never ceased to be surprised at how many of the families he saw while visiting Stephen looked a lot like him. He had always assumed that people in prison looked like the criminal mugshots seen on TV, and that their families probably looked like outlaws too. But this little family, like so many others, looked quite normal—and quite lost.

Skip explained: "They lock the door and don't let people in during the count." The two visitors looked uncomprehending, so he added: "This is one of the two times each day when they count every inmate to account for their whereabouts. I think the prison will open again in about an hour for more visitation. Where are ya'll from?"

"Dallas," the two women said at the same time.

Skip guessed that one of them was an inmate's spouse and the other was probably his mother. Or perhaps the younger woman was a sister.

"We had to get up so early and drive all this way, and now we're not going to get as much time to visit," said the one that looked like a mom.

"Well, you'll have to get used to this type of treatment. The prison system couldn't care less if we see our loved ones." *Wow. That sounded so bitter. Since when do I talk like that?* He was sorry he had said the words, after he saw the pain and sadness in their eyes. And he was surprised at himself for being so rude to strangers. But it was true, sadly. The Bureau of Prisons didn't care how inconvenienced the families were. Their mission was to mete out punishment to every man in their charge. Unfortunately, the families of those men were all being punished, too.

Numerous signs on the premises stated that visitors could not wait in their cars. So, Skip hopped in his truck and headed eight miles back into Bastrop to get a cup of coffee. He bought a cup of coffee and a newspaper at the gas station and asked for dollar bills as his change. With some regularity the prison vending machines took money and didn't vend a product. So, Skip liked to take a large stack of bills to ensure that he could buy Stephen some food, even if some of the machines did not work. As the cashier handed him the bills, he detected a knowing look in her eye, and blood rushed to his cheeks. With this store being so close to the federal prison, perhaps the clerk realized why he was asking for dollar bills as his change? Skip felt a deep sense of shame as he took his change and turned away quickly.

The gas station had two booths where someone could sit down for a minute and eat a snack. Skip availed himself of one because he had almost an hour to kill. He sipped his coffee slowly and scrolled through the news on his phone, because the newspaper was quite thin. Then drove back to the prison. When he drove up, he saw others standing in line, waiting for the door to reopen.

He parked and walked up to the line. He had prefilled his visitation form, because that saved a lot of time once you got through the first set of doors. He noticed not too many people in the line ahead of him had learned to do that. In fact, one woman wore open-toed shoes and one man a hoodie sweatshirt. Skip felt sad for them. They were most likely not going to be allowed to visit their loved one today. Both of those items of clothing were banned. Skip had no idea why they were banned, but he had studied the list of rules on what not to wear provided to him during the first visit. Skip was a rule follower.

Once inside, there were more lines. He was instructed to place his ID and visitation form in a tray and wait on a bench. Two female officers were working the desk this morning and they looked about as excited to see the families as they would have been to see the grim reaper.

The woman took each form out of the tray slowly and squinted at a computer screen for a long time, glancing back and forth between the screen and the form. Skip knew that she was cross-checking the forms with a database. Only people who have preregistered and gone through a background check could visit a federal prisoner.

After about twenty minutes, he was called to the desk and told to go through the metal detector. He removed his shoes and belt and put his truck key and plastic baggie full of dollar bills in the plastic tray and stepped through the machine.

Once a group of ten visitors made it through the screening process, they stepped into a small room with glass doors on one side and metal bars on the other. After another wait, the metal gate was slowly raised, and they were allowed to walk into the prison, following a correctional officer who was calling ahead and notifying another officer of their arrival.

Skip had been visiting for almost three years now, so he knew the drill. Once in the visitation room, there was one final check with a different set of officers at the desk. He entered his time of arrival and a long litany of requested information in a logbook. Then, he was told to sit and wait some more.

Eventually, Stephen came in from a door opposite the one Skip had entered through. They could embrace, but only for a moment. They sank into the plastic chairs. Stephen clapped his hands loudly and rubbed them together at the site of the little baggie. Skip smiled.

"You ready for a Dr. Pepper, already?"

"Nectar of the gods," said Stephen, rubbing his hands together. "And a club sandwich if they have one. My friend Will says that's new in the machine. And some kind of spicy chips if they have any. And ice cream."

Skip laughed and headed out for the machines. Why the inmates were not allowed to get near the machines was unclear to Skip. Stephen had lost a lot of weight and he always ate like a bear when Skip was here. Buying his son snacks allowed him to focus on a positive picture in his mind. It reminded Skip of trying to keep Stephen fed when he was a famished teenager who'd just come in from surfing. The boy had a hollow leg back then.

"I thought you were going to come early?" said Stephen when Skip got back with an armload of junk food from the machines.

"I certainly tried. I got up before dawn and headed out. But some fog on the way between San Marcos and Bastrop slowed me down. I was at the door five minutes before the cut off, but they locked it in my face."

"I'm sorry, dad. I know it ruins your whole day to come over here."

Skip was surprised to hear Stephen acknowledge his sacrifice. Stephen didn't ordinarily notice anyone else's inconvenience.

"Well, you're worth it," Skip said and smiled.

"Anyway, I've been writing to my counselor making a case that I should be moved to a lower security prison. I think I have a good chance. I had no criminal history at all before my arrest. I never used a weapon. There's no evidence in my record that would show that I'm a danger to society and should serve my time locked up behind razor wire."

"So, if it gets approved, where would you go? And when?"

"It could be next week. It could be six months. It could be a year. They won't give me any information right now. I think the most likely place is Three Rivers. It's the closest to my home. And it would be much easier for you to visit."

"Oh, wow. That would be great. How did you know to start this process?"

"Another inmate, named Will, seems to be the best informed about the rules and regulations that govern the federal prison population. He told me."

Skip let Stephen enjoy his snacks and indulged him in some debate over predictions of the upcoming college football season. Since his incarceration, Stephen had become quite well read. Apparently, he read a lot about college sports. He also seemed to be reading a lot about entrepreneurship. Stephen had a great idea for a line of clothing that sounded like it would be a hit with outdoorsy people like Skip.

Skip vowed to read the business books that Stephen was reading, so that they could discuss them on his next trip.

Stephen got up and went to the restroom for a minute and Skip looked around the room. He noticed the pretty lady he had seen in the parking lot earlier and decided that the inmate she sat with must be her son. He looked about Stephen's age. The young woman must be his sister. They didn't appear to be a couple. The couples sat as close together as the bolted-down plastic chairs would allow and spoke in hushed tones, savoring the closeness, many of them with a toddler in their lap. Even after all this time, Skip couldn't get used to seeing children in prison. He continued to be amazed at the number of people who were incarcerated who had small children. He had not been especially close to his dad. But at least his dad had come home every day and been a good provider. He thought how terrible it must be to visit your spouse or your father in prison.

Stephen walked back out of the restroom and Skip watched him walk confidently across the room. Skip wondered if Stephen was more comfortable in this place now. He looked slightly less miserable. Or was he putting on an act for Skip's benefit?

Because Stephen was so tall, Skip was looking upward. For the first time, he noticed the camera in the glass bubble in the middle of the ceiling as Stephen walked beneath it.

"I never noticed that before."

"What's that?" asked Stephen.

"I'm sure I knew that they had surveillance cameras in prison. I guess it just didn't dawn on me that we were being watched, in addition to the two guards at the desk."

I believe that they record conversations as well," said Stephen. "If you look about two feet from the camera, toward the guard desk, you'll notice something that looks like a skinny cord hanging down. I think it's a microphone.

"Well, how useful would that be? Wouldn't all these conversations drown each other out?"

"I could be wrong, but I think they have a way of focusing on particular conversations, and listening in, if they want to."

"Oh," said Skip feeling slightly violated once again. "I have given up a lot of privacy since you came here, so what's one more thing? Right? Our phone calls are monitored. I had to provide my private information and have my background checked to visit. Then, when I get here, I have to go through a metal detector and all sorts of scrutiny. So why am I surprised at this type of surveillance?"

Skip was looking at the camera, hoping someone was listening and feeling a little sorry for him. But, when he saw Stephen's face, he regretted venting his feelings out loud. He could tell that his comment hurt Stephen, even though he insisted no apology was necessary.

For some reason, Stephen never liked to stay until the end of visiting hours. About an hour before visiting hours were over he would get antsy. Skip saw it was about that time, so trying to end the visit on a high note he said, "I guess I better get going. I'll see you soon. And I pray for you every day."

Stephen opened his mouth to say something but paused. Instead he said, "Thanks for coming. I really appreciate it."

Skip hugged him and went up to the desk to retrieve his driver's license. He walked out to the parking lot and opened the truck door, letting some heat escape. He felt a compulsion in his spirit to pray. It was a familiar sensation which couldn't adequately be described with words, but he always tried to comply when he felt it.

He slipped behind the wheel and closed his eyes. "Lord, thank you for this day and please forgive me for complaining about the fog and for the mistreatment by the prison staff. I know that every employee has a job to do and they are just trying to do theirs. Please watch over Stephen and keep him safe one more day. And please allow him to get accepted to a camp if it is your will. I believe it would be good for all of us, and I know you care about the big things and the small things."

He waited to see if anything else came into his heart that he needed to give to God. Nothing did, so he opened his eyes, shut the truck door, and put on his seat belt. Before he could put the vehicle in drive, he noticed a young mother leaving with two young children. The boy looked about eleven and the girl looked about five or six. Skip's heart ached for them. They were just strangers, but he felt sadness for the children to have to live without their father.

He bowed his head again, "Lord, perhaps you allowed me to be late today, just so that I would see that little family and pray for them. Protect them and give them your favor. If they don't know you, please bring someone along this week to tell them the good news about Jesus. Show them this week that you are there for them. May they receive some assurance that even though their loved one is separated from then; *you* will never leave them. Amen."

CHAPTER 34

Skip – Day 1,072

Skip had hoped the day would come when he and Stephen could have an open conversation about faith in God. But the tenor of their recent letter exchange and Stephen's reserved demeanor over the weekend had stopped him once again. He liked to keep their visits fun and encouraging but regretted his failure to direct the conversation. Skip was sure that Stephen would endure prison so much better if he understood he was not alone, that he could have the peace that transcends understanding, just for the asking. His heart longed to speak, but his mouth never cooperated. Perhaps it was easier to have a serious conversation with his grown son on paper than in person. It took a while to find the words, but finally he wrote:

> Dear Stephen,
> I was jogging up a steep trail in Fredrich Park yesterday and I saw something that made me think of you. In your last letter you asked why so many people who say they follow God live a life that isn't consistent with what He taught. You seem to be saying that the failure of Christians to live a good life proves there is no God. Or else you're saying that being a God-follower is so hard

that it's not worth doing. I hope I can persuade you that neither one of those things is true.

The illustration I saw was a beautiful, red oak that had fallen across the trail. It looked alive and it was full of leaves, so I thought it must have been cut intentionally. Then I looked closer at the base of the tree and saw that it was hollow inside. Something had destroyed it from the inside, like fungus or rot or disease. But somehow, it still looked fine on the outside—until the minute it fell over.

In John 15:5, Jesus said "I am the vine; you are the branches. Those who remain in me, and I in them, will produce much fruit."[8] God made us to be alive in body, mind, and Spirit. When we acknowledge who he is, he becomes our root, our source of nourishment. Before we have done that, we look alive on the outside, but we're spiritually empty on the inside. We're like the dead tree that still has leaves.

Acts 2:21 says, "Everyone who calls on the name of the Lord will be saved."[9] The moment you do that, God infuses your human spirit with his divine spirit. Forever after, he gives *fuel* to live on, like the vine. Then, we are really alive. Anyone who doesn't know God can have all the Christian symbols they want—tattoos and cross necklaces, etc.—but they're still dead on the inside until they let God in. So, that's one reason why you might see people who say they know God, but don't act like it.

Also, Christians are still human. If we neglect to listen to God, we are likely to live like the rest of the world and do and say things that are not in line with God's heart. Not every Christian you run into is being a good representative of God or acting in accordance with what they believe. But that doesn't mean that God is not real.

I never said that if you believe in God you will always be happy. But I do believe that if you do, you can always have joy despite your circumstances. There's a difference between happiness and joy. If you want to understand the difference, let me know. I love you, no matter what you believe.

Dad

---

8   John 15:5, NLT
9   Acts 2:21, NLT

CHAPTER 35

Stephen – Day 1,075

The letter made Stephen confused and angry, until the last sentence. His first reaction was to be defensive. But then he remembered that he had, unfortunately, started this conversation. His father's expression of love inserted the possibility that his dad was sending the letter out of love and not condemnation. Stephen needed an explanation that was simple enough for a guy like himself.

Having seen Paul eating breakfast early on several occasions, Stephen decided to search him out at that hour again, rather than waiting to find him on the track. But Paul was not in the cafeteria. Stephen wanted to ask others if they had seen Paul but decided against it for the time being. Even a simple question can start all kinds of unnecessary drama in prison.

The next day he still did not see Paul in the cafeteria, but later spotted him on the track. Stephen sat on a bench until Paul strode by. "Hey," he offered nonchalantly.

"Hey, what's up," said Paul, stopping to take a breather.

"Not much. I've been spending most of my time on schoolwork."

"How's it going?"

"Really well. It's a bit of a surprise how much I am enjoying it. Somewhere in high school I started thinking I was a poor student and gave up, like I usually do with anything difficult. But now that I have nothing else to distract me, I'm finding that I'm halfway smart," Stephen said.

"I'd say you're more than halfway smart. You could be very successful if you want to be. You just have to want success more than you want alcohol."

Paul's rude and intrusive comment shocked Stephen.

How could Paul know anything about my struggle with alcohol?

They hadn't talked about it. Rather than pursue this uncomfortable line of thinking, Stephen launched the conversation in another direction.

"So, have you had a visit from Annie lately?" Stephen knew that Paul's wife Annie worked long hours as a nurse, and sometimes had to work on weekends, which was the only time visiting hours were open.

"Yes, thankfully. My tank was getting low." Paul smiled.

"My wife has only visited me five times in three and half years," said Stephen. "She says she can't stand to see me like this and that it's difficult to get childcare for her boy, my stepson. I am starting to feel that our marriage isn't going to make it."

Stephen was always surprised at how much he was willing to share with Paul. It wasn't like him to overshare. He tried to soften what he just said.

"I just got a new homework assignment but I'm having trouble concentrating. Kylee hasn't been answering my calls and, of course, I can't leave a message. When we do speak it's tense. Sorry to be laying this on you, but I am not sure what to do. My dad is a good guy and always there for me. He would happily give me advice. But he lives in such a different world. Kylee was the one person who fully understood and accepted me. Now I don't have that outlet anymore."

Paul stood with his hands on his hips looking past Stephen into the distance. To a casual observer, they could have been brothers. Stephen was accustomed to towering over everyone, but Paul was equally tall. They both had auburn hair and green eyes.

After a moment, Paul said, "a marriage requires nurture and separation makes that so difficult. Will you go to the library with me next hour?"

Stephen wasn't really planning on going to the library from the exercise yard. He didn't have his schoolbooks with him and he was sweaty from being outside. He wasn't sure exactly why, but he decided to go with Paul. They walked another circle and when the hour notice sounded, they walked to the library and signed in.

Paul went to a shelf and searched around, finally pulling out a book. The paper cover was torn off and the pages were all curled up as if it had been touched by many hands. When Paul opened it and began to flip through it, Stephen realized it was a Bible. Paul pointed to a page that said *Romans* at the top and traced his finger down the page. He stopped on a verse and handed it to Stephen and said, "Read this."

Stephen hesitated, trying to think of an out. He was not a strong reader and he wasn't sure if Paul expected him to read out loud. When Paul didn't rescue him, Stephen read haltingly:

"Those who think they can do it on their own, live only to please themselves, but those who follow after the Holy Spirit find themselves doing those things that please God.

Those who put their trust in God, find that God's Spirit is in them— living and breathing God! Obsession with self is a dead end; but attention to God leads us out into the open, into a spacious, free life."[10]

Stephen looked up at Paul to see if he could quit reading. He felt perspiration soaking the back of his shirt.

"Does that mean anything to you?" said Paul.

"Not really," replied Stephen.

More importantly, how is this ancient book going answer my question about what's happening in my marriage today? And how do I know that God said these things or caused them to be in the book?

Paul was silent for a minute. Then, he continued, "If you read the Bible, one day it will just spring to life. And then it will help you a lot. If you allow God into your thoughts, He will guide your decisions, and all of your relationships will improve."

Stephen turned his head and covered a dry cough. He wanted this conversation to end.

Paul was still staring at the page and didn't get the hint.

Stephen felt completely nonplussed. *How on earth does this answer my question about how to stay married?*

Paul switched gears. "Show me what you've been reading now that you are literate."

Grateful to be done with the Bible, Stephen perused the shelf and located a Doc Ford novel by Randy Wayne White.

---

10 Romans 8:6-8

"Ah, yes. I can see why you would enjoy that," said Paul. "I loved the descriptions of Florida. But, seriously, you need to add something for edification, something that makes you think and not just be entertained."

"Isn't that what I'm doing with my college course?"

"Definitely. But you're ready to add something educational that is *also* entertaining and inspiring. Nothing you're reading right now fits that category." Paul searched the shelves but didn't find what he was looking for. So, he went up to the library attendant and asked him if he had *Crazy Love*, by Francis Chan. The attendant found it in the return cart and checked it out in Stephen's name.

"Let's talk about this when you've read it," Paul said as he handed the volume to Stephen.

"Sure," said Stephen, doubting sincerely that he would read it.

When it was time to head back to the unit to be counted, they parted ways. While standing at attention in the middle of his unit waiting for the count to end, he thought about his conversation with Paul. He knew Paul was trying to help him. He knew that Paul had a healthy marriage, and that gave him some credibility. His thoughts shifted to his dad's last letter. He thought about telling his dad about his conversation with Paul, who had sounded a lot like his dad. But then decided not to. He didn't want to get his dad's hopes up.

CHAPTER 36

Skip – Day 1,103

The wind had shifted earlier that day and was now blowing from the North. A hint of coolness in the air gave welcome relief from the South Texas summer heat. Early September would qualify as fall anywhere else, but in Texas, it was still hot on the first day of dove season.

Skip wore a shirt made of breathable high-tech fabric, camouflaged to blend into the brush country. Over it, he wore a mesh vest which had a deep pocket in the back to collect his kill. He was left-handed, but he could shoot with either hand. His mother found his left handedness undesirable for some reason, so she had forced him to use his right hand. But it didn't change the way his brain was wired.

He stood near a row of mesquite trees, their tiny, lacey leaves providing stingy shade. He wanted to be invisible to the birds as they flew in to roost in the trees. Other hunters stood by large bales of hay in rows throughout the large field they shared for this hunting trip. Skip thought they were a bit too exposed in the open field, and preferred the scant cover and shade provided by the trees. He spotted his target on the horizon. A grouping of nine or ten white-winged dove were headed his way, about 200 yards in the distance. He raised his Beretta shotgun to his shoulder. It felt as natural and comfortable as breathing. He calculated the trajectory of the

12-gauge shot in his gun, anticipating the flight pattern of the fast-flying birds. He locked on to the big bird in front and waited for the right moment.

His most reliable shot would be at a bird flying left to right about thirty yards in front of him. He was more than 90% accurate in that zone. His mind constantly measured and categorized all the elements of the shot. On a day when the birds were sparse, he would take the shot at a difficult angle or a long distance to get the shot. But on a day like today, when the birds were plentiful, he preferred to wait for the easy shot. He did not like to waste shells; shotgun shells were expensive. At least once every outing, he would kill two birds flying side-by-side with two quick shots from his over and under. That was a challenge he enjoyed. It required not only a good eye and quick reflexes, but excellent balance.

He took his shot, and the bird fell in the field thirty yards in front of him. He put the safety on the gun, walked to pick up the bird, and tucked it in the vest pouch. Then he reloaded with a practiced motion while scanning the horizon. The shell fell into the chamber with a neat click. Skip picked up the spent shell casing. He liked to keep the area around him neat and tidy.

When Skip had his limit of fifteen birds, he field-dressed them efficiently. Soon, all that was left was fifteen little dove breasts. One limit of birds fit perfectly in one gallon-size plastic storage bag. Later at the house, he would wash them, lay them flat on butcher paper, and prepare them for the grill. He would insert a piece of fresh jalapeño pepper in the middle of each breast, wrapping the breast and the hot pepper in bacon, holding the bacon in place with toothpicks. Then Skip would grill the *dove poppers* on his barbecue grill until the breast meat was tender and the bacon was crisp.

While he sat on the tailgate of his truck rehydrating and thinking about his supper, his mind wandered to the letter from Stephen. Stephen had been a good shot with a shotgun. Skip had taken him hunting since he was a five-year-old boy. Now, thanks to his felony drug conviction, Stephen could never own a gun again or be caught with one in his possession. This made no sense to Skip since Stephen had never used a gun in a commission of a crime. There were so many things they could never share again.

Skip had been thrilled to get Stephen's letter. He had been sharing his faith with his son since he was born. Stephen went to Sunday school almost every Sunday, unless he was spending that weekend with his mother, which was rare. He had known the songs in the hymnal and had made his father proud about how well behaved he was in the church service. Faith was something they shared, father and son. Or so Skip thought.

When Stephen started getting into trouble as an eighth grader, Skip had been surprised, and devastated. Not that Skip hadn't made a few mistakes of his own when he was younger. But, he had been so sure that it was going to be different with Stephen.

He drove home and put the baggie full of birds in a tray full of ice on the counter. He didn't like to put them in the refrigerator until he removed the last bit of dirt and feathers. He liked to tackle unpleasant tasks quickly and get them over with. But something was stirring in his spirit and he was trying to get it to surface. So, he left his task undone for a minute and reread Stephen's letter. He tended to approach communication like he did every problem: analyze the problem and apply the most appropriate tool or solution. But that approach didn't always work well with people.

Skip was vexed. From the tone of Stephen's letters, it appeared he didn't understand the basic things Skip had tried to teach him for the last twenty-five years. But at the same time, Skip felt hopeful about the invitation to discuss it. Faith became a sensitive topic about the time Stephen went to high school. Skip even sent him to a faith-based boarding school, hoping that if he just heard it from someone else, it would sink in. Instead, Stephen seemed to slip further away from God every single day. Now however, even though hostile, Stephen was asking some excellent questions.

The answer Skip had been praying about all day came to him like a fish striking bait. He sat down at the computer and typed out a letter. He had been told his angular left-handed script was hard to read. So, he had learned to be a good typist. Being ambidextrous had not helped his writing but was a big plus for typing.

Dear Stephen,

Hi. I am looking forward to seeing you on the 19th of this month. In your last letter you made some comments about being in control of your own destiny and implying that Christianity consists of a bunch of rules you don't agree with. I disagree that Christianity is about rules and I am sad if that is all you learned about Christ from me. Don't you remember that the Bible says in Romans that "everyone who believes and calls on the name of the Lord will be saved?" It doesn't say anything about rule following being a requirement. It's just a matter of deciding what you believe and speaking it out loud. God created everything.

So, I don't think he cares how you say it or in what language or where you're standing when you do it. He just wants to hear that you need him.

The Bible says that God is *love*. If you want more love in your life, choose God. Then you will also find your destiny.

Dad

P.S. Being in control of your own destiny led you to: alcoholism, pain, confusion, broken relationships, squandered wealth, and prison. How's that working for you? Maybe you should at least try letting God drive the boat for a while.

CHAPTER 37

Stephen – Day 1,250

Stephen opened his eyes and squinted. His bladder was full and harsh light was coming through the window. From those two facts he deduced that he had probably missed breakfast. He was waking later each day, and his mind was slipping further into despair. His schoolwork was a welcome distraction, so he dressed and headed to the library.

Much to his delight, Will was working. "What are you working on today, M.B.?" Will had taken to calling him "M.B.A." After a while, Will had shorted the nickname simply to M.B., for no apparent reason.

"Math today, Professor. Are you into college algebra?"

"Absolutely. I think I can handle some freshman algebra. Show me what ya got." Will rubbed his hands together and adjusted his glasses. With his close-cropped, fine silver hair—bald at the crown—and slender long fingers that touched the pages when he read a book, he projected the image of a college professor. His eyes twinkled with intellect.

Stephen whipped out his textbook and homework assignment. Will dove into the intellectual challenge with gusto. So much so, he neglected his library attendant duties. Several inmates approached the table, trying to find books. Rather than retrieving the books for them, Will absently pointed in the general direction of a bookshelf. Another inmate brought a book back to have it checked in. "Just leave it over there." Will motioned toward a pile of returned books without looking at the other man.

Everyone in prison is used to being treated poorly, so the inmates who needed help didn't argue with Will's indifference. They just walked away and fended for themselves. Stephen felt special for Will's attention and very appreciative of his help. The lesson probably would have taken him three times as long without Will's tutelage.

"I really appreciate your help. But I hate distracting you from your job.

Will ignored the comment and said, "You don't seem yourself today, M.B."

Stephen felt a powerful surge of emotion and sadness, something he usually kept at bay by staying busy. "I have giant cockroaches crawling on me at night. I turned twenty-nine last week. I should be in the prime of my life, enjoying it with my wife and with friends. But instead I spent the day alone. Kylee didn't even send me a card. I haven't been given any information about my request to transfer to Three Rivers, and I don't know how long I can stand this. I can't stop thinking about my wasted life and what's been taken from me. All for selling some plant products to people who wanted them."

Will was quiet for a long moment, staring at Stephen as if he were listening with his whole body. "I call that feeling the 'dark night of the soul,'" he said.

Stephen sighed, but didn't say any more. Now that he had given voice to his sadness, he felt even more empty. He wished he hadn't allowed his mind to go to the dark place.

Will continued, "I understand completely how you're feeling. Better than anyone you can talk to on the outside, I understand. The dark night of the soul is when all you see is blackness and no light. And you think the light's forgotten you."

Stephen was staring past Will having a difficult time focusing on what he was saying. He looked down and saw that Will had touched his forearm lightly to bring him back to the present. He noted that Will's hands trembled slightly.

"There's still some light out there in the world. Even light that is light years' away eventually makes it to earth and gives us twinkling starlight. So, when you think the night is dark, remember you can almost always find some starlight if you look. I think we should have a party to cheer you up!"

Will's last comment was so out of context, it woke Stephen out of his reverie. "What? You know we can't have a party."

"Why not? I still have the George Foreman grill I bought from Big Mike. We'll make the quesadillas you liked and drink an adult beverage. It'll cure what ails you."

Stephen shook his head at Will's apparent belief that they could somehow pull off such a feat. The absurdity of it made him laugh. And it felt good to laugh. "Quesadillas and an adult beverage sound awesome. But there seems to be a severe shortage of both in this place. In case you've forgotten, we're in the slammer. The ultimate food desert."

"What do you do on Tuesdays after dinner?" asked Will.

"I watch TV, like everyone else. Or I try to do some homework. Why?"

"I tutor Jose. He's trying to earn his GED, but we can't meet in here this week because the library is being fumigated. It's overrun with silverfish that eat the library books. I've been writing up maintenance requests for five months, and supposedly they are finally going to come and spray tomorrow. So, I got permission to meet with Jose in the unit, in the TV room. On Tuesday. He's very appreciative, Jose. He says he's taken his GED about six times, but he believes he's finally going to pass because of me. I told him you and I were leaving for Three Rivers soon. Miraculously, they still have some of their broom-closet moonshine hidden somewhere, and they want to throw us a party!"

"Why'd you tell him we were going to Three Rivers? What have you heard?"

Will shrugged. "We're eligible, and we're model inmates. Why shouldn't we get transferred soon?"

"Haven't you figured out that the BOP doesn't always play by their own rules? They make the rules, and they can change them anytime they want, just to dash our hopes and kill our spirits. And what if we get in trouble for being associated with this party? Don't you remember what happened last time?"

"Why didn't you ask yourself that question before you drove that van full of marijuana over a state line?" Will cocked his head to the side and laughed so hard, he slapped his leg.

A few of the other inmates trying to read jumped at the noise and glared in Will's direction. Will dismissed them with a wave and said to Stephen, "I'll see you Tuesday. Wear something nice, but casual."

At that, they both laughed out loud.

CHAPTER 38

Stephen – Day 1,440

Big Mike Brown walked into the second television room on the Austin unit. This room was where white inmates congregated. He had a task for James Crawley and knew he would be likely to find him there. As he stood in the doorway, Big Mike observed with disdain that even though the television viewers could watch different programs with their headphones, most of them appeared to be watching the same thing: NASCAR.

He didn't want to stay long in this room. He was as out of place here as James Crawley would have been in the room down the hall where Mike and his crew hung out. His eyes surveyed the room and found their mark, a skinny inmate with sallow skin and long gray hair that made him look a lot older than he was.

"Crawley, I need to talk to you," he said.

Crawley's eyes narrowed. He turned his head slightly and stared at Big Mike with suspicion. Big Mike liked the fact that almost everyone was afraid of him. He was one of the last people on earth Crawley wanted to tangle with, and he knew it. Crawley was probably considering which course of action was more dangerous, ignoring his order to have a conversation, or hearing what he had to say. Neither option was going to end well.

Big Mike smirked as Crawley slowly stood up and skulked toward the hallway. Big Mike moved only an inch, forcing Crawley to turn sideways to squeeze through the door. Big Mike didn't take his eyes off the other men in the room until Crawley was well into the hallway. He knew they could feel his presence and his stare, but none of them turned to look his way.

They were not supposed to talk in the hallways, so Mike faced Crawley and got down to business. "You remember that time I got my guys in state jail to provide protection for your brother?"

"Yeah, I remember. I also remember paying you 300 commissary. We're square."

"That job was worth way more than 300. Now is when you provide some payback for a favor you appreciated."

Crawley was quiet. He was sure he wasn't going to like whatever Big Mike was about to ask. But he didn't have any gang affiliations to protect him from the big man's wrath. He had hated asking Big Mike for help and he knew it might come back to haunt him. But what else could he do when his kid brother went to Huntsville? Big Mike had connections in prisons all over the state.

"I want you to hide some contraband in Taylor's stuff."

"What you got against Taylor?"

"What do you care? Are ya'll lovers or sumthin'?"

Mike said it loud enough to be heard down the hall and Crawley got agitated.

"Shut up!" Crawley hissed. "I just don't want no trouble. He's gonna know it was Kip or me and he's gonna suspect me from now on, and possibly retaliate. I don't want to go to the hole for your vendetta."

"I don't care what you tell him if he suspects it was you. Happy sent me word that he hasn't forgotten that Taylor didn't show up in the yard that day when Harley was killed. He thinks Taylor was tipped off and knows more 'n what's good for him. I offered to mess the kid up. But Happy wants the snotty kid to get a shot and not be able to move to Three Rivers like he's been braggin' about."

Crawley said, "How are you gonna get it to me?"

"You and I are gonna skip breakfast tomorrow. Both your cellies always go right on time, like clockwork. You don't always go. So, they won't be suspicious. I'm gonna put it in a book and walk it down to you right after they leave. You put the book in Taylor's stuff right away. While he's down eatin' breakfast, the COs might just get word that there's contraband in your cell. So, this is a heads up for you too. You better get rid of anything you don't want found."

"This is a real bad situation you're putting me in. I wish you'd leave me out of it. Why don't you just throw it on Taylor's bed after the three of us leave the cell?" Crawley said with his hands on his skinny hips.

"Don't care about your situation. I'm gonna throw it on your bed instead if you're not waiting on me. You just be available when I tell you to."

"What's the contraband?"

"That's none of your business. I already told you more 'n you needed to know. Go back to watching your cars go around in a circle."

Crawley walked miserably back to his chair noticing some frowns on the men staring at the TVs.

When Big Mike was out of earshot, Crawley's friend Dwayne said, "You're dancin' with the devil if you're doin' deals for Big Mike."

"He wanted to cut me in on a deal," said Crawley. "But I told him to leave me out of it."

It wasn't a lie. It just wasn't the whole truth.

CHAPTER 39

Stephen – Day 1,441

When Kip and Stephen got up and dressed for breakfast, Crawley pretended to still be sleepy.

"Crawley, you coming?" said Kip.

"Nah, I couldn't sleep last night, with you two girls making so much noise. Go."

"Suit yourself," said the big Samoan.

"Hmph," Crawley grunted and put his arm over his eyes.

When he was sure his cellies were down the hall, he jumped up and dressed in khakis. He peeked out the door and saw Big Mike coming. It was sooner than he expected. He could still see Stephen and Kip headed in the opposite direction.

Big Mike was walking briskly. Crawley felt his pulse pounding in his temple. There were no cameras in the units, but Officer Ornales or another CO could come through the unit door any second. His cell was in view of that unit door. If he got caught with the contraband, he would go to the hole instead of Stephen, for something he didn't do or even want to do.

The huge black man had a book in his hand, as he passed the cell, he lowered his arm to his side and shoved the book at Crawley. Crawley grabbed it with a fast, efficient motion and shut the door. He laid the book on Stephen's bed. Then curiosity got the better of him, and he picked it up again. Although time was of the essence, he had to know what was stashed in the book. When he saw what was inside, his breath caught in his throat. A rectangle the size of a cigarette lighter had been carved out of the middle of the pages of the book.

If you happened to open the book to the first page, you wouldn't see it. But Crawley had opened the book in the middle. Inside the cavity was a fat marijuana joint. Big Mike wanted Stephen to get in very serious trouble.

Crawley wished he could smoke it himself. A fleeting thought went through his mind to pull it out and smell it for a moment, but he needed to hide it in Stephen's things right away. He thought he heard some footsteps outside, so he shoved it in Stephen's laundry bag and headed for the door. Crawley didn't want to be in the cell when the CO came. And he would come. Big Mike would find a way to notify the guards of suspicious activity in their cell. Perhaps he had done it already. The false report would launch a search.

Crawley stood outside the cell, trying to catch his breath. Stephen was a good kid. He didn't deserve this. But what could he do? No one could stand up to Big Mike.

Maybe Stephen will get lucky and the guards won't come.

CHAPTER 40

Stephen – Day 1,442

Stephen had cognitive dissonance (another phrase he learned from Will). He had gotten another letter from his father. And he had read the book Paul had given him in the library. He desperately wanted to believe in something good and positive. His dad, Paul, and apparently Will also, all seemed like smart people. But none of them had overcome his doubts, or his dark thoughts. There was sickness, injustice, and prison in the world, not to mention death. If this mighty God they all raved about was so great and loving, why would he create something so bad? If he was all powerful, why didn't he just fix the brokenness in the world? If someone could answer that question, perhaps Stephen could believe.

It was early, and he was hoping to run into Paul in the cafeteria. Since he had read the book Paul had given him, he wanted to discuss it. The book was easy to read and contained moving stories about God's love. Maybe Paul would fill in the gaps and answer some of his nagging questions. Stephen felt ready to ask.

As he approached the cafeteria, Stephen noticed the CO coming toward him, looking like he was on his way to handle important business. Stephen stepped aside, assuming the man would pass him by. But Officer Ornales stopped him and said, "Inmate Taylor, you need to head back to your cell immediately."

Stephen didn't move. "Sir, what's this about?"

"You put in a request to be transferred to a lower security facility. Your request has been approved. You are leaving in an hour. Get your stuff now, or I will assume that your request has been rescinded."

Stephen sucked in his breath; his heart was racing. He was thrilled, but at the same time, he was devastated at not being able to ask Paul any more questions—or probably ever speak to him again. Inmates were not allowed to call or write to one another. As he turned and headed back to his cell, thoughts flew through his mind?

Who will be there? What if there are more *Happys* over there? Or vicious gangs? What if the move is a mistake? What if the evil you know is better than the evil you don't know? And what about Will? Had Will's transfer been approved?

He went back to his cell, emptied his locker. He couldn't think. He wanted to leave a note or something. He couldn't tell Kip or Crawley to pass along a message, because Paul and Will were both in another unit and Kip and Crawley didn't go to the library, ever.

He bent over to put his shoes in his bag and noticed a book on it: *The Shantaram.* He had borrowed it from another inmate but already read it and returned it to the original owner.

How did it get back in here?

Stephen remembered that he had seen Dion reading it and asked to borrow it when he was finished.

Dion knew I wanted to read it and must have brought this copy by. He was always good to me. I should try to take it back.

He left it outside the duffle bag. He put his shoes in the bag, then his books and letters, followed by his few shirts, neatly folded. Toiletries went on top. He tried to make his stack look neat since all his possessions were visible. The bag was made of mesh netting. On washing day, they put their sheets, towel, and clothes in the bag and delivered it to the laundry. The prison washed it like that, bag and all. Everything came out wrinkled, but it was effective for keeping inmates identical-looking belongings separated.

He peeked out the door. Ornales was standing there, arms at his sides, head back a little, observing the hallway. Ornales cocked his head to listen to something on his radio at his left shoulder. He walked across the hall and stepped into his office and shut the door.

Stephen looked around and realized he still had the library book Paul gave him, and another book that Will had given him. He grabbed a piece of his school notebook paper and wrote: "Will, *Blue Like Jazz* was a great book. Thank you for recommending. I really appreciated it. I wish you well and hope to see you soon. S."

He grabbed the two library books and Dion's borrowed book and dashed down to Dion's cell. The door was closed but the window was uncovered. Stephen rapped on the door quietly and peeked inside.

Everyone was gone. He opened the door and laid the three books on Dion's bunk. He had seen Dion in the library before, so he thought there was a good chance that Dion would take back the library books for him. If the book made it back to the library Will might find his note. It was a small chance the note would reach Will, but Stephen thought it was worth it.

He wrote a note to Dion: "Dion, it's been good to know you. Hang in there and best of luck. I borrowed *The Shantaram* from someone else and it was awesome, so I brought your copy back. I would have enjoyed talking about it with you. Could you please take the other books back to the library for me? – S."

Just as quickly as he arrived, he jogged back. It dawned on him as he ran back that he could possibly have endangered his chances of going to Three Rivers if he got caught in another inmate's cell.

What was I thinking? Why is it always so hard for me to think things through to their consequences?

As he entered the door of his cell, Ornales stepped out of his office and said, "What are you doing?"

"Just looking for you, Sir. I'm done packing."

Ornales looked at him suspiciously and said, "Stand by the bed. Leave your bag on the floor."

They both stepped inside the tiny cell. Stephen complied by standing as close to the bed as he could. Officer Ornales bent slightly without taking his eyes off Stephen and turned the whole bag upside down and dumped the contents on the floor with a few strong shakes. Stephen leaned his head against the bunk and bit his tongue. He owned nothing private. The officer was entitled to treat his meager things like trash, but it still made his blood boil to see his clothes and mementos scattered on the dirty floor.

Officer Ornales rifled through his few things, flipping through books, reaching into the pockets of his pants, feeling the inside of his shoes and inspecting them carefully. Stephen's heart skipped a beat when the Officer began reading his spiral notebook.

"What's this?" Ornales asked.

"A…just a… journal. Sir."

As Ornales slowly turned the pages, Stephen felt exposed, like the day Denise left him standing naked. After what felt like an eternity, Ornales threw it on the pile. Finally, he picked up Stephen's jar of instant coffee and a packet of ramen noodles. Stephen's heart sank as Officer Ornales opened the little plastic jar of powdered coffee and emptied it into the trashcan. Then, he also threw the plastic coffee can and the noodles in the trash. Stephen was heartbroken to lose the coffee. It was so expensive in the commissary and he could not afford to replace it anytime soon. He tried to remember something positive from one of the books he had just read, but as he watched the coffee go in the trash, all that hopeful stuff about God's "Crazy Love" seemed like just so much rubbish.

"Get your stuff and let's go," said Ornales.

"Yes sir." Stephen knelt and started folding his things once again.

"Come on. Let's go," Ornales said with more force.

Stephen shoved his things back in the bag and they walked out the door and down the hall.

Ornales led him down the hallway and through the offices in the front building. It was the same building he had walked into four years earlier. They checked out some paperwork and the CO led him to a bus, waiting just outside the door. It looked like a school bus that had been painted white. He went up the stairs, ducking his head to enter and looked around. He hoped Will had also been approved and maybe they were traveling on the same bus. At first, he didn't recognize anyone, but then, about two thirds of the way back on the left side of the bus, he saw Sean. Whatever they were about to discover on the other end, they would discover it together.

PART III
"SWEET RIVERS"

CHAPTER 41

Stephen – Day 1,453

There was a mattress on the bed—a regular twin bed, not a bunk. Stephen had been in Three Rivers for a week and was still in awe of how much better it was than Bastrop. The mattress wasn't very nice, but it was infinitely better than the plastic mat on his bunk bed in Bastrop. Will had been right about that. And he had been right about many other things, too, such as the freedom to move around the facility without being locked in one area for an hour. The biggest thing missing was Will, himself. Stephen missed his friend and could not understand why he was not transferred at the same time. They both were eligible. But he was hopeful that Will would arrive soon, maybe on the next bus. Or had he been offered a different camp, closer to his home?

Stephen's sleeping area was called a quad. It consisted of four twin beds, four lockers, and a low table, all surrounded by modular walls which did not extend all the way to the ceiling but served to provide a little privacy. His quadmates were decent. There was a different class of federal prisoner at the federal prison camp than at the medium-level security prison. Camp was a model of incarceration designed for low-level offenders who were not considered a threat for escape. There was no razor wire. In fact, there was no fence around the property at all. The complex was several miles from town and sat far off the road, but any of the inmates could have walked away at any time, provided they weren't fearful of being sent to a higher-level prison to finish their sentence.

Although Three Rivers was nicer in every way than FCI Bastrop Medium, one thing was not as nice. There was no library. And there was no one to recommend books for him to read. Will and Paul had exposed him to things he never would have read and sparked his interest in reading. So, Stephen asked family and friends to send magazines that contained book reviews. When he saw a review of something he thought he'd like to read, he would write to his mom or dad and ask them to send it to him. His uncle Sam was also very thoughtful about sending books. Reading not only filled many hours and kept anxiety and dark thoughts away, Stephen was also able to trade the books after he read them for commissary items or for other books.

He read *A Long Walk to Freedom* by Nelson Mandela and learned about apartheid and world history. Mandela's prison experience was so terrible that it put Stephen's situation somewhat in perspective. After finishing *The Last Lecture*, by Randy Pausch, Stephen hoped he would not get some terminal disease and die at a young age, especially since he was going to lose at least eight of his prime years to incarceration. Stephen related to Eckhart Tolle's book, *A New Earth: Awakening to Your Life's Purpose*. He thought Tolle's description of human dysfunction, selfishness, anxiety, and the inhumanity humans inflict on each other, as well as mankind's failed attempts to find meaning and purpose through material possessions and unhealthy relationships, was spot on.

Stephen was learning so much, but he wished he had someone to talk to about what he was reading. Sean was a great listener and a good conversationalist, but he was not very interested in reading the same types of books. So, Stephen had no one to share his newfound interest with, until he met Ramon.

One afternoon a bunch of young guys asked Stephen to join a basketball game. He was tall, a pretty good shot, and an excellent blocker, but a bum knee made him a little bit slower than the younger guys. One of the guys coached him throughout the game and seemed more educated than the others. They started practicing together on a regular basis and became instant friends when Stephen discovered that Ramon had read the Tolle book. But the joy of finding a new friend was tempered by the loss of an old one.

Stephen soon had an opportunity to apply his self-help education when he received a soul-crushing letter from his old childhood friend Arnie.

Dear Stephen,

I got your letter telling me that you are now in Three Rivers and asking if I would like to be on your list of approved visitors. I don't wish to be on the list and I would also ask that you not write to me anymore.

Since you went away, I've learned quite a bit about your life between high school and prison and it's not the type of activity I want to be associated with at all. I have graduated from college and have a good job at a bank. I'm about to be married to a great girl, and I don't think I want to be explaining to her why I'm getting letters from a pen pal in federal prison. I also don't want anyone at the bank to associate me with a felon. They run background checks regularly and I don't want to do anything that would unwittingly damage my future career.

I wish you well. I really do. I hope your life after prison is very different.

Best wishes,

Arnie

Stephen sat on his bed and wiped away a few tears. He and Arnie had been friends since grade school. They had done a lot of crazy things together. And now, Arnie was so ashamed of what Stephen had done that he didn't even want to get a letter in the mail from him. He had lost so much because of his poor choices. Why had he never counted the cost? He threw the letter in the trash.

His father's voice echoed in his mind.

Son, every choice you make matters. If you compromise in a little thing today, you'll make a bigger compromise tomorrow, until you're caught up in something you never thought you would do.

A lot of things his dad said were probably right. But he would never, ever want to face Skip and admit to it. It felt better just to be angry.

CHAPTER 42

Stephen – Day 1,490

"We get to do the sweat box today!" Stephen was so eager her could hardly stand it.

"Why are you so excited about going with Ramon for the ceremony?" asked Sean.

"Why do you say I am excited?"

"Because you did that thing you do when you're excited, clap your hands together and then rub them back and forth."

Sean always seems to notice unusual details about other people. *I wonder what other predictable habits I have.* Stephen thought.

"Of course, I'm excited about it. When was the last time we ate sausage?"

Ramon was Lakota Sioux. He had petitioned the prison warden for permission to engage in a religious ceremony common to his ancestral people. He had been denied several times because his request was quite outside the norm. But he appealed up the chain of command using terms like *religious freedom* and *discrimination* and was finally granted the right to engage in a native American sweat lodge ceremony.

He explained to the prison administrators that he could not do the ceremony alone, because it involved a healing circle of prayer. He was granted the right to take two inmates with him, provided he chose inmates with no infractions of the rules. He chose Stephen and Sean, and this was the big day. Stephen was especially excited because the ceremony required a "feast" at the culmination and Ramon had been told that he would be given a link of sausage to take with them, quite a rare treat.

"I don't believe we have ever been served sausage," Sean said. "I hope you're not participating just for the food."

"Actually, I really like Ramon and I want to support him. He's a deep thinker, and he's interesting."

"I've been reading up on the sweat lodge ceremony," Sean said. "It is a ritual designed to produce purification and balance of body, mind, spirit and emotions. It represents a transformation of the Old Self into the New Self. I'm trying to take it seriously.

"How on earth have you been reading about the sweat lodge ceremony? We don't have the internet or a library."

"I asked Ramon for some information and he shared a little book with me. And I told my mom. She sent me some internet research about it in her last letter."

"Hmm," Stephen said, impressed with Sean's level of interest and support. "That's cool."

The sweat lodge ceremony was set to take place at 3:30 p.m. and they would be given one hour. By scheduling it at this time, they would be forced to return in time for count. Ramon came by Stephen's quad just before lunch and told him to wear something very light.

"It's gonna be hot, man. But you're gonna really like it. It's very special."

Now that Sean had prepared him a bit more, Stephen said, "Yeah, I'm drinking a lot and trying to prepare my mind for something new." Stephen could tell that Ramon liked that answer.

Time dragged so slowly that day, Stephen felt like he was moving backwards. But when the appointed hour arrived, Stephen walked to a special side door where they had been instructed to meet Ramon. Ramon had a jug of water in each hand and a paper sack full of other items.

Stephen's excitement intensified. "What is all that stuff? This is so amazing that they're letting you do this."

"They're letting *us* do this. I've been given some supplies that I asked for to per-form the ceremony. I think we have everything we need. Are you ready?"

"Did they let you have the sausage?"

"Yes. I have it right here," Ramon held up the bag.

Sean gave Stephen a look of disapproval. Stephen pretended not to see it.

"The prison doesn't even provide shampoo or toothpaste, yet they let you have sausage. I still can't get my head around it," said Stephen.

They walked out the door under the watchful eye of the CO. Across the parking lot from the front door, off to one side, Ramon built a tent out of poles and a plastic tarp. The tent had no floor, just bare dirt. Stephen entered cautiously, surprised there was nothing in the tent. Apparently, whatever they were going to do, was in that paper sack.

Ramon removed a gallon Ziploc back full of charcoal briquets and a little metal grate. He carefully laid out some other small baggies and got to work, using the grate to dig a hole in the center of the tent. It was already hot in the tent in the afternoon summer sun. Even without any heat source, they were sweating. Stephen started to tell Sean about the letter he'd received, but Ramon cut him off.

"In the tent we will talk only about spiritual things. We will give thanks primarily. So, please remain in quiet contemplation and think of things you are thankful for."

Ramon continued setting out his items. He placed the grate inside the shallow hole and then arranged the charcoal on top of it. When he had them neatly stacked he pulled a box of matches out of the sack.

Sean and Stephen both exchanged looks. Matches would be a valuable barter item, and they both wondered if they could borrow some. Unfortunately, there were only two in the box. Ramon hesitated before striking the match. He cupped his hand around the box to protect it, although there wasn't a breath of wind inside the tent.

The charcoal was apparently the quick-light variety because it caught fire. Ramon piled some round smooth river stones on top of the charcoal and stared at it intently for a few quiet moments. Then, he removed another baggie from the larger sack. It looked like it contained spices or dried leaves. He invited Sean and Stephen to hold out their hands and he poured some of the dried leaves in their hands.

"This is tobacco and sage. We're going to put it in the fire, but not yet. I'll go first and then invite you to follow my example."

It was getting very hot in the tent. Sean and Stephen were sweating profusely. Ramon opened one of their three bottles of water and poured a little bit of it on the hot stones. A cloud of steam drifted upward. Ramon sprinkled his tobacco and sage over the rocks and the tent filled with the aroma.

"Grandfather Creator and Mother Earth, we put these natural elements back into the Earth and invite you to give us wisdom and power. I am grateful for supportive family members who will welcome me back home soon." Ramon looked at Sean and Stephen and said, "Everyone on Earth is related to each other through our relationship to our Mother: Earth. I invite you to speak some words of gratitude and say a prayer. Please sprinkle your tobacco when I pour the water, so that it will enter the steam."

Sean and Stephen were both a little nervous.

Sean said, "I'll do it." He reached out his hand slowly. Ramon poured a little bit more water to raise the steam and Sean poured his handful of leaves on the steam. "I'm grateful for my wife and the fact that she got a good job." He paused for a while, looking at the hot stones. "And for friends," he added.

It was Stephen's turn and he really didn't know what to say. So, he just decided that he would be honest. It seemed important somehow not to be false. So, he held out his hand and released his leaves into the steam. "Something is on my mind that is hampering me from opening myself up to good and healthy thoughts. Someone I thought was a lifelong friend no longer wants to be part of my life. But now that I am focusing my thoughts on being positive and thankful, I am grateful I had the chance to know him. He made my life better." Stephen nodded a few times. It felt right to release his sadness into the steam. He wanted to voice another thought, so he placed his hand back in the steam and brushed in a few more tiny leaves from his palm. "I wish him well in his life."

After their prayer circle, Ramon let them take a quick break outside the tent. Although it was hot outside, they felt a chill as they exited the tent. Ramon explained that they would reenter the tent one more time, he would refresh the fire by adding more charcoal and rocks, and he would complete the ceremony by singing a song.

Ramon's song was in the Lakota Sioux language and was hauntingly beautiful. When the song was over, Ramon pushed the rocks to the side, pulled out the link of sausage, placed it on the grill and allowed it to sizzle for a few minutes.

Stephen's mouth was watering. He hadn't eaten sausage, other than Slim Jims from the commissary, in five years. Ramon sliced the sausage in three pieces with a plastic fork and knife and handed a piece to Sean and Stephen speared on the end of a plastic fork. They did not have any plates or napkins, but they didn't care.

Stephen took one small bite, and delicious hot grease ran down his chin. "I'm really grateful for this," he said with a smile, pretending to be adding leaves over the fire.

They all smiled, chuckling through their chewing.

CHAPTER 43

Skip – Day 1,610

t was Saturday. Skip should have been planning to have friends over to watch college football, or working on a home improvement project, but he was getting ready to visit Stephen in Three Rivers Federal Prison Camp. While Three Rivers was so much better than Bastrop, it was still horrible. He wrestled with resentment at having to give up his Saturday to visit his son. Skip worked long hours during the week, and Sunday was filled with church activities. So, Saturday was his only day off, and he spent one of those precious Saturdays every month driving to see Stephen. Even sweeping out the garage would be more pleasant than visiting the prison.

Still, his heart went out to Stephen, who didn't have the option of mowing grass or any of the things Skip could do. He knew he was Stephen's most faithful visitor, and it seemed right. It had mostly been just the two of them for so many years. Why shouldn't he be the one to keep Stephen encouraged now?

He double checked his list. He had printed the visitors form and completed all the questions (No, he did not have any weapons in his possession, etc.). He had his baggie full of coins and $1 bills for the vending machines, which didn't work any better than the ones in Bastrop.

Skip checked his clothes in the mirror. He decided to change his shirt, because it might look too much like khaki, a color which was not allowed. He also needed his driver's license as identification. The check-in officer would keep it until it was time to leave again. He scrounged around for more quarters. The ritual of preparing for the visit was complicated, but he had it down now.

The two-hour drive was uneventful. Three Rivers was a wide spot in the road that one could pass and not realize they had missed anything at all. As he drove into the parking lot he saw that, as usual, it was full. He couldn't remember a time when he was not competing with crowds of other visitors.

Skip glanced down at the little leather portfolio he carried with him. It contained a yellow legal pad on which he kept copious notes about work projects and other important matters. As he was planning out the visit list last night, he had written down some comforting scriptures and thoughts to help him through the day. He looked at what he'd written:

"But those who wait for the Lord's help find renewed strength; they rise up as if they had eagles' wings.[11]"

What does it mean to *wait upon God*?

To wait on God means to put all my trust in Him, believing that He cares about what is happening in my life and knows how to use it for my good.

To wait on God also means to put my hope in Him, not in human endeavors or material things.

Daniel is a great example of what it means to wait on God. He was taken captive and lived in a foreign land, yet he never lost hope. While he waited on God, Daniel exhibited these attributes:

He protected his mind and body by refusing the King's food.

He worked hard at everything he was asked to do.

He fostered a strong friendship with three other faithful men.

He prayed constantly.

Skip looked at the words on the page. He was doing three of the four items he'd written down pretty well—all but the third one. He had begun to isolate himself

---

11 Isaiah 40:31, NET

from friends. He made a note in the margin to call his friend Ken and reconnect. Then, he closed his eyes and prayed, "God, you are still good, even when things are bad. You see the big picture, and I cannot. I dedicate this day to you and I ask you to give me words of hope and encouragement for Stephen."

He got out of the truck and took his place in the long line. At Three Rivers, visitors stood outside in the elements while the officer inside let in one or two at a time and checked to be sure they were on the approved visitation list.

Skip was glad that he had reread the story of Daniel the night before. While he waited in line in the cold and rain to visit his son, it felt like waiting to be thrown into the lion's den. At least, Skip knew that story had a happy ending.

CHAPTER 44

Stephen – Day 1,747

Stephen woke in the middle of the night to the sound of someone crying out in terror and loud thunder-strikes of fists hitting flesh. Momentarily, he thought it might be a nightmare, but the sickening thuds sounded all too real. His next thought was it could be a sexual encounter. He had hoped to avoid ever being exposed to that, although he heard references to it happening. After lying frozen a moment longer, he realized that someone was being viciously beaten.

With his heart racing, he thought about getting up to see what was going on. What if it was Sean being attacked? With only three COs at night to guard 300 men, no one was likely to respond. But he had been in prison long enough to know that he didn't dare cry out or call for help. If Stephen left his quad to try to intervene, and a CO did show up, he would be punished for having something to do with it. When something bad happened in prison everyone got punished, and those involved, including onlookers and those who notified the COs, received harsher punishment than those who kept to themselves.

The inmate being beaten apparently went unconscious with the next blow and most of the noise stopped, except for a few more punches. The attackers dispersed quietly to wherever they had come from and everyone nearby let out a breath. It took a long time before Stephen could relax enough to breathe normally. He cleared his throat quietly a few times to see if any of his quadmates would talk about what they thought happened, but nobody responded.

In the morning, everyone was somber, dressing quickly and hoping to avoid the fallout sure to come. Stephen planned to follow suit, but two COs came rushing by his quad, just as he was trying to escape to breakfast. He could hear bits and phrases. The victim was Joe Valdez, sleeping just two quads away. Stephen laced his shoes and walked as quickly as he could toward the cafeteria. Two prison employees who did not look familiar passed him, going in the opposite direction. One of them may have been a nurse.

He went through the cafeteria line. As he turned and tried to locate a place to sit down, he realized that the cafeteria was more crowded than usual. It was as if every inmate in Three Rivers had decided to dress and eat early. Yet the normally noisy room was quiet, with most inmates staring at their trays. He spotted one free table across the room, close to the door he had entered. As he neared the door, he saw the COs and the two other employees pushing Joe on a gurney. Stephen got a very quick glance at the man. The side of Joe's head had a gaping wound and one of his eyes was pulverized, a swollen purple-and-red mess. Stephen wondered if it was going to be reparable.

After Joe was taken to medical, the rumor mill began. Sean always seemed to have sources, so Stephen sought him out after breakfast. "What do you know about Joe?" said Stephen without a greeting as he stepped into Sean's quad.

"Some members of the Tejas Familia think he stole some of their contraband," said Sean. "Joe works as a groundskeeper. From what I hear, he might have come across a bag in the bushes. The story is that he took something out of that bag."

Stephen nodded his head, slowly sipping his coffee, holding the mug in both hands for warmth. It was impossible to hide anything or keep something secret in federal prison.

"What was in the bag?" asked Stephen.

"Rumor has it, it was steroids."

After a thoughtful pause, Stephen changed the subject. "Dewayne is making tamales this week. You want some?"

"No thanks," said Sean.

Sean never wanted any of the tasty food that some of the Three Rivers inmates were able to make from the commissary ingredients. Stephen didn't know if it was because Sean didn't have a lot of money to spare, or if he really didn't like the food. Stephen had come to like it a lot. Dewayne's tamales were tasty.

Dewayne would buy a bag of Doritos at the commissary, crush the chips, and mix them with water to make the *masa*. Then he would take Slim Jim beef jerky sticks and shred them up into tiny pieces to make the filling. The final step involved wrapping the tasty meat pies in wet paper towels and steaming them in the microwave. Stephen thought they were delicious and well worth a packet of Mackerel—the currency of Three Rivers.

Stephen had another request for his *How to Survive in Federal Prison* guide, so he excused himself and headed back to his quad. He had made a bit of extra money selling copies of it to new inmates. The problem was that he didn't have a way to copy it very easily. Obviously, inmates didn't have access to photocopiers. So, he had to buy a new notebook at the commissary and hand copy his advice into the first thirty or so pages. He thought about paying someone else to copy it for him, but that cut into his profit too much.

He decided that he needed to modify the guide now that he was in Three Rivers. The camp experience was completely different from the medium security prison in Bastrop. A lot of the inmates at Three Rivers had never been to a higher security prison. They were low-level offenders who got two to four years' incarceration as their sentence. The guys who had graduated down from a higher security level were in the minority, and they all knew how nice it was in comparison. They didn't have much sympathy when one of the camp inmates complained about their surroundings. Stephen and Sean, who *did* know how much better it was, had taken to calling the Three Rivers Federal Correctional Institution, "Sweet Rivers."

As he flipped through his guidebook, Stephen realized that he had included nothing on how to deal with violence, like what happened to Joe. He wasn't sure how to address it because there wasn't much an inmate could do to guard against a sneak attack from two guys with a lock in a sock. Then, he thought of something useful to share:

At FCI Three Rivers you may be surprised at how much contraband is brought into the Camp. This is because the Camp is near a highway where people can easily leave a duffle bag full of contraband (favorites are drugs, alcohol, food items, and cell phones) in the bushes nearby. Because Camp inmates are not locked in, they can sneak out to the bushes at night and find the bag. If you find a bag, do not touch it. Do not report it. Get away from it fast. Don't mention it to another inmate. Don't be associated with it.

As he put down his pen, he realized his hand was trembling. The sound of Joe being beaten had pushed its way into his thoughts and traumatized him a second time as he wrote. He stood up, laced his hands together behind his neck and stared at the ceiling. He was suddenly grateful that as curious and impulsive as he could sometimes be, he'd never stumbled into something in prison as dangerous as Joe apparently had. He was grateful for that, and for Sean's company and Dewayne's tamales. He rubbed his hands together and took off down the hall to find those tamales.

CHAPTER 45

Stephen – Day 1,755

Today was a good day and Stephen decided to celebrate. He had just received his final grades in Spanish II and Biology and was now a college sophomore. Considering how hard it was to go to college in prison, this was something to celebrate indeed. Of the hundreds of inmates he'd met over the last five years, only two others were trying to go to college. That was not a surprise when considering the BOP employed people like Janet Johnson.

Janet Johnson was the education coordinator at Three Rivers FCI, and evidently hated her job, or Stephen. He wasn't sure which. She made it almost impossible for Stephen to go to school, when in fact it was her job to try to assist him. Apparently, the BOP kept statistics on how many inmates took the graduate equivalency exam or GED. So, that was where Janet focused her time. She planned to spend her time on activities measured by her boss, and not one thing more. GED classes were offered, but Stephen's desire to take college courses didn't fit in with her plans. Several times, when Stephen's textbooks arrived, rather than allowing Stephen to have the textbooks, she returned them to the university without explanation.

Stephen requested an appointment with her and tried to explain that college tuition was very expensive, and he needed the textbooks to take the courses for which he was registered.

"I'm busy," she said. "I don't have time to review the books you ordered to see if they're allowed in the prison system."

"You're the education coordinator," he pleaded. "Don't you want me to get an education?"

"I really don't care if you get an education," she said with contempt. "You're a criminal. Why do you deserve to go to college?"

Stephen was dumbfounded by her attitude. He did not like to file grievances, because he worried about retribution from the staff; however, in Janet's case he made an exception. His grievances were never acknowledged, and her motivation never improved.

Stephen should have finished his two courses in five months, but it took him almost a year. Whenever he completed sufficient assignments for a test, he had to set up an appointment with Ms. Johnson to proctor the exam. Stephen learned not to get his hopes up because the likelihood of her showing up was quite low. When she did show up, it was her job to watch him take the test and send it in to the university. On several occasions, his test sat on her desk for weeks without being returned to his professor, which resulted in him not being able to get a new assignment for long periods of time. With all these added obstacles, it was borderline miraculous he had ever finished.

Janet Johnson wasn't the only challenge. He had a terrible time finding somewhere to study because there were almost no places available that had a writing surface and were also quiet. So, when he got a job as the chaplain's assistant, he was delighted at the prospect of using the little chapel as a place to study. The chapel at Sweet Rivers didn't require much upkeep, and it was quiet. Because he was diligent and efficient about his work duties, the chaplain agreed to let him remain in the chapel to study after he finished working.

So, today he was celebrating the fact that he had become a legitimate college sophomore. Stephen and Sean had purchased bean dip and crackers from the commissary and they were planning to make snacks and watch football. Sean wasn't as interested in football as he was, but he was being a good sport in celebrating Stephen's victory over his educational hurdles.

Sean showed up in the common room with a can of cheese whiz and a box of crackers. Stephen had the bean dip. A piece of cheddar cheese would have made the treat complete, but real cheese was not available, only highly processed, shelf-stable products. At least they had the all-important microwave. Because they didn't have any dishes on which to microwave their food, they tore the cracker box apart and used it as a tray. They were eating bean dip-and-canned-cheese cracker treats and toasting with little plastic cups of water when the CO walked in and put a damper on their festivities.

"Both of you have certified letters to pick up. Put this stuff in the trash and go to CO Schultz and sign for your letter."

They looked at each other. Neither one of them was expecting any correspondence from their attorney and couldn't imagine what else would come certified.

"Sir, we just have a few more bites to eat," Stephen said. "And we saved our money a long time for this snack. Can each of us go independently, instead of at the same time, and that way we don't have to throw away the food?"

The CO pushed his chin forward for a moment. He looked perturbed at their response.

Stephen stood up straight and tried his best to look respectful. He knew that the CO could require them to do anything he asked. But, he also knew the COs had a degree of appreciation for inmates that rarely made any trouble.

"One of you can stay for five minutes. The other needs to go and come back. We don't have time to keep up with your mail or store it for you."

Stephen turned to Sean, "Do you want to go or stay?"

"I'll go first," Sean said and disappeared. "I can't stand to wait. I have to know now."

Stephen paced in front of the television for a few minutes, fending off requests from other inmates for one of their snacks. When Sean returned, he asked, "What was in your letter?"

"I don't know yet. I wanted to get back in here for you. I brought mine with me." He had a large white envelope in his hand. It looked like something from a lawyer's office.

Stephen took off. On his way out, he said, "Go ahead and eat all the snacks if you want, but don't give them away. I'll eat them if you don't."

Stephen walked quickly down to CO Schultz's office at the entrance to the facility, just outside of the visiting rooms. This was not an area that he was normally permitted to be in outside of visiting days. He hoped it would not get him in trouble.

When he approached CO Schultz's office he cleared his throat a few paces back and stood up straight and with a respectful tone said, "Sir, I was told to see you about a certified letter, sir."

Without a word, the CO handed him an envelope, a logbook, and a pen.

After he signed, Stephen passed the log back to the CO. "May I be excused?"

"Get back to your unit, Taylor."

When Stephen reentered the common room, he knew that Sean had gotten bad news. His tender-hearted friend was staring at the TV glassy-eyed, with his letter in his lap. Stephen slipped in beside him and asked, "What is it?"

"You open yours first," said Sean.

Stephen tore open his envelope. It was from an attorney in Austin he had never heard of. He had to read the first paragraph twice. It began: "Please be advised that I represent Kylee Taylor in the matter enclosed herein…"

Kylee was divorcing him.

He took a deep breath and picked up the little cardboard tray of snacks that they had worked so hard for and walked over to some other inmates watching football and gave them the snacks. Sean did not protest. Neither of them felt like celebrating anymore.

He sat down beside Sean and said, "Kylee's divorcing me. I guess I shouldn't be surprised. But I am. I hope your news is better than mine."

"No. Same."

"What?"

"I got a divorce petition, too."

"What? Seriously?"

Sean nodded.

"Let's go for a walk."

They went outside to the exercise area and began to walk around the little track, still carrying the papers in their hand.

"I guess I knew things were not good," said Stephen. "But it still feels like a shock. And a loss."

"I think my situation is more tragic than yours."

"Why?"

Sean looked miserable. His eyes were red, and his breathing was labored. "You're going to be inside for four more years. You weren't expecting to be reunited with your wife soon. I'm going home in six months. I was looking forward to being welcomed home by someone who loves me. Now I find out that there will be no one waiting for me when I get out."

They walked around the track until their legs ached, taking some of their grief out on their own bodies. As they returned for the evening count, Stephen realized that losing Sean in six months' time was going to be almost as painful as losing Kylee.

CHAPTER 46

Skip – Day 1,817

Tamara looked radiant crossing the stage. Her blonde hair was curled stylishly and her smile beamed pride in her accomplishment. Skip was proud of her and he told her so. Skip had known Tamara since she was a young girl and he was pleased to be invited to something as special as her high school graduation. She posed for pictures with her parents and siblings before she asked her father, Ken, if she could go for a celebration dinner with her friends.

Skip put a hand on Ken's shoulder after Tamara and her friends ran to the parking lot. "You should be proud. She's an amazing girl and she is going to be the CEO of some company in the not-too-distant future."

Ken pursed his lips and nodded, apparently worried that his voice might crack if he spoke. The parents of one of the other graduates came over to offer their congratulations and Ken recovered.

As Skip observed this happy moment, bitterness threatened to crowd into his thoughts. Seeing beautiful, sweet, Christian kids like Tamara and her friends was heartwarming and heartbreaking at the same time. He was genuinely happy for her to have such a bright future. She was smart. She was disciplined. She had a good head on her shoulders. She was certainly going to be very accomplished at whatever field she chose in college.

What did Ken and Debbie do right, that I did all wrong?

Earlier that day he had seen the familiar, *No caller ID* message flash on his cellphone. When he answered, he heard the mechanical robot voice say, "You have a call from a federal prison, if you choose to accept the call, press 1 now." Stephen had come on the line and shared with him that Kylee had filed for divorce. It was so hard to try to comfort someone in a two-minute phone call that cuts you off mid-sentence. Skip was sad, even though he could hardly blame Kylee for her decision to move on.

Skip had not visited Stephen this weekend. He stayed in town to see Tamara graduate. Next weekend he would drive the 200-mile round trip to visit his son in prison. It would be expensive. It would be exhausting. And it would not yield anything especially useful, except the opportunity to share his love with Stephen, who was rejecting almost everything Skip believed in and stood for.

Am I accomplishing anything at all in this life? What kind of legacy will I leave?

These soul-crushing thoughts stole his joy. He felt so out of place at church, he had started finding reasons not to go. Everyone else's children seemed to be doing well. It made Skip feel like a complete fraud in their presence. Skip hugged everyone again and slipped out quickly. Halfway to the truck he heard Ken call his name.

"Hey, we're volunteering at Meadowcreek next week. Our life group is adopting the boys in the Oak Cabin. We're gonna make them a nice dinner every couple of weeks and make sure they have toiletries and stuff. We could use your help. Can you come grill some fajitas next Thursday?

"Let me check my meetings that day, and I'll text you if I can come."

"All right. I hope to see you there. These young guys could really use some fatherly influence. Most of them don't have dads. Or worse, they have a dad who hurt them.

"I can see where you would be a great fit for that," Skip said.

"You would be too."

"Thanks, Ken. I'll let you know."

Skip turned and hopped in his shiny truck. He turned the key in the ignition and laughed to release some feelings that were threatening to turn into anger and self-pity.

I'm sure they do not need me volunteering with orphaned and abandoned children. If they knew what a loser I am as a dad, they would not only not want me as a volunteer, they would put me on the blacklist and ban me from the grounds.

CHAPTER 47

Stephen – Day 1,828

Stephen experienced a roller coaster of emotions for several days: anger, sadness, nostalgia. After they ran their course, he decided that he wouldn't make the divorce difficult or ask Kylee for anything. It bothered him that Kylee would keep all the nice furniture and gifts his parents had purchased for them as wedding presents. But what choice did he have? He had no money to fight, and he had no grounds. Part of him realized that he had abandoned her five years ago, just as she was abandoning him now. He hadn't intended to. But he made choices that resulted in it all the same.

Sean had gone into hibernation for a few days and was still not in the mood to talk. Stephen had dropped by his quad to check on him three times. Sean was sitting cross-legged in his bed, drawing on his tablet. Beautiful, but fractured, images bled from the pages.

Stephen wished that he had such a therapeutic outlet for his pain. He told his father about the divorce petition, and Skip had been a bit more sympathetic than expected, but it was difficult to receive much encouragement in a two-minute phone call.

Will and Paul would have been wonderful to talk to in his current situation. Both would have been encouraging and thoughtful, and probably found a way to make him laugh. It was a shame that inmates were not permitted to call or write to each other. He thought about his friends as he walked to the CO's office to check out a key to the chapel. It was Thursday morning and it was part of his work assignment to go to the chapel to clean up from the previous evening's activities and get the space ready for the next gathering.

"Sifuentes has the key," said the CO.

Stephen cocked his head back, perplexed. Gilberto Sifuentes was head of the Tejas Familia gang in the Three Rivers prison and seemed like an unlikely person to need a key to the chapel.

"What? Sir, why would Sifuentes have the key?"

"You are welcome to ask him yourself," the CO said dismissively.

Stephen walked to the chapel to see if it was open. It was, but it was full of gang members. He stood at the open door for a minute, confused.

"What do you want?" Sifuentes demanded.

"I'm supposed to clean the chapel now and arrange the chairs for a meeting tonight," answered Stephen uncertainly.

"Well, you can see that the space is in use. Now, get out."

Stephen backed up and shut the door but stood looking at it for a moment. Everything about that exchange was wrong. Even though he had not come to believe everything his dad believed, he still felt a sense of reverence for the chapel. He thought about his grandparents and how they dressed in their Sunday best for church, treating it like a holy place. Gang members shouldn't be using it to plot strategy. He determined to talk to Pastor Jim about it and see what could be done.

Stephen left. After dinner, he tried again to acquire the key and found Chris Benson there, asking for the same key. Stephen was happy to see him. Well-groomed and handsome, Chris was tall like Stephen, and probably a few years older. Chris was an attorney by training and made a living putting together business deals. He had been convicted of income-tax evasion.

Chris led a men's Bible study on Thursday nights and had invited Stephen several times. Stephen wasn't quite sure why, but he had resisted. He liked Chris a lot; he just wasn't quite sure if he wanted to hear about the Bible for a whole hour. It didn't sound like fun.

"I was about to go clean up the chapel for you," said Stephen. "I tried earlier and there was…another group using the room."

"I was going to go study my notes for tonight," Chris said as he signed for the key.

They walked to the chapel together. Stephen unlocked the door and they both looked around, stunned.

The place was a mess. Potato chip bags littered the floor, and someone had knocked over a soda can and left the sticky soda to dry. Soft drinks were not available outside of the locked visitation room, and food was not allowed outside the cafeteria or the common room. Stephen was surprised that Sifuentes' crew had gotten their hands on forbidden food and didn't even try to hide it. Apparently, they had decided to start using the chapel as a place to meet, under the pretense of a religious gathering, but there was nothing holy about whatever they had been discussing.

Chris started to pick up trash, but Stephen stopped him. "You go ahead and study your notes. I'll get this."

Chris hesitated a moment, then set out his Bible on one corner of the chaplain's desk and began to write notes on a notepad. Just before 7 p.m. other guys started to come in. Stephen decided it was clean enough and was about to say goodbye to Chris and leave, when he saw Sean slip in quietly.

"Have you been coming to this?" asked Stephen.

"Once or twice. After getting my divorce petition, I thought I could use some encouragement. Or at least a distraction. Are you going to stay?"

Stephen was planning to say no, but it didn't come out when he opened his mouth. He thought for a moment and considered whether he might stay and listen, just once? Just to support Sean. He shrugged and sat down next to Sean.

The other guys had Bibles and notebooks and he realized that he might need something to write on, not because he wanted to take notes, but so that he could doodle and daydream if he got bored. He looked around and saw that he had left one of his school notebooks in the chapel from a previous study session. He got up and grabbed it and a pen off the chaplain's desk.

He was now in the habit of taking notes from his schoolwork. So, during Chris's lesson, he absent-mindedly took notes. He was surprised at how interesting the lesson turned out to be. It was not at all what he was expecting. It had lifted his spirits and it really seemed to be helping Sean, who, for once, wasn't doodling.

Later, before bed, he flipped open the notebook and took another look at what he had written:

God has given you a sound mind to use: 2 Timothy 1:7.

You become what you think about: Proverbs 23:7.

You have the power to control what you think about: Romans 12:2.

God encourages you to think about positive things: Philippians 4:4-13.

Your plans will be successful if you commit them to God: Proverbs 16:3.

He stared at the paper for moment, willing his heart to believe. Wouldn't it be great if it were all true? If God would just wipe your slate clean. Erase your mistakes. Give you a sound mind. Open doors for your success. Unicorns and rainbows. He tore out the page and threw it in the trash. A few minutes later, he decided to retrieve it. He dug around in the bottom of his locker and found the leather Bible his dad sent him four years ago. He folded the sheet of notes and put them in the front of the Bible. Maybe he would visit Chris's class again sometime. Just to support Sean.

CHAPTER 48

Stephen – Day 1,839

Stephen was under the Bob Hall Pier, sitting on his surfboard with his arms wrapped around his knees. A late summer storm was blowing, and he was waiting out the rain. A slight chill to the air made him shiver. It was probably the first cold front of the fall and it was beautiful. Clouds roiled in the sky. Angry waves throbbed and punched the air. The rain blew sideways, so he was almost as wet under the pier as he would have been out surfing, but the pier protected him from the fierce wind.

He was anxious to get back out in the water. The game warden and the beach park ranger had already driven by once. He was fifteen and tall for his age. Out on the waves, he could pass for someone not truant from school, but if they got a good look at him....

When the rain passed south and the sun broke through, the sky was glorious. Magenta, gold, and lavender clouds floated in the blue heavens like sails. The storm had passed, but the wind was still earnest, and the waves pounded the shore. His heart pounded, too. On a surfboard he was the whole of himself. It was hard work paddling in the big surf, jumping up and guiding the board with his legs and toes, bending it to his will. His legs and lungs ached, and the salt water stung his eyes.

The feeling of flying across the water was like nothing else. Sometimes when he felt this way, he thought to himself that he would gladly jump off a bridge if he could be assured that heaven felt like this.

There were other things that felt almost as good, but not quite. His mother's third husband, Dan, had a 60-foot sportfish. A few times, Dan had let him steer. The power of the engines and the sea air on his face as he piloted the *Hercules* through the gulf felt amazing.

Gliding over the water on his surfboard, cutting through the wave, making it carry him against its will, was thrilling. Each wave he conquered gave up all its energy to him. When he finally sat down on the beach to rest, he was spent in a way that felt marvelous. He could hardly catch his breath from the exhilaration.

Something hit him on the shoulder from behind. It stung. What was it?

"Shut up over there!"

Stephen sat up on his elbow and realized where he was. He was dreaming again.

"Sorry. Bad dre—nightmare," he said.

"Yeah, right. Was your nightmare named Amber?" Danny, one of his quadmates asked sarcastically. The two other men laughed and mumbled obscenities.

Stephen was embarrassed. He was still breathing heavily. He took a deep, long breath to quiet his mind and slow his heart rate. Amber. That name hadn't entered his conscious thoughts for a long time. Had he said her name in his sleep? He turned over and stared up at the ceiling, trying to remember her.

They had gone through middle school and two years of high school together, before his parents had shipped him off to boarding school. She was a year younger, but they were in the same grade. They had become school chums, cutting up in the back of the room while everyone else was listening and studying. One day he talked her into skipping school with him to go to the beach. They swam and ran up and down the beach. She even had her own surfboard, much to his surprise. She was not as good as he was, but she held her own.

The reawakened memory was now so fresh it seemed like yesterday. She had packed sandwiches for them that day. After surfing for hours, those baloney and cheese sandwiches had been delicious. Amber was one of the only people he confided in during those years. He had shared his deepest insecurities, and she had not run away.

"I would never have done this on my own," she had said. "But I'm sure glad to be missing Ms. Gonzales' algebra class."

"I know. Everyone seems to get it, but me."

"And me!" she agreed.

Stephen felt relieved.

Amber shared, "My parents are worried about my grades. So, they took me to the doctor and now I have some prescription medicine. It helps me do my homework, but when it wears off about dinner time, I can't even keep my eyes open. I feel like someone hit me with a brick. I don't like to take it. It makes me feel hyper-alert all day and then it steals my evening when I want to do things with my friends. My brain can only stay alert so long, apparently."

He pulled out a joint. "This is my medicine. You want some?"

She wrinkled her nose. "I don't know."

"Just try it," he said as he lit the marijuana cigarette. "You have to take a deep breath and hold it. Like this." He demonstrated.

She shook her head no and stared out at the waves, ignoring him.

"I got this from my mom's house. Her society friends do it all the time. You're just going to feel relaxed."

She reached for it gingerly, but inhaled heartily. She sucked in a cloud of smoke and almost choked to death. They laughed until their sides split.

They finished the joint and lay back in the sand, their bodies still wet from the ocean. The sky seemed intensely blue. The wind was a soft, warm blanket massaging their limbs.

After a long while, she rolled onto her side and smiled at him. "I see what you mean. The weed does calm my crazy, wild thoughts a little bit."

Stephen smiled and stretched his arm out where her head had been. She was either going to have to rest her head on his shoulder or move. She lay her head on his shoulder.

Her body was tiny, tan, and athletic. She wore a bikini top and board shorts. Her toenails were painted yellow and he thought they looked wonderful with her tan skin. Little water droplets beaded up on her arms and legs, resisted by her oily sunscreen.

He felt such a deeply satisfying feeling for her that day. Protective. Not entirely sexual. She was too young to think that way. They both were, really. He was no longer a virgin, but she probably was.

They lay there in the sun for a long time, sharing deep secrets of the heart. They both felt different from the other kids at school; the kids who wrote papers, cross referenced their sources, and understood algebra. Stephen just couldn't make all that stuff stick. He tried to do the assigned homework. He'd read the same paragraph over three times, each time gleaning almost nothing from it. He had never understood why he could recall the lyrics to every popular song but couldn't retain the material from his textbooks. He was clever enough to keep his classmates in stitches constantly with his jokes, so why couldn't he find the hidden meaning in *Moby Dick*? His quick wit and good looks were probably the only things that had kept him from flunking half of his classes.

If only he could have back for just an hour the sweet way he felt about Amber that day. It was so innocent and real. They were always friendly after that, but she never skipped school or smoked pot with him again. Instead, she took her medication, stayed serious about school, and did well. He continued his downward spiral of skipping, smoking, and surfing. When he moved from the Island to go to boarding school, they didn't keep in touch. He kept up with her through friends and was glad to know that she had become very accomplished.

When he went off to boarding school and moved away from the Island, he had not found another activity which was quite as satisfying as surfing. He tried jogging and scuba diving. But it just didn't give him the mental high and physical satisfaction that surfing had. After high school, athletics started taking a backseat to drinking and smoking. Gradually, drinking replaced almost everything that had once mattered, including exercise, friends, and family.

During his crazy days in El Paso, those days when he had money to burn, he added sex to his growing list of addictions. At the peak of his involvement with the drug organization, he didn't control his daily schedule. So, his opportunities to meet someone new or plan a real date became quite limited. Instead, as he traveled, he created a network of beautiful women in every city. He kept a special phone on which he kept their contact numbers. In his line of work, he had to get a new cell phone number regularly, but he kept the second phone so he could always stay in touch with his women. There were many. They had an arrangement that passed for a relationship. He would text when he was in their town and they would hook up at a hotel. Later he would send them a note, and jewelry. That way it seemed more like a date than paying for sex.

During one of his many back-together times with Kylee, she had discovered the phone inside a duffle bag in his car. One look at some of the names on the device sent her fleeing back to Austin, sobbing, in the middle of the night.

He stared at the ceiling thinking about Kylee. How beautiful she was. How fragile. He knew she didn't like to be alone. The fact that she took the initiative to seek a divorce probably meant that she had found someone else. He released the anger he had over the divorce and her decision not to stick by him. To his surprise, he hoped she would find happiness. He had certainly never given her any. In the morning, he would sign the documents and send them back.

Stephen let out a long sigh. He had totally messed up love back when he had something to offer. What on earth was he going to do four years from now, when he walked out of this place with nothing? Who was ever going to want him then?

CHAPTER 49

Stephen – Day 1,882

Chaplain Jim was not coming back. When Stephen went on Thursday morning to get the chapel key the CO told him his cleaning services were no longer needed. No one was going to be using the chapel for a while.

"I'm supposed to set up for Bible study tonight."

"There won't be any Bible study in the chapel tonight, or any other night. Go find your counselor and see what your next work duty is going to be," said the CO.

"Can I ask why we can't use the chapel?"

"No. You may not," the CO said and turned his back to Stephen.

Instead of reporting to his counselor, Stephen sought out Chris Benson to find out more. "I haven't heard this," said Chris. "I still thought we could use the chapel. But, I had a feeling something was wrong. I was looking for the schedule of who's preaching this month, and I noticed that it was not posted this week."

Chaplain Jim was responsible for organizing church services for more than one federal prison, so he wasn't in the Three Rivers office every day. He did not conduct these services himself, but instead organized a calendar of visiting pastors. Most were Christian pastors, either Catholic or Protestant, but Chaplain Jim also allowed the chapel to be used by other faiths.

When Stephen first met him, Chaplain Jim seemed sad and disillusioned. But after Chris Benson started coming to church services and teaching a Bible study, the chaplain was energized and showed new interest in his job. Now he was gone without an explanation and the chapel was off limits. Stephen had noticed that Chaplain Jim hadn't been around much after the Tejas Familia gang started using the chapel for their meetings. He wasn't sure if the gang members had taken over the chapel because the chaplain was no longer present, or the other way around.

Stephen felt angry and disappointed. Chaplain Jim had abandoned him without saying goodbye. They had worked closely together for several months and Stephen enjoyed his company.

"So, how can we have Bible Study tonight?" Stephen asked. "There's no place to meet."

"Well, perhaps we can think of another way to meet," Chris replied "I was just thinking of having some coffee. Would you like some?"

"You have coffee?"

"Yes. Just got this from the commissary this week," said Chris holding up a small container of instant coffee.

"Yes! Hook me up. You don't mind?" Not very many inmates would share a commissary item with another inmate without trading something for it. But Chris was just that nice. They made instant coffee by using tap water from the bathroom and heating it in the microwave. They walked out to the exercise yard where there were several benches and sipped the coffee.

"What do you think happened to Chaplain Jim?" asked Stephen.

"I think he might have gotten fired."

"Why?"

"I don't know for sure, so I don't want to say."

"Well, you obviously suspect that he did something un-chaplain-like. I can hear it in your voice, even though you don't want to say. I thought he was a Christian?"

"Just because he's a Christian doesn't mean he can't make a mistake."

"What's going to happen to my job cleaning the chapel? It's just going to go away isn't it? Like all the desks in Bastrop. Like all the fruit in the commissary. Like Kylee. Like Arnie. Like Will." Stephen was getting louder and more agitated.

Chris interjected calmly when Stephen took a breath. "If you put your faith in people or circumstances, you're always going to be disappointed at some point.

That's why I have decided to put my faith in God. He will never let us down. Don't get disillusioned about Chaplain Jim and quit coming to Bible study."

"How could you tell that's what I was feeling?"

"I can just tell. You never share anything in Bible study. You just write in your little notebook. I can tell you have questions and doubts. But you never voice them. What's your story?"

Stephen was silent for a moment. He stared at his hands.

"I was raised with a dad who believes in God and grandparents that believe in God. They took me to church, but it never resonated with me the way it does with them. I like the way you teach. When you teach I can almost believe, but then my doubts win out."

"What part do you doubt? That God exists? Or that He loves you?"

It felt good to finally admit to his doubts. Stephen was glad they were alone. "I just can't believe all that stuff in the Bible. I've been reading a little bit about different religions and spirituality, trying to open my mind to what you're saying and what Ramon says. But it bothers me that there are so many conflicting messages about faith. How can I know for sure that you're right about God and everyone else is wrong?"

Chris continued, "If you have doubts, God understands. All you have to do is ask Him to help your unbelief. That's what I did. I just told Him that I really wanted to believe and asked him to make Himself real to me. And He did."

Stephen remembered Paul saying the same thing with the same conviction.

"You need to stop doing so much research, and do some more knee-search," said Chris. "You'll get your answer."

But what about guys like Ramon and my friend, Hussain? They are good people but they don't believe the same thing you do."

"I'll have to pray on that one before I can give you an answer," Chris said. "All I know is that when I surrendered my heart to God, I had a unique experience that's hard to describe, except to say that He made himself real to me."

Stephen was ready to go back inside, but there was another question he wanted to ask. "Chris, when you pray, you sound like you are talking to a friend, someone you know. How did you learn to do that?

This time Chris was silent for a few seconds. He took a deep breath and he had a serious look on his face. Stephen thought perhaps he had offended him.

Chris finally said, "It's funny you would say that. When I pray I *do* feel like I am talking to someone I know. It's like the other inmates in the room disappear and I am talking only to God. I feel His presence when I am praying, and other times throughout the day. Do you want me to pray for you right now?"

Stephen shook his head. "I guess my relationship to God, whoever he is, is still private. I'm still waiting for him to make the first move."

"He already has. But I'll pray he shows to you in a tangible way that he is there for you."

"Thanks for the coffee," said Stephen. "It was a treat. Do you want me to try to round up the guys and see if they want to have Bible Study in your quad?"

"Not today. We just had one."

CHAPTER 50

Stephen – Day 1,899

New men arrived weekly, and some familiar faces left. On a cold Wednesday in March, Sean carried his small box of belongings down the hall to be released from prison. Stephen and Sean shared more in the last six months than many friends do in a lifetime. Hopes. Dreams. Encouragement. Although he was certainly happy for Sean, Stephen felt the loss deeply.

"You better write me because you know how special it is to the guys inside to get a letter. Tell me about how good you're doing and all the women you're dating," Stephen said with a laugh as he slapped Sean on the back.

"I've got some ideas for what my pen pal name is going to be. Obviously, I can't send you letters under my own name, since we met in prison. But I will write to you and you will know it's from me." Sean said.

Stephen wanted to give his friend a hug, but it was frowned upon inside the fence. So, they clasped hands and bumped shoulders, which passed for affection.

"I know you're gonna make it. Of all the people I've met in here, you're the one I know for certain won't be back," said Stephen.

Sean didn't say anything, but his intense blue eyes spoke the words that would not come out.

After Sean left Three Rivers to return to the world, Stephen went back to his quad and sat on the bunk. He wanted to cry, but there was no privacy in prison, and no safe way to show emotion. He struggled to hold it inside, but the emotions almost let go when he found a little drawing inside his textbook with a note from Sean.

It was a beautifully drawn sketch of a seashell sitting on top of a surfboard. The note said, "We've been tossed around a bit. But we're gonna wash up somewhere perfect and that new place is going to be better. We're not going to just survive. We're going to be better and stronger than before."

Stephen had assumed that there was nothing from federal prison that he would want to keep when he got out. This note was worth keeping.

Sometimes in prison months would go by and not one interesting thing would happen. That was not so on the day that Sean left. On that very same day, Alex Trevino arrived. Stephen knew Alex from Bastrop. A mechanic from Del Rio, Texas, Alex was in his late twenties, with a wife who visited faithfully and two small children.

Alex wore his hair short and was not covered with tattoos. Like Stephen, he had tried to get away from his involvement with the drug organization but was rounded up in a sting. Stephen was happy to see that he had become eligible for the lower level incarceration of a camp. Surely it would be easier for his wife and kids to visit.

"Hey Alex. Bet you're glad to be here," Stephen said when Alex showed up at dinner.

"Ah, man, I can't tell you, how glad I am to be out of Bastrop. That place sucked and it was getting worse every day."

"Tell me about some people. What's going on with my cellies?"

"I rarely talked with them, but I think they were doing okay. They got a new cellie after you left. Quiet guy."

"What about Dion?"

"Dion got transferred to camp too. He went somewhere else, not here, though."

"I'm really happy for him. He was a good guy. I hope he gets a better cellie situation than having to be near Big Mike all the time."

"Yeah that guy was a piece of work. Mean as a snake. He got sent up."

"What?"

"Yeah, no camp for Big Mike. Somethin' bad went down. I never found out exactly what it was. About the time you came here he went the other way. High security somewhere."

"Whoa. If medium was horrible, I can't even imagine what high security does to your soul. You don't have any idea what happened?"

"Contraband of some sort. I heard they found it sitting right on top of his bunk. But, you know how rumors are in prison. Surely, he wasn't stupid enough to leave drugs on top of his bed. Although, he was pretty cocky. Who knows?"

"What about my friend Will? He applied to come here. He should have been eligible. I can't figure out why he's not in here with me."

"Will?"

"Will Blankenship. You know. The guy with the little goatee and glasses that taught GED classes and worked in the library?"

"Older guy with short gray hair?"

"Yes. That's him."

"He got in some trouble too. I don't know how long you will be here, but you might not see him again."

Stephen deflated. "Wow. That tears me up. He was such a good guy. Helped me with all my homework, taught dozens of guys to read and write. Introduced me to all kinds of books and authors I would never have considered. What on earth could he have done that got him in so much trouble?"

"According to what I heard, he got caught with a George Foreman grill in his cell and some food we're not allowed to have. Yeah, he became ineligible to come to a camp for eighteen months. He'll have to stay in that hellhole a while longer for that."

Stephen let his weight fall back against the wall he was standing near. The news was like a kick to the gut. "Why would they punish him so severely just for wanting to make something to eat? They practically starve you in there. It's not like he had drugs."

"The warden wanted to make an example. You know. Decrease the contraband."

Stephen shook his head vigorously and pounded his fist on his thigh.

I hope it wasn't my party that got Will 18 more months in Bastrop Medium Prison and kept him from going to a Camp.

Will had never failed to encourage him. Stephen hoped that someone would come along that could do that for Will, perhaps reminding him to look for that light in the darkest night.

CHAPTER 51

Stephen – Day 1,916

Stephen didn't recognize the handwriting or the return address on the envelope.

Very curious.

He opened it and still didn't know who it was from. Still confused, Stephen skipped to the bottom to see the signature. It was signed, "Gary Blankenship."

Will found a way to write me!

Dear Stephen,

My dad asked me to write to you. There are some things that he really wanted to share with you. He has cancer. And it looks pretty grim. They have moved him to a prison in North Carolina.

He told me to write you two things. First, he wanted to tell you not to settle for easy or mediocre things in life. Do the hard work and you *will* succeed. He said of all the people he met in prison, you were the most likely to have a happy future. Second, he wanted me to tell you that the answer to many questions you have about Christianity can be found in Isaiah 53. You might not see it at first, but read that chapter of the Bible and think about it. I hope that he can send you another update himself very soon. Please pray for him and for our family. This is really hard.

Gary Blankenship

Stephen slammed his fist into the wall.

This is so unfair.

His mind churning with emotions. He did random chores around the quad and walked down a few halls aimlessly, trying to process the letter. Half of him wanted to read Isaiah 53, but the other half was angry at God and didn't want to open the Bible ever again.

The letter was so odd. Why didn't Will start the letter with "I wanted to let you know that I've been diagnosed with cancer and here's what's going on with me...?" Why would he waste a stamp on such useless advice to Stephen, when he must have more important things going on in his life? Unfortunately, after reading the letter, none of the other things he'd planned to do that day seemed worth doing.

The leather Bible his father had sent him hadn't gotten much use since he'd used it as a resource for his early homework assignments, but Stephen decided to try to find Isaiah 53. He found the listing in the Table of Contents and flipped through the pages. The chapter wasn't long, and it seemed to track stuff his dad had told him about Jesus.

One part read:

"Yet it was our weaknesses he carried;
it was our sorrows that weighed him down.
And we thought his troubles were a punishment from God,
a punishment for his own sins!
But he was pierced for our rebellion,
crushed for *our* sins.
He was beaten so we could be whole.
He was whipped so we could be healed.
All of us, like sheep, have strayed away.
We have left God's paths to follow our own.
Yet the LORD LAID ON HIM
THE SINS OF US ALL,"[12]

---

12 Isaiah 53:4-6, NLT

This isn't helping me. I already know what the basic Bible story says. I just don't know how I can be sure it is true. Maybe somebody made it up. How could Will think this would somehow answer all my questions?

Stephen felt crushed in his spirit. The Dark Night of the Soul, the feeling that Will had described, threatened to take control of his thoughts.

I need Chris. I don't know why, but I know he can help.

CHAPTER 52

Skip – Day 1,950

"I brought the fajita meat. What do you have?" Skip called out to Ken as they both pulled up in front of the little cabin at Meadowcreek

"We brought all the drinks and paper goods."

"I think Mark and Staci are bringing the beans and rice. I'm not sure we have tortillas, salsa, and cheese. Do you know if someone was bringing that?" asked Skip.

"Well, hopefully someone has that assignment. If not, I'll slip out and get some," said Ken.

The boys' cabin sat quite a distance from the parking pad, so carrying the groceries in was going to be a bit of chore. As they began to unload, a polite young man came out to greet them, pulling a wagon.

Skip held out his hand. "This will sure help. Thank you. I'm Skip."

"I'm Jonathan. Thanks for coming. I'll show you where to go." They loaded their groceries and supplies into the wagon and walked toward the cabin. Oak trees surrounded the cabin and a barbeque pit sat in the grassy area between the older boys' cabin and the cabin for middle-school-age boys.

Meadowcreek was a state-subsidized home for children who had been removed from their homes by the Texas Department of Family and Protective Services.

Through some required training, Skip had learned that children became involved with the DFPS for a variety of reasons, including abuse, neglect, and the death or incarceration of a parent.

Several members of their church life-group volunteered at the facility, planning dinners, birthday parties, and special events for the kids. For a few months Skip resisted going but offered to contribute money. He knew that children were often removed from homes with nothing but the clothes on their back. The state provided the basics, but there was always something to be purchased or repaired. He thought donating was enough, but eventually Ken convinced him to get involved personally. He was glad that he had.

This night they had twelve boys, a few more than usual. One boy joined them mid-dinner. He had a black eye and looked like he was fresh from a fight. Skip's first thought was that he'd had a bad scuffle with another boy in the cabin. Then, he realized that this boy might have been taken from his home this very day. It broke his heart.

As Skip finished grilling and slicing the fajita meat and sausage, the young man who had brought the wagon approached him.

"Do you need anything?" he asked

"You can help me clean up the pit," he said. Skip thought most boys did better when they have a task.

Jonathan followed instructions well and he was fastidious about his work habits. Skip liked that. They picked up the trash and moved into the kitchen and began to collect the empty plates and load the volunteers' supplies back in the wagon.

"So, what grade are you in?" Skip asked.

"Eleventh," said Jonathan.

"What's your favorite subject?"

"Probably math. Maybe science. I'm pretty good at both."

"Really? That's great. I'm good at those, too. I don't like English quite as much."

Jonathan shrugged. "I'm pretty good at all my subjects. Meadowcreek is making me go to the charter school on campus. But I want to go to Kendall High until my mom gets better. She's sick right now. But when she gets better we're going back to San Antonio. I'll graduate from there."

"How long have you been here?"

"About twelve weeks."

"You seem kinda young to be so mature and already in eleventh grade. How old are you?"

"I'll be seventeen next week." Jonathan puffed up a little when he told Skip his age.

He feels like he's about to be a man. That's a good thing.

"What do you think you want to be?"

"I'm not sure. I think I would like to be an anesthesiologist. The other thing I'm thinking about is engineering. I might do that since it cuts out eight years of expensive schooling.

Skip raised an eyebrow.

I wish I had thought so logically about my future when I was this kid's age.

"I believe God will make a way for you to achieve your dreams," Skip said. "I really do. God can make things that seem impossible, possible, because He made it all. Hang on to this determined attitude you have. It will pay off. My life group comes out to Meadowcreek about once a month. I don't know if you'll be here when I come out next time, but if you are, maybe we can visit again. I'd like to hear about your classes," he said.

"Sure," said Jonathan.

Skip sensed a little hardness in the boy's answer.

He thinks I'm just being nice and that I have no intention of returning. Some adults in his life have let him down.

On the drive home Skip called Ken. "Hey, you know the young man who helped us with our groceries? The one who brought the wagon?"

"Sure. I remember him."

"It's his birthday next week. Do you think we can do something nice for him?"

"Mike Murray coordinates that for the Oak Cabin. I'll check with him to see if they already have Jonathan on their list. If they don't, we can all pitch in."

"Great. I want to help."

CHAPTER 53

Stephen – Day 2,008

Stephen needed to find Chris. Stephen had not returned to the Bible study since Sean left. But he heard that Chris had put together a new Bible study group that met in the cafeteria. Stephen headed down there and was happy to see Chris sitting in a corner studying.

"Hey, Chris. Are you busy? Can you talk?"

"I've got a few minutes before the rest of the group arrives. What's up?"

Stephen sat down beside him. "I got some terrible news yesterday that I can't reconcile with all the stuff you have been telling me, and I was wondering if you could help me sort it out."

"I'll try. What is it?"

"When I was in Bastrop, I made friends with a guy, an older man named Will. He read the Bible and I thought he was a Christian. He was good to me. I wouldn't have passed some of my college classes without his help. I just found out he has cancer. If God is good, and my friend was a Christian, why did he get sick?"

Chris shook his head. "I can't tell you why your friend got cancer. But what I can tell you is that if your friend knows the Lord, then God can and will help him through it, and something good will eventually come of it. Going to prison is the worst thing that's ever happened to me. But my life is going to be better because of it."

Stephen wasn't convinced. Chris's answer sounded like something Christians might say when clearly there was no good answer.

Chris asked, "Is there something else that's bothering you?"

"Yes. My friend sent me a scripture reference to look up. I read it. But it didn't solve anything for me. I wrote it down." Stephen handed Chris a piece of paper with the words "Isaiah 53" on it.

Chris squinted at it for a minute and then smiled slightly. "I think I know why Will sent this to you. You need to study who Isaiah was and the time in which he lived. Then, come back and we'll talk. Are you going to stay for Bible study?"

Stephen shook his head. "Maybe soon."

Stephen left the cafeteria disappointed that Chris seemed to know the answer and didn't want to tell him.

What? Is it a mystery? Why can't he just tell me?

CHAPTER 54

Stephen – Day 2,100

Terre Haute, Indiana; Waseca, Minnesota; and Yankton, South Dakota all sounded like cold places. Freezing cold places. Nevertheless, Stephen was willing to be transferred there, and the sooner the better. He spent many months researching the Residential Drug Abuse Treatment Program, also referred to as RDAP. Not all federal prisons offered the RDAP program, but Stephen learned that if an inmate is selected for it and completes the program, he can reduce his sentence by twelve months, spending six of those months in a halfway house or under home confinement instead of a federal prison.

As soon as he was eligible, Stephen submitted his application. He applied for the program at every federal prison in the country other than Beaumont, Texas. Beaumont was the only place he did not want to go. He had heard that it was full of gangs and violence.

Unlike state prison, a federal inmate cannot shorten his sentence with good behavior. So, the RDAP program was Stephen's only hope of going home early. He watched the mail every day, hoping for a response to his application.

Today there were two letters in the mail. One from a T. Lannister, with an address in Austin, Texas. He recognized Sean's handwriting and the reference to *A*

Song of Ice and Fire, by George R.R. Martin. Sean wouldn't discuss any of Stephen's books with him, so Stephen had finally consented to read something Sean was interested in and became a huge fan of the series. Sean and Stephen had nicknamed several of their fellow inmates after the characters in the books.

The other letter was from the BOP.

This must be the response to my application.

He tore open the envelope and read it with mixed emotions.

> Federal Inmate Taylor # 83297-260,
> You have been approved for the Residential Drug Abuse Treatment Program (RDAP). Your eligibility pertains to participation in Beaumont, Texas. To be accepted into the RDAP program you must initiate a transfer to FCI Beaumont Camp prior to December 1. Your counselor will provide you with additional details.
> Sincerely,
> Bureau of Federal Prisons

Stephen was happy—and disappointed. He'd been accepted into the program, but he'd have to do it in the place he was most afraid to go—Beaumont.

He'd heard terrible things from inmates who'd come from Beaumont Medium Security. On the bright side, he was going to a camp-level facility.

Perhaps the camp won't be as bad as medium. I've made it through some rough stuff so far. How much worse can it be?

He turned his attention to Sean's letter, and enjoyed it immensely. So much so, he wrote back to Sean right away. He told him he would likely be transferring to Beaumont and starting the RDAP program, and hopefully returning to Austin in less than two years instead of the full three years that remained on his sentence.

With nothing to do before dinner, Stephen decided to try to unravel the mystery Chris had given him. He didn't have a computer, or the internet, or a library. How was he supposed to find out more about Isaiah? He decided to call his father.

There was a short line at the pay phone for a change. He entered his information into the keypad and waited for a connection. After the phone made its automated speech, he heard his father's voice.

"Hey, nice to hear from you."

"Yeah, you too. It's been a while. What are you up to?"

"Well, Sam set up this cool fishing expo through his church out at the fish hatchery, for single-mom families and underprivileged kids. I spent most of the afternoon teaching kids how to hold a fishing rod."

"That *is* cool. Hey, I hope you don't mind. I only loaded two minutes on the call. If you don't have time to answer my question over the phone, will you send me a letter?"

"Sure. What is it?"

Stephen was suddenly, irrationally nervous. He didn't want to launch a full-on sermon from his dad. *How could he ask about Isaiah without the lecture?* He bought time.

"First, before the phone hangs up, I wanted to let you know that I got accepted into RDAP."

"Oh, Son, that's awesome! When do you start?"

"I'm not sure. Probably around December. But it's in Beaumont."

There was a long pause.

"I'm not sure I can see you once a month when you move to Beaumont. That's a very long drive. But I will send you letters and books and magazines."

"I understand. I'll send you more information soon."

"I sure appreciate you letting me know. What was the other question you had?"

Before Stephen could think of a way to ask his question about Isaiah, the phone went dead. The automated phone system had disconnected the call. For the very first time, Stephen was glad.

PART IV
THE LAST PLACE ON EARTH

CHAPTER 55

Stephen – Day 2,150

No one else in Three Rivers was going to Beaumont, so Stephen wouldn't be going by prison bus. Instead, to his great surprise he would travel on a commercial bus line. When the big day arrived, he was told to put on sweatpants and a white T-shirt and fit all his personal belongings in one cardboard box. The prison gave him a one-way bus ticket to Beaumont, Texas, and twelve dollars for meals. He was instructed that he would be met by a prison representative at the Beaumont bus station. If he did not arrive on schedule, he would be considered a fugitive.

The ticket indicated he would change buses in San Antonio and would have a layover. He got an idea. His uncle Sam worked in San Antonio, not too far from the bus station. He called Sam from the payphone. Stephen was very pleased that he answered, because he couldn't leave a message.

"Hey, I can't talk long. I'm headed to Beaumont today. I'm transferring buses in San Antonio around 12:30. And I'll be in Beaumont around 6 or 7 p.m. I won't have phone privileges though for a day or two. Just wanted to say hi and tell you that I wouldn't be calling for a while."

"That's great news. I appreciate you letting me know. Be safe."

"Will do. Talk to you later."

"Yep."

Sam was a man of few words and not a great phone conversationalist. But Stephen really hoped he had gotten the hint that he wanted to see him at the bus station. Stephen knew the system recorded the phone calls, and he hoped that he hadn't been too obvious. He didn't want to get into trouble. But Stephen hoped Sam would supplement his food situation. Twelve dollars wouldn't go far for lunch and dinner. He wasn't sure what food would be available at bus stations, and he wouldn't get to Beaumont until after dinner had been served.

An inmate who had earned special privileges, called a *trustee,* drove him to the bus station. He was a nice guy and wanted to know more about where Stephen was going and why. The trustee dropped Stephen at the bus station, watched him go in the building and then returned to the prison in Three Rivers.

Stephen went up to the counter and showed the attendant his ticket.

"Do I need to do anything else," he asked?

She looked at the ticket, then back at him, and shook her head.

She knows.

Stephen felt like a marked man. He was sure everyone on the bus would realize he was an inmate, and he felt ashamed to be riding with them.

The bus was late, so he sat in the waiting area. As he waited, a fleeting thought crossed his mind.

I could just walk away.

When the bus arrived, he and one old woman boarded. She sat on the second row, but Stephen sat toward the back of the bus. He thought they would drive directly to San Antonio, but the bus stopped at several small towns and picked up three other people on the way. When Stephen got off the bus in San Antonio he was thrilled to see Sam standing there.

"How long until your next bus?"

Stephen pulled out his ticket and looked at it. "It looks like it doesn't leave until about 2:45 p.m."

"Can you go get some lunch?"

"What? Leave the bus station?"

"Are you wearing an ankle monitor or something?"

"No. Is there something close by?"

"The best hamburger in San Antonio is twenty minutes away."

"What if it takes too long?"

"We'll get it to go and you can eat it in the car."

"A hamburger would be awesome. Let's go."

Stephen felt a thrill of happiness at the prospect of eating a hamburger, and abject terror at the thought of being arrested as a fugitive. His stomach won the battle. Twenty minutes later they pulled into Chris Madrid's restaurant. Stephen wore a smile as wide as Texas.

They ordered giant cheeseburgers and hand-cut fries. The place smelled terrific.

"You want a beer?" asked Sam.

"You're too much! You want me to get thrown back in the pokey forever?"

"I just know you haven't had anything decent to eat in almost six years and beer goes with a burger. It'll wear off by the time you get to Beaumont."

"I'm gonna have to draw the line at being AWOL and eating a real hamburger."

When their burgers arrived, Stephen almost wanted to cry. He inhaled it, literally and figuratively. Nothing he'd eaten for six years had tasted anything close to this.

"I think I could eat another one."

"You want more?" asked Sam.

Stephen looked at his watch and shook his head. "We don't have enough time."

They dashed back to the bus terminal. Stephen almost expected to see federal correctional officers waiting to take him somewhere terrible and punish him for eating a hamburger. But no one was there. He hugged his uncle tightly and they chatted for a few more minutes.

"Thank you so much. You don't know what it means to see you today. I haven't been outside in the real world for six years. Just riding on a public bus made me nervous. I needed to see a friendly face and remember what I've got to look forward to and why I applied to the RDAP program. When you look at concrete walls and angry men all day long, sometimes it's hard to recall the things that make life worthwhile. In fact, it seems to be stealing my memories of the outside world. I don't even dream about getting out anymore. All my dreams contain images of prison. So, this day was very special. It reenergized me."

"You only have two more years to go. Just stay on track. When you get back, we'll get hamburgers often, if you want. Or fry some fish. You know how much your dad likes to do that. I'm the better cook, but don't tell him that. You know he thinks he is."

Stephen laughed. Suddenly, he felt ready to face the next leg of the journey.

CHAPTER 56

Stephen – Day 2,191

Stephen transferred to Beaumont FCI with the hope of getting into the RDAP program, but it wasn't a done deal yet. So, he tried to do everything he could to position himself to be admitted. He followed the rules. He put his shoes in the locker correctly. He checked his bunk and locker area regularly to be certain no one had hidden any contraband near his things. He made his bed. And when the first opportunity came to discuss work, he told his counselor that he had kitchen experience at Three Rivers. He knew volunteering for a work detail might look good in his file. Washing coffee cups wasn't exactly kitchen experience, but he was sure he didn't want to end up cleaning toilets.

A few days later, his counselor told him to report to the kitchen at 5 a.m. the following morning. After almost six years in prison, he had finally gotten on a circadian rhythm that allowed him to be alert at that hour. Prior to prison he hadn't had much knowledge of what goes on in the world at 5 a.m.

Today, he had been instructed to find Charlie in the kitchen and do whatever he was told. It was rare to get kitchen duty so soon after arriving at a new prison. The opportunity to steal and sell food made it a coveted job. Just the thought of having access to more food made Stephen perk up and walk with a smile. When he arrived in the kitchen, all the lights were on and people were going about their tasks.

"I'm here to talk to Charlie," he said to no one in particular.

"Over at the griddle," an inmate replied in an unusually friendly manner.

The presence of a griddle was a nice surprise. Stephen hadn't seen much more than oatmeal and bug-infested cereal for years. Stephen noted that almost everyone in the kitchen wore a hair net, something else not seen at Bastrop or Three Rivers. Stephen regularly found hair in his food. Charlie was not wearing a hairnet, but his long, gray curls were tied back with a rubber band.

Charlie adjusted the heat with one hand as he flipped pancakes with the other. Although intent upon his task, he also kept an eye on the battalion of busy beavers working in the kitchen. This well-oiled machine was apparently under his direction.

Charlie turned to Stephen and looked him up and down. Stephen knew it wasn't going to be easy to land a job in the kitchen, so he gave it everything he had, padding his resume a little.

"I worked in the kitchen at Three Rivers Camp for the last year. I know how to do dishes, make good coffee and I read instructions well." He just thought of that last part on the way over to the kitchen. The large pails of food that the BOP provided often had instructions on preparation. Quite a few of the inmates at Three Rivers had not been able to read.

"You can serve in the tray line this morning and we will talk after breakfast," said Charlie.

Stephen wandered over to the tray line where a young guy in a white apron was pouring oatmeal out of a pot into a tray.

"Hey, I'm supposed to help you this morning. Where can I get an apron?"

Instead of just pointing or nodding in the direction of the aprons, the young man put down his pot and reached into a shelf under the metal serving line, pulling out an apron.

"Thanks," said Stephen.

"My name's Rob. You?" said the young man, resuming his task. He had one visible tattoo, on the inside of his forearm and short, close-cropped red hair. Even though his hair was very short, he still wore a hair net. Stephen's hair had grown long, and he had remembered to wear it in a ponytail, like Charlie. So, he rather hoped that he wouldn't be asked to wear the hair net. The elastic looked uncomfortable.

"Stephen," he answered. "How long have you been in the kitchen?"

"'Bout six months. It's a good job. Charlie runs it real well. And it's not corrupted, if you know what I mean?"

Unlikely.

Stephen looked up and saw that the clock read 5:50 a.m. It was almost time for the cafeteria doors to open.

Rob filled the trays in front of him with pancakes and found Stephen a pair of tongs. "Two pancakes for everyone. Got it?"

"Sure, no problem." Stephen held up his tongs and pinched them together in the air, pretending to serve invisible pancakes all around.

"Ok," Rob laughed. "Put 'em down for a minute. We have to pray."

"What?" said Stephen.

This isn't church, why would they be praying?

Rob turned on his heel and walked toward the pantry at the back of the kitchen. Stephen turned and saw that all the other kitchen workers were standing in a circle. Charlie was talking to them. He was the last to reach the circle and stepped up cautiously.

"Let's bow our heads," said Charlie to the group. "Lord, thank you for this day. Thank you for this food. We offer up our best service to you this day, Lord. Help us honor You when we serve others. Amen." Charlie finished with conviction.

"Amen" echoed most of the group. Stephen noticed that most of the guys in the group looked young. And most of them showed more enthusiasm for their work than he had ever witnessed from any inmate.

He walked back over to his food station pondering this as the doors to the chow hall opened and dozens of inmates entered and queued up. He dutifully put two pancakes on each plastic tray, as Rob served up the oatmeal in one of the smaller wells of the tray.

After breakfast was over, the workers laughed and joked with one another as they placed their aprons in a mesh bag to go to the laundry room. There was a bit of food left over and they shared it equally. In a place where inmates often fight over the tiniest item, Stephen found their camaraderie unusual.

"Stephen, you're new, why don't you take that last pancake?" Rob said.

"Are you sure?" Stephen asked, doubtful but hopeful.

"Sure." Rob smiled.

Stephen gobbled it hungrily and got a few grins and head nods from the group.

I could totally get used to this.

CHAPTER 57

Stephen – Day 2,212

There was someone new in the cafeteria this morning. A well-groomed older gentleman with wavy, salt and pepper hair and a nice tan stood near the line. A white ring circled his left wrist, where a watch had probably been until a few days ago. He looked like he just walked off a golf course. He also looked confused and completely out of place.

Did I look that lost on my first day?

Stephen felt compassion for him and, when he had a free moment, went over and introduced himself.

"You just get here?" asked Stephen.

"Last night," he said. "I'm Mark Escobar."

"My name is Stephen. I'm kind of new here myself. I've been here for six weeks, but I came from another prison. It's hard at first, but it gets easier."

Mark looked miserable.

"The counselor said I would be assigned a job. What type of job is he talking about?"

"Almost all the work here is done by the inmates, with the correctional officers supervising. You could be assigned to clean the unit, do the laundry, mow the grass." Stephen could see the doubt on Mark's face, and he laughed.

"You look like you're used to having a personal assistant who takes your clothes to the dry cleaners and a lawn service that mows your lawn," joked Stephen. "Here you'll scrub toilets and push a lawn mower." Stephen was goading him now a bit and he wasn't sure why, probably because Mark was so easily horrified. It was clear that Mark had never cleaned a toilet or pushed a lawn mower. He was going to have a difficult adjustment.

"So, do you know who I am?" Mark asked.

"No. I was just joking with you because you look like you just came off the cover of a business magazine with your tan and nice haircut. Are you a congressman or something?"

"Just a county commissioner. And attorney. At least I was." Mark laughed nervously. "My case got a lot of media attention in El Paso. I thought perhaps it was on the news over here. What about you?"

"Spoiled trust-fund baby who fell in with the wrong crowd," said Stephen.

They sized each other up for a minute and started laughing.

"My advice to you is, don't tell anyone your story yet," Stephen offered. "Be a little bit mysterious. Everyone in here is eager for something to gossip about. I think it will help you if you just stay aloof. Tell your counselor right away that you're hoping for an administrative task as a work assignment. Sometimes there are clerk-type jobs that need doing and they often need educated men to teach GED prep. Has anyone from a gang approached you, yet?"

Again with the miserable and transparent face. This guy really wears his emotions on his sleeve.

"Not yet," said Mark. "Is that going to happen?"

"Probably. Soon. Just tell them that you want to remain independent. And try to look cool and confident. Right now, you look disgusted and offended. That may not go over well with some inmates."

"How do I get some shower shoes? The shower is gross. When I went into the restroom last night, I noticed some guys in there had shower shoes."

"You will have to wait until commissary day and they will cost about $25. Often, they don't have any. If you put out the word that you want some, other inmates will offer to sell you theirs for the right number of stamps. So, buy stamps on commissary day if they don't have the shoes. Actually, buy stamps even if they have the shoes. And buy Mackerel. You can trade both of those items for most of the things you will need."

They talked for a while after breakfast.

"I've put together a guidebook for new inmates, and I think you're the perfect candidate for it."

Mark chuckled. "I've read every book ever published about federal prison. I think I can survive without the guidebook for eleven months.

Stephen felt a twinge of guilt when he realized he was sad that Mark only got eleven months. He knew they were going to become friends.

CHAPTER 58

Stephen – Day 2,260

Stephen learned he had been selected to join the breakfast detail. He felt honored. Charlie ran a tight ship. Oddly, all of Charlie's crew wanted to do a good job, even though their "customers" had no choice at all in whether to patronize the establishment and would have eaten sawdust, if it were offered to them.

In the first few days, though, Stephen was sure he was going to get fired. He got everything wrong and always lagged a step behind the rest of the team. One day, when he burned a whole tray of toast and set off the smoke alarm just before the doors opened, he was certain his days on kitchen crew were numbered. But instead of taunting or insulting him, one of the other guys jumped in to help him.

The little, tight-knit group did their prayer thing every single day before they served the meal. It still made Stephen feel awkward and uncomfortable, but he always said "Amen" along with the rest of the gang. After he'd been at it about three weeks, he found that it was one of the highlights of his day to work alongside people who were happy. Outside of the kitchen, everyone was either complaining or trying to hustle you.

One morning Stephen arrived a few minutes early. It was still dark outside. Charlie was alone in the kitchen with all the lights on, humming under his breath and arranging frozen potatoes onto a tray. Stephen studied him as he approached. Charlie's light, blue-gray eyes were striking. There were a lot of wrinkles around them, but he wore them well.

"So, how long have you been working in the kitchen?" Stephen asked.

"About five years." Charlie nodded toward another empty tray. "How long will we have the honor of your presence?"

Stephen started spreading potatoes, following Charlie's example. "I hope I will only be here eighteen months. I've served almost seven years already. My sentence was nine. I transferred here to try to get into the RDAP program."

"I've seen a lot of guys get into that program. I hope you get in soon."

"Thanks," said Stephen, a bit surprised. "I'm a little worried about getting in. There's quite a few hoops to jump through. They'll place me in a separate unit soon, and then if I pass inspection every day I may get accepted in three months. The program is nine months long. Why are you smiling?"

"I've been through the RDAP program once. I know how it works."

Stephen digested that for a few seconds. "What?"

"I'm in here for my drug habit, like you are, apparently. It just happens to be my second time, so I'm no longer eligible for RDAP. I will have to serve my entire fifteen-year sentence this time."

"That's tough," said Stephen. "I wish we had more access to rehab programs in our country. My parents tried to get me treatment a few times. And they had the money to pay for it, unlike most people. But I wouldn't go. Now, of course, I wish I had just done it."

Charlie nodded but said nothing. The other guys were filtering in and starting their routine. Charlie said, "Put these in the oven. He smiled. "And keep a better eye on them than you did the toast." He walked off and gave instructions, jokes, and encouragement to the other guys.

Charlie had a nickname for everyone. *River City* hailed from San Antonio. *Specs* wore glasses. *Bones* was quite thin. Charlie nicknamed Stephen *Colgate*, apparently because of his million-dollar smile. Stephen thought it was an odd choice but felt an odd sense of belonging when Charlie shouted it out every morning.

Kitchen duty counted for all his work credits. So, Stephen had the rest of the day to himself. He signed up for one more college course, hoping it would be his last behind bars. It was much easier to study in Beaumont. Like in Three Rivers, he had a twin bed and a locker that doubled as a desk. With no bunk bed overhead, he could sit up on the bed and study. He could also pull up a chair if no one else in the quad was using it, and he could put his books on top of his locker cabinet. There was no education coordinator at Beaumont, which ironically made it much easier to succeed in college. His counselor, Frank, was happy to proctor his exams and send them back to the school.

Frank came looking for him after breakfast. "Inmate Taylor, we should be able to transfer you to the RDAP unit in a few days. That doesn't mean you are accepted into the program. Let's talk about how this will work."

Stephen stood up from his chair and said, "Would you like to sit down? I can move to the bed."

"No. I'm fine. When you move to RDAP unit, I will remain your counselor. As you get closer to your release date, I will make arrangements with the halfway house. To get in to the RDAP program you must exhibit satisfactory behavior in the unit for ninety days. Near the end of that time, you'll get a letter telling you if you're in. If you do not get accepted the first time, then you will stay on the list as long as you continue meeting all the rules of the unit. Guys who transfer here from other prisons to take the RDAP program who have a release date sooner than yours will get priority over you. While on the unit, you will need to keep your bed made and your area clean at all times, attend every required training, and not get written up for an infraction of any kind. Do you understand?"

"Yes, sir. I'm ready."

"Well, not actually. The fact that your boots are sitting on the floor beside your bed, and not in your locker, would be an infraction when you get to the RDAP unit. And that snack-food wrapper lying on the desk and not in the waste receptacle would be another. Do you have any questions?"

"Who will explain all the program rules? Will that be you? Or someone else?"

"Your RDAP program counselor will explain more when you get there."

Stephen felt hope beginning to well up inside him from a very dry, dusty place.

CHAPTER 59

Stephen – Day 2,300

Stephen was spending less money on snack food now that he was on the breakfast team because Charlie gave them the leftovers after breakfast. Stephen liked getting there early so that he could earn an extra helping of whatever was being served. In other prisons he had eaten food that tasted awful and was often spoiled. At the camp in Beaumont, Charlie worked hard at keeping the food fresh and at preparing it. Some of it was pretty good.

Charlie had petitioned the BOP and been successful in obtaining improvements to the food and the food storage areas, including several large refrigerators. He had made a case that it was a health and safety issue.

One morning when they were alone in the kitchen before the din cranked up, Stephen asked, "Why do you put so much effort into making us breakfast?"

Charlie said, "When I was on the outside and had a chance to take care of the things God gave me, I didn't do it. I had a family. I had a house. I had a job. But I put getting high first on my list. That was a bad choice. In my lowest moment in prison, I rediscovered my faith. Taking care of what God gives you is one way to honor Him. As an inmate, I don't have much, but I have the responsibility for feeding the guys in this prison. So, I try to do it in a way that tells God I am doing it for Him."

Stephen frowned. "I guess I never thought about God being interested in the way we flip a pancake or serve oatmeal. Doesn't he have better stuff to do?"

"I'm pretty sure He does care about the little things as well as the big things."

Stephen smirked and said, "What makes you so sure?"

"Genesis."

"What about Genesis?"

"The story of Joseph is in Genesis. I am in prison because of something I did, but Joseph was falsely accused and thrown in prison. Can you imagine how bad that would be? But *four* times…" Charlie held up four fingers with a little flair, "the Bible says, 'And God was *with* Joseph.' Joseph had a spirit of excellence in everything he did, even in prison. And God took care of Joseph. So, I figure that's what I'm gonna do. I'm gonna try to be excellent. Right where I am."

Stephen thought it seemed a bit naïve, but there was something about Charlie that made you like him. Made you trust him. Made you want to join him in his campaign to work hard and be your personal best. But as soon as Stephen was out of Charlie's presence and back in regular population, it was hard to think like that. But suddenly Stephen got an idea. He had never gotten to have another conversation with Chris because of his transfer to Beaumont.

"Hey, what do you know about a guy in the Bible named Isaiah?"

"He was an Old Testament prophet."

"A friend of mine from a different prison who knew I was struggling with believing in God, told me to read Isaiah 53. I've read it, but I don't see why he thought this passage holds any answers."

Charlie smiled. "What is the distinction between the Old Testament and the New Testament?"

"The Old Testament is older, I guess."

"Go back and reread that chapter, and we'll talk about it again tomorrow."

Stephen sighed and left the kitchen, thinking *"If I ever find out what Will was trying to tell me, it will be a miracle."*

The next morning, Stephen woke even earlier and headed to the kitchen. He was determined to beat Charlie in there one day and win some brownie points. But despite rising earlier and earlier, it had yet to happen. He thought this would be the day, but no luck. Charlie was already there, hard at work.

Stephen got a cup of coffee and sat on a stool to watch Charlie work.

"Ok, I get that Isaiah 53 is a description of Jesus. What's newsworthy about that?"

"Isaiah wrote that 700 years before Jesus was born."

"So, it's not about Jesus?"

"It's clearly about Jesus," Charlie was getting a little bit frustrated. "There are like twenty separate prophecies about Jesus in the Book of Isaiah. They all came true. That scripture that you read was written 700 years before Jesus' time, but it described the crucifixion very specifically didn't it?"

Stephen had to let this sink in. "So, you think that's what my friend meant?"

"Yes, I do."

"But how can Christians be so sure they are *right*?" Stephen could tell that he was keeping Charlie from important business, but Charlie seemed willing to listen, so he pressed further. "What about Muslims, Jews, Hindus and all the people who have some other religion?"

Charlie looked around the kitchen and nodded and smiled to a few crew members as they came in. "Jesus said, 'I am the good shepherd, and my sheep hear my voice.' That's really all I know. There came a day when I felt like *I* heard his voice. I said the sinner's prayer. After that, the words of the Bible kinda leapt off the pages and I was sure that there is a God, and that He is the God of the Bible."

Charlie tapped Stephen's chest. "Listen to your heart. Instead of being so offended by the fact that God only made one way to Heaven, why don't you try being grateful that the one way is open to *everyone*?"

Stephen opened his mouth to argue, but Charlie told him to get to work and walked off to help a newer crew member.

CHAPTER 60

Stephen – Day 2,349

After breakfast, as Stephen was walking back to the quad from the chow hall, he ran into Mark. They would often meet midmorning in the TV Room or on a bench in the covered area by the exercise yard. Mark was a well-educated and successful businessman, and Stephen wanted to make the most of his access to someone who had done exactly what Stephen wanted to do with his life: own a successful business.

"Let's talk," said Stephen as they sat down on a bench. "I need to learn this. Starting my own business when I get out is the best option for me. If I try to get a regular job, who will hire me? So, I've taken several college business courses while I've been—"

Mark interrupted. "You're not likely to learn anything all that useful in your college business courses. I took a ton of them before I went to law school. All I learned was how to manage someone else's business or be a good employee."

Stephen was puzzled. "What can I do, then?"

"When I first started out at the law firm, I was doing a bunch of work for a client who owned an insurance adjustor service. He didn't have a college degree; he just had a knack for mobilizing adjusters after a storm. He would track hurricanes, and when one hit, he was ready to drop 100 adjusters on an area. It was clever. He saw a need, and he filled it. The large insurance carriers can't afford to keep an army of adjusters on hand. So, this client built a network of independent contractors who he could mobilize on short notice. He made vulgar amounts of money doing this. I had seven years of education. The client had almost no education and he was making a lot more money than me. It got under my skin.

"I figured out I could make more money doing a business deal than I might make in several years as an associate attorney working my way up the partnership ladder. So, I saved some money and went in with one of my clients to buy a small apartment building. At first, we ran it ourselves, even taking the calls in the middle of the night to fix plumbing problems. But soon, we were making enough to hire a maintenance supervisor. We used that property as collateral to buy another one. Then we leveraged both properties to buy another one. In about four years, I wasn't practicing law anymore, except to paper all my own transactions. When I couldn't get a property rezoned that I saw great potential in, I ran for county commissioner. The rest, so they say, is history."

"What happened?"

"I still own it all. What do you mean?"

"I mean, why are you here, in federal prison, instead of buying another piece of property?"

"A developer offered to purchase a piece of property that I owned at a very decent profit. The developer planned to build affordable housing on it if they were selected for a federal government grant. I feared that the surrounding neighborhood residents might raise a ruckus if they found out about the subsidized housing project. So, I pulled some strings at the city to get the project renamed and pushed to the bottom of the agenda. The city council knew that affordable housing was desperately needed, so when it came up for their approval they were all in favor of it. Except of course, the councilwoman whose district it was in, just down the street from her gated community. It passed. But she voted against it. Then, she probed and snooped and my contact in the city planning office ratted me out for downplaying it on the agenda. Because I stood to benefit from the land sale, the Texas Rangers said it was an abuse of state power."

"How'd you end up in federal prison instead of state?"

"My attorney said federal prison camp would be better than state prison. So, he used the connection to the federal grant that would subsidize the project to get the matter removed to federal court."

They sat in silence for a moment.

Stephen said, "This place is pretty bad. Can you imagine what a state prison is like? At least we're in here with drug lords, money launderers and Medicare fraudsters. In a state prison, we'd be sitting next to murderers and rapists."

"I guess that's a good point," said Mark. But he did not look comforted. "I just have to endure the next ten months," he said sadly.

Stephen cocked his head to the side and gave Mark a look of disgust.

"Oh, sorry," Mark said. "Sometimes I forget that you came down here from a higher-level prison and you've been incarcerated a long time."

"Yeah. A very long time, for doing a business deal, like you. So, I have an idea for a *fruiteria*. I want to make it hip for Austin because that's where I want to live. If a guy's gonna get a second chance, it's probably there."

"So, what's unique about fruit cups?"

"My idea is to market it as locally sourced. They love that in Austin. I have an idea for a Hawaiian theme logo." Stephen showed Mark a Tiki-masked character that he had sketched." I want to call it "Hurricanes." One type of fruit will be a Category 1, mixing two fruits, Category 2, 3, and so on. And if you want a smoothie, we will call that *Hurricane Style*. Get it?"

"Yeah, that's clever. I can see that going over well in a place like Austin. But what you want to do is get it up and running. Use social media to get some buzz. Then franchise the idea. Or sell it."

Stephen felt a little let down but also a bit energized. Mark was funny and worldly. Stephen hoped to stay in Mark's good graces and continue to get this invaluable business advice.

"Yeah, that's what I was thinking. Maybe have one brick 'n mortar location that is trendy and popular and then branch off into some food trucks. When the buzz is really big, franchise it to other cities?" He said hopefully.

"I like it," smiled Mark. "How will you raise the capital to lease your first location, buy your inventory and hire your employees? I like to use other investors' money, mostly. But you need to raise enough so that you could operate without any income for the first five or six months. Nothing takes off as quick as you think it will."

"Six months of working capital? I'm not sure right now. I've been reading about this crowdfunding stuff. You make a video and sell your idea and if other people like it they invest. Small amounts mostly, but hopefully large numbers of people."

Mark smiled again, with his movie-star teeth, "I forget you've been in prison for quite a while. I'm quite familiar with crowdfunding. The problem is that you're giving away your idea often before you've operationalized it, so someone else can steal it and do it better. Also, I've rarely seen those campaigns raise all that much money. Some do, sure. I've seen some movie projects get funded, because they have a theme that resonates with a wide audience, but a restaurant idea rarely gets the funding it needs. We already have lots of choices of places to buy food. But, it can still be part of your marketing, and raise a little bit of your needed cash. Your locally sourced pledge might resonate with some investors, though. But it's been done quite a bit already."

Stephen wanted to pump Mark for more ideas, but Mark wanted to get in line to use the phone.

"Speaking of crowdfunding," he said. "I lost my commissioner seat when they sent me here. But I still have some friends and influence. Sasha, my wife, is hosting a fundraiser at a friend's home for a local candidate that is a friend of ours. I want to talk to her about how to approach some of the people and how to handle questions about me."

"So, since you're in prison, you're trying to use your remaining influence to fill your council seat with someone friendly to you?"

"Exactly."

CHAPTER 61

Stephen – Day 2,403

Stephen had two great mentors in Mark and Charlie. Mark was well-educated, well-spoken, charismatic, and rich. Charlie was uneducated and would be in prison for a long time, but something about him made Stephen feel that there were invaluable lessons to be learned from him. Sometimes it was difficult to choose which man to spend time with, but this morning it was easy. Stephen had gotten some terrible news, and he knew Mark would not be the best person to burden with it.

Charlie wasn't always chatty, but occasionally he would let Stephen make a big cup of coffee with cream and sugar and sit on a stool and talk. Charlie rarely sat, and his hands were usually busy. After the breakfast service was over, Stephen asked Charlie if they could talk.

"You know I've been listening to the stuff that you're telling me. But anytime I start considering believing in God, more bad things happen. Shouldn't it be the other way around? If God is *love*, why would he let terrible things happen to people who are trying to do what's right?"

Charlie was wiping a big ladle with a dishrag. He concentrated on the utensil as he replied. "Sometimes, we go through something so bad, we can't see how anything good can come from it. The Bible is full of stories where that's exactly what happens. Whenever something difficult and painful happens, that is when we need to press deeper into our faith, deeper into our dependence on God. Tell me your bad news."

"I was number thirty-seven. Can you believe it? Thirty-six men are allowed into each new class of the RDAP program, and I missed the cut-off by one number. I went by the rules. I did everything I was supposed to. But now I can't start the program for another three months. I would never have come to this godforsaken place if I had known I wasn't going to get into the program. The harder I try to be good, the worse things get. I even asked God to help me get into RDAP. He didn't hear me—or he didn't care."

Charlie shook his head. "Nothing I can say to you right now is going to take the sting away. But the Bible says that God's ways are higher and more sophisticated than our ways. He might be working out something bigger and better for you than just getting into RDAP. He's not a genie. He is the God of the universe."

Stephen pressed for more. "Sometimes I think I'm not seeing good things in my life because of my doubt. Do you think it is possible for me to believe in God, but just not believe in all the pieces that I doubt?"

Charlie surprised him by saying quietly, "Yes. Yes, I think that is something God understands. Who among us came to Him with any real understanding? In fact, Jesus said that little children are more likely to understand God than Bible scholars. Jesus said you only need a mustard seed of faith to be saved." Charlie held up his thumb and forefinger as if he were inspecting a tiny seed.

Charlie continued, "There's a story I really like about a father who asks Jesus to heal his son. He says something like, 'If you can, please have compassion on us and help us.' Jesus answers, 'What do you mean, "If I can?" Anything is possible if a person believes.' The dad immediately blurts out, "I do believe, but help me overcome my unbelief!' And Jesus healed his son right there on the spot. Do you get why I think this story answers your question?"

"Not really," said Stephen honestly.

Charlie took a deep breath. He looked like something was hurting him.

Stephen felt guilty for pressing the issue, but he was tired of having questions and not getting answers he could understand.

Charlie said, "Don't you see? God meets us where we are. Even if our faith is tiny, if we just want to believe, He gives us more faith. No matter how many doubts you have, if you just keep watering that tiny mustard seed of faith, it will grow."

"I can tell you're getting tired of me," Stephen said. "I'm trying to understand. Yesterday when I got this awful news I went down to the TV Room and came across a preacher on TV. I tried to listen to see if it would make me feel better. But it didn't. He was kinda shouting, and it seemed theatrical. It just didn't ring true. I have a hard time reconciling your Jesus with all this stuff other Christians say."

Charlie bristled. "Yahweh God is ancient and eternal and mysterious. Just because you didn't like one guy's preaching, doesn't mean you should write off God. You don't have to agree with every preacher to be close to God. Jesus saved a condemned thief, crazy naked men, and prostitutes. None of them was in church, but they each had an authentic experience with the savior."

"I would like Jesus better if he would just show up for me once in a while."

"Well, you'll either believe or you won't," Charlie said sharply as he got up to walk away.

"So, you're giving up on me?" huffed Stephen.

"I'm tired of fighting with you about something I feel strongly about. But just know that even if I give up, God never will. God must have something big for you to do because He is so obviously pursuing you. And you are running away as fast as you can, just like Jonah. A story you told me you dislike because it seems so impossible. I hope He doesn't throw you in the belly of the whale to turn you around. That's all I can say."

Charlie's words wounded Stephen deeply and he lashed out. "You're not quite as encouraging when someone asks you the hard questions, are you?"

Charlie kept his back to him and walked away. For once, Charlie left a cup on the counter.

CHAPTER 62

Skip – Day 2,460

Skip's flight to Houston arrived late. Now he was trying to make up the time by pushing the rental car over the speed limit. He still had to drive ninety-five miles from Houston Hobby Airport to the Federal Correctional Complex in Beaumont. It was a lot of traveling, but he hadn't seen Stephen in three months.

The prison complex in Beaumont was imposing. Skip found it nerve-racking merely driving into the prison complex. He passed the tall, razor-wire fences and guard towers of the maximum-security prison first, then the medium-security prison, finally arriving at the camp-level prison. A seasoned visitor now, Skip had his paperwork ready along with his identification and car keys in the plastic bag.

He walked into the lobby, placed his paperwork in the appropriate basket at the desk and went to sit on the one of the benches. After about forty minutes, the prison employee at the desk called Skip's name. When he walked up to the desk, she shoved his paperwork at him and said, "I'm sorry. You can't visit today."

Skip was so shocked, he couldn't speak for a moment. He stammered, "Well, I, uh… I can wait if it's time for the count or something. I flew in from another part of the state and then drove a long distance. I spoke with him on the phone yesterday and he is expecting me. There should be no reason why he can't have a visitor today."

"You're not hearing me," she said loudly. "You are not going to have a visit today. Goodbye. You have to leave now."

"Well can you at least tell me what's going on?" Skipped tried to modulate his voice.

"Sir, I cannot and will not tell you anything further. If you don't leave right now, I will have security escort you off the premises, and you will never be allowed to visit again."

Skipped looked at her for a long moment, but he held his tongue. He walked out of the building as dejected as he had ever felt in his life. As Skip learned long ago, prisons answer to a higher governmental authority, not to the inmates or their families. Sometimes Skip felt like they saw it as their duty to make the inmates and their families completely miserable.

Skip's heart went to a bitter, broken place. He was so shaken up that he couldn't seem to find his way out of the parking lot. He felt a thrill of panic when a correctional officer pulled a white truck right in front of him and stopped, blocking his progress. The officer jumped out of the truck and approached Skip's vehicle. Skip kept both hands on the wheel not knowing what to do. "Sir, what is your purpose here?" the officer said.

"I'm just trying to find my way back to the front gate. I'm here to visit my son. But they wouldn't let me see him. I don't know why."

"Please provide your identification."

Skip handed over his drivers' license with a shaking hand.

The officer looked at the drivers' license and at Skip and said, "Sir the sign clearly says, 'No vehicles beyond this point.' If you don't wish to be in further trouble, you'll need to turn around and head directly to the front gate, which is that way."

On the long drive back to Houston, he complained to God. "Lord, you know that I got up in the middle of the night to make that plane. You alone know what's going on with Stephen. Somehow let him know that I was there and tried to visit but was turned away. Please send him a friend."

Skip hadn't cried in a long time, but hot tears stung his face as he drove. "Please show me why this is happening to me. I hate being treated that way. I hate that it's so expensive to visit and to talk on the phone to him. I hate that he's in that terrible place."

When Skip arrived at the airport, it only got worse. The earliest flight home didn't depart for four hours. He got a cup of coffee and sat down to wait. He opened his small travel bag and took out some work-related journals. When he did, a note dropped out. Skip picked it up and looked at it. There was a colorful, hand-drawn picture of a masked superhero on the front. It was a thank you note from Jonathan Carter. He ran his hand over it and flipped it open. It read:

> Thank you so much for the TV, movies, clothes, and gift card. It meant a lot to me that you remembered my birthday. I have enjoyed our visits. And while I hope to be gone next time you visit, I still hope you will come.

How did that get in there?

Skip read the note and felt an immediate heart-tug of emotion. It felt like a message directly from his heavenly father.

Skip and the others in the life group had organized the birthday party for Jonathan at the Meadowcreek Children's home. Skip bought him a small television and the other group members added a DVD player, some movies, and a bunch of clothes. Although the supervisor of the Oak Cabin had been a little bit upset with Skip for purchasing such an expensive item, saying that it was not fair to the other children in the home, she agreed to let Jonathan keep it. Skip had pointed out that Jonathan would be leaving soon and his exemplary work in school deserved a reward.

Jonathan wrote each group member a thank-you letter. Seeing the note softened Skip's bitter feelings. Something about Jonathan touched Skip's heart.

He's a good young man. I hope he accomplishes all his dreams. He deserves it.

Alone at the empty gate, Skip put on some headphones and lay the magazine in his lap. He had his elbow on the armrest of the chair and his forehead in the palm of his hand. To someone walking by, he might have been reading or napping. He closed his eyes and prayed.

Lord, my heart is just broken right now. Please forgive me for my bad attitude.

Skip had been begging God to change the situation, to change Stephen's heart. But nothing seemed to be improving. In fact, the situation seemed worse than ever.

Skip laid his fingers on the card.

Lord, as I see this thoughtful card from Jonathan. I feel like you might be inviting me to seek out other people's sons and daughters, to mentor and to help them, while I wait on my son to come home. I feel totally unequipped for that task. I can't even parent my own son. If this is your will, please show me where you want me to go. As my pastor sometimes says, please make it big and obvious.

A loud cry interrupted Skip's prayer. He turned and saw a young mother with a baby in a stroller. A large shoulder bag, slung over one of the handles of the stroller, had slipped halfway off and dumped its contents.

Skip dashed over to the woman and helped her pick up her items.

"Oh, thank you so much," she said as she unbuckled her frightened baby and soothed him.

On his knees, Skip reached under one of the waiting-area chairs to retrieve a pacifier, and then walked around picking up crackers, a banana, diapers, and other items that had spilled on to the carpet.

"I appreciate you so much," said the woman rocking and shushing the baby. "Seriously, you're a Godsend to me right now."

When she said that, Skip straightened and stared at her. Then he said, "Well, that seems big and obvious."

"Excuse me?" She said confused.

"Oh, nothing." Skip smiled. "I mean, it's no trouble at all. I have a long layover, and you have your hands full."

"Well, bless you. You're an angel." She said as she snapped the little one back into the stroller.

After handing the mother's bag back to her, Skip sat down again. He picked up Jonathan's card and looked at it.

I let the pain of what I've been through with Stephen drain all my emotional energy. I've been begging God to fix my broken family. Could he be asking me to do something to help fix other broken families while I wait on Him?

Skip leaned his head back for a minute and rubbed his temples and forced himself to completely let go of his resentment over what happened earlier that day.

This is how I'm going to deal with this grief in my soul: I'm going to choose to love God even if He never answers my prayers for Stephen. I am going to use the gifts and talents that God has given me to try to be sure that some other parent's prayers for their child get answered. I will be a Godsend.

CHAPTER 63

Stephen – Day 2,551

Stephen wondered if he had made a terrible mistake leaving the kinder, gentler Three Rivers prison. If he could take a year off his sentence, it would be worth it. But if he remained in the general population, unable to take the RDAP class, it definitely was not. He was alone with his thoughts, walking on the track. He passed some other inmates he did not know.

Are they staring at me?

He thought of Dion, and his warning to be more alert to his surroundings. He had let his guard down a bit at Three Rivers. Now he felt a sudden need to be inside. He looked over his shoulder and didn't see anyone. He let out a tense breath when he rounded the last curve and was nearing the door.

A lightning bolt of pain shot through his left ear.

He tried to raise his hand to that ear, but his arm felt like jelly. He wanted to turn around to see what was happening, but his knees buckled.

Why is the track rushing up so quickly? Where is the door?

And then the lights when out.

***

Stephen didn't know where he was. He was vaguely aware that someone was carrying him.

Am I on a stretcher?

No one was checking his vital signs or tending to him in any way.

Oh God. Please don't let me die in this place.

He felt tears streaming down his face.

If I can feel tears, maybe that means I'm not dead.

He awakened in a small room that looked like an office. From the pain he was experiencing when he was conscious, surely some medical help was on the way. He touched his ear and his hand came away bloody. He could only open one eye. He lifted his head a bit to look down and saw thick blood down one side of his shirt. His thoughts were garbled and he heard a ringing in his ear. Someone shouted his name. Angrily.

"Inmate Taylor!" It was Officer Rodriguez.

"Yes, sir." His speech sounded slurred.

"Who did this to you?"

"I don't know."

"Yes, you do. And you're not leaving here until you tell me."

"I don't *know*," Stephen said. "I'm hurt pretty bad. Can you take me to medical?"

"You're not going anywhere until you tell me what happened."

"I don't know what you are talking about. Why am I not receiving medical attention?"

"You were found unconscious on the track with a wound to your head. I believe that someone targeted you and you know who that person is. And you will be punished if you do not tell who it was."

"*I* am going to be punished?" Stephen asked with genuine shock and despair. "I don't know. I didn't see anyone. I may have just tripped. Maybe I'm having a stroke. My head hurts bad."

"I think you're lying."

Stephen felt an irrational urge to cry but tried to control himself. Federal prisoners don't cry. But the unfairness of the situation unleashed a wave of self-pity that crushed his spirit.

What if this keeps me from getting into RDAP?

He'd been waiting over a year, but all it would take was one bad report from Officer Rodriguez to get him kicked out. He couldn't stop the tears. Seven years of emotional pain and suffering forced them to flow.

"Sir, I truly don't know what you're talking about. I have no memory of seeing anyone do anything to me at all. But I really need medical attention."

Officer Rodriguez didn't say anything, and Stephen's hopes rose.

Officer Rodriguez spoke calmly, "I will ask you one more time who did this to you. If you don't tell me, you are going straight to the hole."

Although Stephen's tears only made Officer Rodriguez angrier, he couldn't control them. "Please don't do that sir. I promise I am telling you the truth. I don't know anyone who wants to hurt me or why they would. I always try to mind my own business and follow the rules."

He wanted to sound sincere, but he couldn't modulate his voice. It sounded frantic and emotional in a way that made him feel ashamed. He was hyperventilating, and suddenly the room began to swim. "I'm gonna be sick!"

Officer Rodriguez watched him vomit without offering a trash receptacle or calling for medical attention. It was a Saturday and no medical personnel worked weekends. So, the officer would have to call an ambulance and transport Stephen to a local hospital if he thought it was warranted. He didn't. He spoke into the radio on his shoulder, "Officer Jones. Code Blue. Officer needs assistance. I'm gonna need you to escort Inmate Taylor to solitary confinement. Taylor, you will stay in the hole until you tell me what I want to know."

Officer Jones arrived, and Stephen said one more time, "This is wrong. I shouldn't be punished for this. I did nothing wrong. I'm hurt. I should be receiving medical attention."

In front of Officer Jones, Officer Rodriguez' demeanor changed. "I'm not segregating you from the population to punish you, but to protect you until we discover who did this to you. Now stand up."

Stephen stood up, feeling woozy. He couldn't believe that he was being sent to solitary confinement in this condition. He reached up to touch his forehead and he could feel gravel and sticky blood.

"Can I take a shower and get fresh clothes?"

"You can do neither of those things," said Officer Rodriguez.

As they walked down the hallway, each inmate they passed stopped what he was doing and stared.

I must look bad.

Stephen tried not to look cowed.

They exited the camp building and walked through the exercise yard. Officer Jones used his badge to open a locked metal door. The door clicked open and they entered the medium-security building. They passed door after door, all metal, all painted dark gray. Each door had a small window. He could see eyes peering out at him.

They stopped at one of the doors and Officer Jones unlocked it. Stephen expected to see a sparse cell with a cot. He was shocked when the door opened and the cell was not empty. An enormous Black man, even bigger than Big Mike, lay on the little cot. A significant portion of his body hung off it. He had tiny tears tattooed all over one side of his face and neck.

"Inmate Johnson, this is Inmate Taylor. He has been assigned to stay in this cell."

"Step inside, Inmate Taylor," said Officer Jones.

"Where am I supposed to sleep?"

"Guess you'll have to fight over the cot," Officer Jones said with a laugh.

Stephen did not move immediately. He just stared agape at the little room and big man inside of it. "Why am I not being put in solitary confinement by myself?" said Stephen, genuinely fearful.

"All the cells are full. Now get in there before you get more time added to your sentence," said the officer.

Stephen stepped inside. He felt the vibration of the metal door as it slammed shut. All the air seemed to have left the room.

"What happened to your ugly face?" demanded the other inmate.

"Fell on the track."

"You wouldn't be in here with me if you fell on the track."

"You sound like Officer Rodriguez."

"I sound like someone who doesn't want to hear any more from you. If you say one more word to me, you might find your face more permanently rearranged." The big man crossed his enormous arms across his larger chest and stared up at the ceiling and slowly closed his eyes.

Stephen slid down the wall and put his long legs out in front of him. His cell-mate had impressive scars on his hands and over one eye. Written in ballpoint ink on one of his tennis shoes was the word, *Bear.*

CHAPTER 64

Stephen – Day 2,552

Stephen heard footsteps coming down the hall and soon the metal plate over the hole in the door slid open. A CO handed two paper sacks through the opening. After the metal plate closed and the footfalls drifted away, Bear snatched Stephen's bag out of his hands.

"Hey!" Stephen yelled.

"Shut your mouth."

"You can't take my food!"

"I can, and I will."

"You'll get punished. You'll go up the ladder."

"You think there's something worse than this?" he said through a mouthful of sandwich.

"And if I tell the CO when he arrives the next time?"

"I'll kill you. Slowly. By stepping on your neck. I've done it before. It's not a good way to die."

Stephen seethed. "I'd rather suffocate than starve. At least the BOP will punish you."

"Suit yourself. I like my odds on that one. You'll go home in a box, and I won't have to look at your ugly face no more."

Stephen lunged for the bag, but Bear caught him on the chin with his elbow. Stephen's head snapped back, and he fell against the wall. His ears rang, and he didn't know what to think or do. The man was huge.

Stephen sat down and tried to think about the positive things he had heard and read while in prison. He thought about things he'd learned from his dad, Paul, Will, and Chris. As day turned into night, his stomach growled loudly, and he hoped that Bear would let him have the dinner meal. It didn't happen. It was the same the next day. Hope faded a bit more every time the window opened, and Bear claimed both Johnny sacks.

As he lay on the floor with hunger eating his insides, Stephen considered making up a lie about what happened in the yard. Officer Rodriguez said he would get out of the hole when Stephen told him what he wanted to know. But if he did that, someone else would get in trouble. Officer Rodriguez would take nothing less than a name.

On the fifth day without food, every cell in Stephen's body screamed for fuel. His head pounded and his stomach ached. He decided he might give up his own mother to stop the pain. When he heard the food cart moving down the hall, he glanced up and saw Bear smirking at him.

"I'm telling him today," said Stephen.

Bear jumped off the tiny cot with surprising speed and jerked Stephen to his feet by one arm. Bear put an arm on either side of his head, palms flat against the gray cinderblock wall and said, "Pray I kill you quick when I break your neck, because it might just make you a quadriplegic instead."

Stephen was weak and disoriented. He barely had the strength to stand. His head swam, and he lost his footing, falling heavily back against the cell wall. "Go ahead. Hit me."

"Just you wait. I will mess you up."

They heard the cart stop. Bear let his arms drop and faced the door.

Stephen stayed where he was, slumped against the wall and waiting for the end. A million things went through his foggy brain. The CO might not believe him if he told him that Bear was eating all his food. If that happened Bear would kill him. He knew it. Even if the CO *did* believe him, Officer Rodriguez was sure to write up the incident in such a way that would cause him to lose the opportunity to be in the RDAP program. So, all hope was lost anyway. He was pretty sure that he couldn't go on. Just eighteen months from going home, he was somehow certain in that moment he would not make it to the end.

Charlie's God, I'm pretty sure you're not real, but if you are, I need a miracle.

The CO opened the window. A voice in the hallway said, "Inmate Taylor, on your feet."

Hunger and fear had depleted Stephen so completely, he could not reorient his mind, and for a moment could not speak. Slowly, he stood up.

The CO said, "Are you ill, Inmate Taylor?"

"Something like that."

The door opened.

"Step out."

He could hardly summon the strength, but he stepped out into the hallway.

"Officer Rodriquez wants to speak with you. Come with me," said a young CO Stephen had not met before.

As they approached Officer Rodriguez' office, Officer Rodriguez was waiting for them in the hallway.

"Thank you, Officer Ganshowitz. I'll call you when I'm through with Inmate Taylor."

Stephen blurted out, "Wait. I request a witness to this conversation."

"I get to decide if we have a witness to this conversation," said Officer Rodriguez with undisguised hatred.

Office Ganshowitz, obviously new and outranked by Office Rodriguez, took a slow step backward.

"I haven't eaten in six days!" Stephen shouted frantically. "My cellie has stolen every item of food that has been brought to me. I plan to tell Officer Rodriguez this, but I have good reason to believe that he will put me back in the same cell and let me die, because he believes I am hiding information from him, which I am not."

Officer Ganshowitz flashed a questioning glance toward the other CO.

Officer Rodriguez cracked a smile and rolled his eyes. "Inmate Taylor has moments of hysteria. I'll take care of it."

Officer Ganshowitz nodded, turned on his heel, and left.

"Are you feeling inclined to tell me what happened on the yard?" asked Officer Rodriguez.

All at once, Stephen understood. Officer Rodriquez knew Bear was eating his food. That was why Bear wasn't worried about being punished.

"Are you going to tell me who targeted you?"

"I can't tell you because I don't know. When they do an autopsy, they're going to know you starved me."

"I've made a few notes in my nightly log that you have been refusing food and have claimed you're on a hunger strike."

"Aren't you supposed to take me to the hospital and force-feed me?"

"It's not for you to decide what I'm supposed to do. You're the criminal; I am the correctional officer. Besides, if you choose to starve yourself to death, most Americans would consider that a community service."

"I can't make something up, just so you can fill out your report. I don't know what happened."

Officer Rodriguez got up from his desk and said, "Let's go."

Stephen knew that Officer Rodriguez was going to put him back in the cell with Bear and that Bear was going to kill him.

Officer Rodriguez unlocked the cell and laughed spitefully.

Stephen knew he was walking into certain death. He considered assaulting the officer to get himself injured and sent to the hospital. At least there he might get food. But if he survived the scuffle, Stephen knew he would eventually be sent to a higher-level prison for a long time, a worse fate than being suffocated by Bear. So, he stepped through the door holding his head up.

Stephen had no fight left. He stood there, waiting for the inevitable.

"Sit down," said Bear.

"No. If you're going to kill me, you'll have to knock me over. I'm not gonna lay down for you."

"Sit down and shut up."

Stephen sat down on his mat and stared at the wall. Bear didn't move. After a few minutes, Stephen realized he didn't intend to. *I guess he's not going to kill me yet.*

It wasn't until the evening Johnny sacks were delivered that Stephen understood. Bear had not killed him because he wanted to keep getting double portions at every meal.

CHAPTER 65

Stephen – Day 2,557

They got two meals a day in the hole. Stephen's only hope was that at some point a different guard would see him lying there, emaciated, and call for medical attention. The lunch sacks arrived and Stephen didn't get up. He let the guard hand them both to Bear. The guard could see Stephen but didn't question him. Stephen heard Bear unwrapping his sandwich and chomping with gusto.

Stephen lay on his mat with his face to the wall, wondering how long it took to die from starvation. Then something hit him in the back of the head. Seconds later, Stephen felt something else hit him in the head. Whatever it was, it didn't hurt. He didn't bother to look to see what Bear had thrown.

"Eat your chips, stupid," said Bear.

Stephen rolled over slowly and saw a bag of potato chips on the floor, right in front of his face. Was Bear toying with him? Baiting him? He reached for the bag slowly, expecting Bear to step on his hand, just for sport. But it didn't happen. He snatched the bag, tore it open, and put a handful of chips in his mouth.

Bear leaned back against the wall, looking smug, as if he were watching a dog eat.

Stephen emptied the rest of the bag in his mouth in one motion, before Bear could snatch it away. The salty chips didn't taste right. They tasted like metal and stung his tongue.

Without a word, Stephen turned back toward the wall, tears streaming from his eyes. He needed to shut down the tears. He didn't want Bear to see how much he had humiliated him. As he tried to focus, he noticed the crumpled paper bag that had bounded off his head and landed in the corner. Something was written on it. Stephen took the wadded-up paper sack, uncrumpled it, and flattened it. On the bottom were the words: "God is our refuge and strength; He is always ready to help in times of trouble. Psalms 46:1"

Stephen had prayed for a miracle the day before. He was still alive, even after telling the CO about Bear stealing his food. Then, Bear had given him a morsel to eat. Now Stephen was reading a message that said God was ready to help him in times of trouble. Was it a coincidence?

"What does it mean?" Stephen heard Bear's voice.

"I'm not sure."

"Is that from your gang?"

Stephen didn't know how to answer. Maybe if Bear thought he had a gang, he might be more reluctant to kill him. But then again, couldn't Bear see that it was a Bible verse? How likely was that to be from a gang?

"I can't be sure. Maybe the bag was for someone else. Maybe the message was for you?"

"What's it say?"

Stephen held it out to him. They sat opposite one another in an eight-foot-by-eight-foot cell.

"What's it *say?*" said Bear, staring at Stephen instead of the bag.

Suddenly, Stephen realized that Bear couldn't read. He tried to recover naturally. He didn't want to embarrass Bear and incur his wrath.

Stephen looked down at the crumpled paper. "It says, 'God is our refuge and strength; He is always ready to help in times of trouble. Psalms 46:1.' It's a quote from the Bible. I think I know who wrote it. If I'm right, it was meant to encourage me and make me feel better."[13]

"Who do you think sent it?"

---

13 Psalm 46:1, NLT

"Before I was put in here, I was working in the kitchen with an old man who—"

"Charlie?" Bear interrupted.

"Yes."

"He's all right."

"Yes. He's a pretty good guy," said Stephen, nodding. It was the friendliest exchange they'd had.

***

When the CO delivered dinner, Stephen stood up. He did not know whether Bear would let him eat, but he decided to take advantage of their two-minute exchange earlier and act like it was going to happen. When the CO opened the tiny hole in the door, an idea popped into his head. He yelled at the hole in the door: "BOP rules say that we can have reading material in solitary confinement. And we can have a pen and paper for writing letters while we are in solitary confinement. You are violating our civil rights by not allowing us to have them."

"Take it up with the warden."

"I will. Please provide me with a grievance form and a pen."

The officer ignored him.

Bear asked, "Is that true?" as they both grabbed the second Johnny sack.

"I don't know. I was bluffing. But it might be," Stephen said, keeping his hand on the sack.

"It'll be a cold day in hell when they bring you a grievance form."

"Yes. Most likely."

Bear gave Stephen a curious look and let go of the bag.

Stephen sat down to eat but stopped chewing when he felt Bear's glowering stare. He held his sandwich midair but didn't take a bite.

"You ever been hungry before?" Bear asked.

"Before the last five days?"

"Yeah."

Stephen shook his head no.

"We used to go days without eating when I was little. It hurt so bad."

Stephen didn't know what to say. He believed Bear was telling the truth, but that didn't give him the right to starve someone else. He put another bite in his mouth and chewed it more slowly. Then he remembered to check the bottom of the sack. Someone wrote a note on this bag, too. It said, "Be strong and courageous! Do not be afraid and do not panic before them. For the Lord your God will personally go ahead of you. He will neither fail you nor abandon you. Deuteronomy 31:6."[14]

Stephen tore the message off the bag and put it on the floor beside his mat. He could tell by the way Bear was looking at him, that he expected Stephen to read it but didn't want to ask. Stephen pretended he didn't see the look, "Did you see this? There's another note on my sack." He read it.

"My sack has a note too." Bear held it up toward Stephen to read.

Stephen acted as if he was reading it out loud to himself instead of reading it to Bear for his benefit: "The most difficult thing is the decision to act, the rest is merely tenacity. – Amelia Earhart.

"That's another good message," said Bear. "Do you still think these notes could be from Charlie?"

"Yeah. Maybe.

Bear tore the note off his bag, too.

He put it under his pillow.

14 Deut. 31:6, NLT

CHAPTER 66

Stephen – Day 2,581 (30 Days in Solitary)

Apparently, Stephen wasn't going to die of starvation, but he thought he might die of boredom. He missed chatting with Mark and Charlie. Bear wasn't much of a conversationalist. They were allowed out of their cell for one hour of exercise, every other day. He could shower every third day. He wondered what his family thought about why he couldn't call. Were they worried about him?

Agonizing weeks passed, and the only real encouragement Stephen received came from the notes on the Johnny sacks. Not every bag had a note, but many did. Sometimes it was a scripture. Sometimes it was a wise saying. Stephen wasn't sure that Charlie was writing the notes, but it was a logical assumption. The food came from the kitchen. Charlie oversaw the kitchen. Whoever was doing it was taking a risk. Although the messages looked benign, if a CO saw it and thought it was a coded message, the sender could get thrown in the hole, too.

Why would he risk it?

As his list of collected verses grew, for the first time in his life Stephen actually wanted to look something up in the Bible. He thought of all the Bibles lying around his grandparents' house and his dad's house and how he had ignored the book all those years in church. Now that he couldn't read it, he wanted to. The scriptures on the bags suddenly seemed significant.

The next time they were being escorted to the yard to exercise, he said the CO, "I have a constitutional right to the free exercise of religion. I cannot go to any worship services in solitary. I need a Bible to exercise my religion. Please bring me a Bible and some writing materials."

The officer said nothing, but that night when the Johnny sacks arrived, the CO shoved a small Bible at him. Paper for taking notes had not been included, but still it was a huge achievement.

He ate his baloney sandwich with one hand and flipped through the Bible with the other. He stopped in the Psalms and looked up some of the ones on his collection of bags. When he put the last bite of sandwich in his mouth, he heard Bear say, "Read it."

"Which part?"

"Any part."

"Charlie likes the book of Genesis, so I'll start there." Stephen started reading.

Apparently, the sound of Stephen's voice made Bear sleepy because he closed his eyes and his breathing became regular. Stephen stopped reading but, eyes still closed, Bear said, "Read."

Stephen wasn't the strongest reader. Some of the words were unfamiliar. But fortunately, he had been given a modern translation of the Bible, so at least he didn't have to contend with King James English.

Over the next few days, they read about Noah, Abraham, Jacob, and Joseph among others. Reading the stories in context made them a lot more real and interesting. Stephen was excited to be reading it aloud. He discovered that he understood what he was reading better. When he read silently, his mind wandered and he could only read a few lines. But when he read to Bear, the stories came alive to him.

Bear appeared to be engaged, too. If Stephen put the Bible down and stopped reading entirely, Bear did not complain or ask him to read. But if he picked it up and flipped through it, he heard, "Read."

After Stephen finished Genesis and Exodus, he began to get frustrated with the unfamiliar foreign names and places. So, he flipped over to the Gospel of John. His dad had always told him to start there if he ever decided to read the Bible. It was a familiar story, but Stephen heard it with fresh ears this time.

The days dragged, with no phone calls, no cafeteria line, no commissary day. But having the Bible to read made all the difference in the world. It was the difference between having hope and having none. And there was one regular event in his life. Once a week, Officer Rodriguez would have Stephen brought to his office. Officer Rodriguez wouldn't even look up when Stephen entered his office. Still reading paperwork on this desk, the CO would say, "Are you going to tell me the truth?"

Stephen would answer, "I've told you everything I know, Sir. That is the truth." The other CO would take him back to the hole.

CHAPTER 67

Skip – Day 2,594

Something was terribly wrong. Skip hadn't heard from Stephen in forty-two days. He had tried calling the prison in Beaumont, but that was a terrible ordeal. The prison system didn't have a customer service line and wasn't set up to take incoming calls. The only number he could find was a voicemail, with a recording that said he could leave a message. But the mailbox was always full. He called repeatedly. He wrote letters to Stephen every other day. No response. He searched online on the Bureau of Prisons website which lists the location of every federal prisoner. Instead of "FCI Beaumont" beside Stephen's, name, the location box was now blank. Skip had never seen that before. It was like Stephen had vanished.

Skip was in an executive meeting when the familiar "No Caller ID" alert popped up on his smartphone. He jumped out of his chair and dashed out of the room. They were supposed to turn their phones off in meetings, but Skip didn't want to miss a call from Stephen, because he could not leave a message.

"Hello?"

"Dad?"

"Stephen, what's going on? It's been forty days. Why haven't you called? I flew to Beaumont and they turned me away. Are you all right?"

"No. I'm not all right. I've been in solitary confinement, but I didn't do anything wrong. I blacked out one day on the exercise track. Or I fell, or something. I just woke up with blood all over and no memory of what happened. They won't let me out of solitary because they think I'm lying and that someone attacked me."

"Is that legal? Can they do that?"

"That's what I'm hoping you can tell me. Apparently, after thirty days you earn a phone call. But they made me wait forty-two days. I called you right away. It might be another thirty days before I get another chance. Will you please call an attorney or do some research on prison rules and see if they can hold me in solitary confinement when I've not been accused of doing anything wrong and haven't broken any rules?"

"Yes, I will. Have you gotten any of my letters?"

"No. They're not letting my mail through. Will you check on that, too? They put me in solitary with another prisoner who threatened to kill me. He hurt me worse than the fall did."

"Did he assault you? Are you injured?"

"I'm better now. He's bigger than me, if you can believe that. He stole all my food for quite some time."

"What made him stop?"

"I don't know. You always tell me that you're praying for me. I'm sure I've never needed your prayers more than I do right now. I'm really, really worried about missing the RDAP class. Whatever you do, try to keep that in mind. If there's a chance for me to get out of the hole and not get kicked out of RDAP, that's what I need prayer for."

"Do you want me to pray right now?"

The mechanical voice broke in, announcing that the call was about to end.

"Well, yes, but I guess I won't hear it. I love you. Just in case I don't get another call for thirty days, I wanted to tell you."

The connection ended.

***

Skip did not return to the meeting. He went back to his office and got on the internet to research federal prison rules and regulations. His head was spinning. He felt happy that his son knew that his dad cared about him and prayed for him. Yet, he worried that Stephen might be lying about not knowing whether he had been attacked. It sounded suspicious. Skip still had a lot of faith in law enforcement and officers in authority.

Surely, they would not put him in solitary confinement for falling on the track. And not intentionally with another violent inmate.

Based on what he found online, it did not appear that the prison system had a right to put an inmate who had not been accused of any wrongdoing in solitary confinement, unless there were legitimate concerns for the inmate's safety from other inmates. Skip grew angrier the more he read, but he wasn't sure who he was angry with.

Skip looked up the name of the warden of the Beaumont federal prison complex. He drafted a professional letter, citing the prison regulations and asking the warden to investigate the circumstances immediately. He suggested misconduct on the part of the officer or officers involved and requested a response. He copied the pages of the rules and highlighted the relevant sections and included them with his letter. Finally, he printed a FedEx label and inserted the well-prepared packet into an overnight envelope.

Skip walked the letter down the hall to the front desk, where overnight deliveries were picked up. As he was walking back to his office he thought about whether he should return to the meeting he'd left so quickly. It was probably about to wrap up and it would be embarrassing to answer questions. He'd have to say it was some sort of family emergency, which busy executives weren't supposed to have.

Did I do the right thing? Will the letter even get to anyone who might care?

Suddenly, he realized that he knew someone who would absolutely care, someone he had neglected to contact. He returned to his office, shut the door, and started to pray.

CHAPTER 68

Stephen – Day 2,628

They'd read through the New Testament. Parts had been hard to understand, but most of it had been amazing. What was it Paul had said to him all those years ago in Bastrop? "Read the book and it will come alive."

Stephen wasn't sure whether Bear was having the same reaction. Bear wanted him to read all the time, but rarely asked questions or shared his thoughts.

Now that they had finished the New Testament, Stephen was rereading some of the books he had enjoyed. He had just read James 5: "Confess your sins to each other and pray for each other so that you may be healed. The earnest prayer of a righteous person has great power and produces wonderful results." As he started the next sentence in the book of James, Bear interrupted him.

"I know what happened to you."

Stephen didn't understand. "What are you talking about?"

"When you got hurt. When you got in here"

"All this time you've known, and you didn't taunt me with it? What do you know?"

"I can't say. Because one of 'em will kill me. Happy or Big Mike. One of 'em will."

Stephen put the Bible down on the mat in front of him and stared at Bear. "Why are you telling me this now?"

"Because the book says to confess your sins so you can get healed."

"Are you going to tell me what happened?"

"No. I'm going to tell God. I guess he already knows, but I'm gonna tell him, maybe when I'm out walking."

"Were you involved?"

Bear looked at him for a few seconds, then said, "I can't talk about it. And neither should you. Being in the hole is bad but being dead is final."

Stephen had never wanted to know what Bear was in the hole for, until now. "Why have you been in here so long? What did you do?"

"You better keep reading."

Apparently, confession time was over.

***

It was one of the days when Stephen and Bear could walk for an hour. It was muggy and hot, but the sunshine still felt wonderful. As Stephen walked and felt the fresh air, stories he had read from the Old and New Testament came into his mind. He glanced behind him, a habit that was ingrained now. He saw Bear talking to the air and wondered if he was telling God what he would not tell Stephen. Stephen wanted to tell God a few things, too.

"Lord, if you're really there, I want to know you. I don't care about all the stuff I can't answer or don't understand about the Bible. I don't want to be like the Israelites, wandering in the desert and never appreciating what you've given me. If even half of the promises in the Bible are true, I want those things. Please, please, please if you are real, let me know."

He saw a bench and sat down. Something his father had written to him, which hadn't been very persuasive at the time, came flooding back: "Whenever you need God, focus on the beauty of his creation. He inhabits even the small things: the wonderful smell of coffee, rain, the ocean breeze on your face, beautiful music that makes your heart soar. God created all those things. Jesus said that if the people did not worship him, even the rocks would cry out. I feel closest to Him when I look at the things He has made and appreciate them."

As Stephen felt the sun on his skin and saw the beauty of the creation around him, he realized that the whole world was shouting at him that God is real, but he had been walking around blind.

CHAPTER 69

Stephen – Day 2,644

Ninety-two days and nine hours after being placed in solitary, the door to Stephen's cell opened. This time it wasn't the little metal food door and it wasn't just long enough for a walk or a shower. It was opening to an exit.

Officer Wilson stood in the open door and said, "Taylor, get your things. You're going back to Camp."

Stephen was sitting on the floor, with the Bible in his hands. He looked around. *What things?*

He stood up and started to follow the officer. At the door, he looked back. Bear sat on the bunk with his arms crossed, staring at the wall. Bear glanced his way but Stephen couldn't read his expression. Stephen stepped back into the cell and held out the Bible.

Bear took the Bible without a word and laid it on the bunk beside him.

As Stephen walked back to the camp facility with Officer Wilson, crazy thoughts flew through his head. *What is going to happen to me now? Is someone waiting to hurt me out here? Will I be allowed to start RDAP? The next class probably starts in three days.*

When they walked inside, Stephen was directed to a new quad. Apparently, they had given his bunk away.

Stephen asked the officer, "Do you know where my things are: my schoolbooks and my family letters and photos?"

"I have no idea." Officer Wilson turned and walked away.

Stephen would have loved to find Mark, but he wanted to find his counselor first. He asked around, but the answer in every case was "Return to your quad. Your counselor will find you when he needs to tell you something." Stephen eventually found Mark, talking to some other inmates. Mark was surprised to see him.

"No one would tell us what happened to you. We figured you went up for some reason."

Stephen told him everything.

"That's awful. I'd have called my lawyer for sure."

"I'm just thrilled to be out. That is without a doubt the worst thing that has ever happened to me."

Later, Stephen tried to call his dad to tell him, but the phone informed him that he had no money on his account. So, he returned to his quad and borrowed a piece of paper, and a pen. He wrote a letter to his father explaining that he was out of solitary and needed money placed on his account immediately. Then he realized that he did not have enough money to buy a stamp and had nothing to barter with. His new quadmates would not let him borrow the all-important stamp, so he went in search of Mark.

***

Stephen never thought that he would feel happy in prison; however, the day that his counselor told him he had been selected for RDAP, he felt genuine happiness. He was going home in nine months instead of eighteen. He'd never wanted anything more. Only a few days out of solitary, and now he was moving to a new wing of the facility, reserved for men in the RDAP program.

The RDAP unit housed ninety-four inmates. Every ninety days, thirty-six new men entered the unit and an equal number graduated out of the nine-month program. They had their own eating area and their own exercise yard.

Stephen hit it off particularly well with Brad. They both lived in Austin and were huge football fans. Brad had only served eighteen months in prison prior to getting into the program, substantially less than Stephen's seven years.

"So, you were a successful businessman before you got thrown in prison?" asked Stephen. "I thought everyone in this program was going to be someone who committed a drug crime."

Brad handed him a dish as they cleaned up the eating area. "No. You don't need to have committed a crime involving drugs. A substance abuse problem that led you to commit a crime also qualifies."

"So, did you?"

"What?"

"Have a substance abuse problem that led you to commit a crime?"

"That's what I put on my application. I oversaw marketing for a small oil company. The company had raised some money from investors for some speculative wells, but we were not using all the money that we raised in the way that we told investors we would. The owner and some of his partners told me exactly what to say, and I knew how to make it look like the money had been used correctly. I foolishly thought that they would be the ones to get in trouble if the scheme were discovered. But, when the regulators got wind of the fraud, the owner made it sound like it was all my idea. I had a terrible drinking problem at the time, so I didn't get my own lawyer or try to protect my interests, until it was much too late."

There was something amazingly positive about Brad. He didn't complain about prison conditions like most inmates did. One day Stephen saw Brad's girlfriend visiting him and understood that Brad had a lot to return to.

At first, Stephen didn't share everything about his past with Brad because he was embarrassed. Eventually Jay, their RDAP instructor, was able to draw out much of the truth. He made them work hard, share their stories, and confront the wrong thinking that led them to prison. Some of them had harder truths to face than others.

There was another man named Stephen in the group. Like Brad, he had been a businessperson, and he had a good family and a short sentence. They nicknamed the second man "Stephen Too," which they thought was a funny variant of "Stephen #2." Brad shortened it to "Stu."

Stephen felt privileged to be accepted into their group. Everyone in the RDAP class anticipated returning to the world, being successful, and never coming back. It was the opposite of what most inmates believed.

***

On the forty-fifth day of RDAP, a large cardboard box arrived with the afternoon mail. It contained all Stephen's things that had been missing since he was sent to the hole. He dug through the box eagerly and found his textbook, his glasses, his letters and photographs, his radio, and even his shower shoes. A large stack of unopened mail was also in the box. Most of the letters were from his dad. He flipped through them quickly, looking at the return addresses, but stopped when he saw the name, G. Blankenship on an envelope.

The letter had been addressed to him at the Three Rivers mailing address but was dated after he had been transferred to Beaumont. He tore it open, hoping to learn that Will was still alive. The cover page was short.

Dear Stephen,

I'm sorry to tell you that my dad passed away about two weeks ago.

I'm taking care of his affairs and discovered that he left a letter for you. I found it in some of his things. Since he took so much obvious effort to write it, I felt compelled to send it. I hope it has the intended impact on you.

Gary Blankenship

Behind the letter from Will's son was another letter, this one in Will's handwriting.

Stephen,

Now that I know that my time is short, I have some things I want to share with you. I know you were seeking answers about faith when you were in Bastrop. I felt that I should have talked with you about it then, if I had been a better friend.

Instead of using the gifts and talents God gave me to make an honest living and have a pleasant life, I took short cuts to get what I wanted. I tried to fill the empty place in my heart with material things. I regret it. And I don't want you to make the same mistakes. You shared with me that you struggled with alcohol. Alcohol addiction is just a variant on the lie that I fell for. Your brain thinks, "A drink would make me feel better right now. It would help me not to feel depressed, worthless, angry or scared." You and I both know it's not true. Drinking makes everything worse. But there is a feeling better than drugs and alcohol, and it is peace. You will never find that peace if you get involved with any of the stuff you did before prison when you get home.

I sure hope you get this letter and I sure hope that you find peace and your special place in the world.

God bless,

Will Blankenship

The next page of Will's letter contained a list of principles to live by, and several scriptures to support each one. In some cases, Will included additional book titles to support his principles. Stephen scanned the list and thought it looked like excellent advice. He felt so special that Will had thought of him and was amazed that Will's son would take the time to send this letter.

The RDAP class required him to study every night. There were books to read and reports to give. On several occasions, Stephen drew from Will's sage advice to add substance to his class participation.

He thought of home every waking minute. Who would be standing there waiting for him when he walked out the door? Where would he live after he got out of the halfway house? Would he ever be able to get a job? How much had the world changed while he was in prison? If only Will had lived and been able to continue to give him advice. Stephen knew his father would want to give him counsel on how to get back into the civilized world. But his father had never tried to explain an eight-year gap in his resume. He was too busy with RDAP and its related chores to read any of the scriptures or books that Will had recommended, but he kept the letter and looked at it often.

One day when I'm settled, thought Stephen, I'm going to read all these references he took the time to send me. I'll be reading his book suggestions for years to come. He's gotta be laughing about that up in Heaven.

CHAPTER 70

Stephen – Day 3,052

In seven days, Stephen would be going home. The RDAP class had been hard work, but very educational. Today, Jay gave them all some paper and colored pencils, and asked them each to draw a picture of something that depicted the wrong thinking that led to their substance abuse.

"You have twenty-four hours to work on it," Jay said. "Be creative."

Stephen sketched a tall skinny building. Then he drew a little stick figure with a big smile and a can of beer in his hand falling headfirst off the top of the building. Little dashed lines showed the trajectory of his fall. Finally, he inserted a dialog bubble to show the falling character saying, "I can handle this. Everything seems to be going just fine."

The next day, Jay asked each group member to show their drawing and explain what it meant. When it came to Stephen's turn, he held up his drawing and everyone laughed. Stephen always enjoyed making people laugh, but this afternoon, he was trying to be serious.

"I have an amazing way of ignoring the red flags around me and convincing myself that something I want to do is acceptable." Stephen pointed to the stick figure. "Obviously, in this picture, the old Stephen could ignore the fact that he was upside down and falling, and not even realize he's in danger. When I get out I hope I can pay attention to the obvious warning signs that something is unhealthy and likely to lead to a bad outcome. I tend to believe that I can handle anything. So, I let myself walk right into harm's way. In the future, I'm not even going to get close to the edge. I hope."

Everyone clapped.

They continued around the circle, sharing until everyone had described his picture.

Stephen still had the drawing in his hand when he walked into his quad. He threw it in the trash can, believing that the RDAP class was over. The wall calendar showed seven days still unchecked. He should have been excited but felt as though a dark cloud hovered over him. He would be free, but what would he be? He was a thirty-three-year-old man with no college degree or accomplishments. He'd spent almost eight years of his life in federal prison. He was a felon, a label he would wear for the rest of his life. What chance did he have of realizing any of his dreams?

Stephen stared at the picture in the trash can and the image on it burned through his soul like a fire. His skin prickled.

This picture isn't just a metaphor about drugs. This is a picture of my life. I could be headed for destruction if I don't get serious about God. Prison didn't cure me. RDAP didn't cure me. Only God can cure me from the condition that I'm in.

Stephen reached into the trash can and plucked out the picture.

Kneeling by his bed Stephen said softly, "Jesus, you may not remember me. I haven't talked to you for a while. It's usually just when I'm in trouble or in need. I can feel it in my soul this instant. I'm hurtling through space toward someplace I don't want to be. I read the scripture that says, 'If the Son has set you free, you are free.' And that's what I need more than anything, to be free. Free from sin. Free from addiction. Free from fear. So, I ask you, right here in this moment to set me free."

Something light and lovely entered Stephen's mind. It didn't have a form or a face or an explanation. But everything he had said felt right, confirmed, accepted. It felt like salve on a burn. He knelt in silence for a moment, feeling as if a weight the size of Texas was lifted from his shoulders. A slight, almost imperceptible breeze blew across his face. The room was cooling down and feeling comfortable for a change. He got up off his knees and lay across the bed. He felt exhausted, like he had just finished a marathon. He decided to close his eyes for just a moment.

In his mind's eye Stephen saw a beach and felt the waves. It was a memory of the last place he felt free and happy. He spoke to God with his thoughts: *Thank you. I feel set free in my spirit from dark things that have kept me from talking to you. I thought I had to do something good before you would take me back. My mind tends to go down dark paths and rationalize my selfish behaviors. Right now, I remember a happy memory I haven't had in a long time. Perhaps with your help, I will have the power to guide my wrong thoughts in the right direction when I get home, like I used to go against the current on a surfboard. Please help me stay on course.*

When he opened his eyes a few minutes later, the room was darkening. An hour had passed, and no one had bothered him, something almost unheard of in prison. When he stood up to get started on his RDAP coursework he paused and explored a new feeling inside of him. He was happy. The fear and anxiety that prowled his mind, waiting to devour him, was gone.

***

Seven days later, when Stephen finished giving his graduation speech, the entire group stood and applauded. He hadn't seen that happen before in RDAP, and he considered it an honor. He walked back to his quad and cleaned out his locker. He found the journal that contained his "How to Survive Prison" handbook.

What should I do with this?

On the back page he wrote a one-page story of his faith journey and a scripture: "For I know the plans I have for you," says the Lord. "They are plans for good and not for disaster, to give you a future and a hope." Jeremiah 29:11 Then he flipped to the front of the notebook and wrote above the first line, "Start at the back!" He considered the title, then made one change: "How to Succeed ~~in Prison~~ *in Life*."

He got permission from his counselor to leave the unit for twenty minutes. He walked over to the cafeteria, but it was closed. So, he tore out one of the blank pages of his notebook.

Dear Charlie,
Thank you for teaching me how to cook, and for tolerating all the burnt toast. I hope you'll keep trying to get through to knuckleheads like me. You had more influence on me than you know. Please consider sharing this guide that I wrote with someone who seems like they might need it. – Stephen

He slipped the notebook and the note under the kitchen door. He returned to the common room of the RDAP unit where he found Brad, Stu and a few of the other RDAP graduates toasting with Tang orange-flavored breakfast drink. Brad held up a cup in his direction and said, "I know you're going to make it, Stephen." Then, he motioned in a circle toward the whole group. "We will all make it."

"I believe that." Stephen said.

And he did.

***

Stephen was only allowed one box to take his things home. It didn't matter. There wasn't much he wanted, anyway. He'd given away most of his books, his shower shoes, his radio, and his toiletry items. He placed the Bible inside the box along with the pile of photos and letters that he'd kept through the last seven and a half years. Mark, Brad and Stu had added new notes of encouragement to the pile.

Stephen carried the box like a shield and began walking down the hall and away from the RDAP Unit. The guard nodded at him at the front gate. He walked out into the sunlight, searching for the face that would take him home.

Thirty-six inmates would leave today, released one at a time. The families had to wait in their cars and not leave their vehicle until their releasee got near. So, Stephen had to scan the lot. Then he saw a smiling face. A face that had welcomed him into the world. The face that had come to see him almost every month for the last ninety months. A face he had failed to appreciate for thirty-three years. But just now, it looked like a face he might like to know better. Stephen had never thought that they'd looked anything alike. Everyone always told him he favored his pretty mother. But for the first time, he could see a little bit of himself shining in his father's eyes.

Epilogue

Skip and Stephen – Day 1

Skip stood at the front desk of the halfway house waiting to take his son home. Today, there was no one at the desk. Skip rang a buzzer on the desk that separated him from the vast building behind the desk. Finally, a slight, frazzled-looking man approached the desk and said, "Can I help you?

"I'm here to pick up my son, Stephen Taylor, he's being released to home confinement today."

"Can I see your ID, please?"

Skip handed over his driver's license and watched the man's face as he typed Skip's name into the computer terminal at the desk. After what seemed like an age, the man stood up and lifted a bar between the desk and the wall that separated Skip from the space where the man stood. Then the man punched a code into a keypad that unlocked the door behind him and held it open.

Skip felt nervous when the door shut behind him and he found himself alone. He thought he would be escorted. He had never been behind this door, and had no idea where Stephen was. He followed a short corridor to a room the size of a basketball court, full of metal bunk beds. Many of the bunks had men lying in them, most sleeping or reading. He scanned the cavernous room, and finally spotted Stephen's auburn hair.

Skip sensed the collective gaze of the other men in the room as he walked toward his son. It made him uncomfortable, but he resisted the urge to look around. When he reached the center of the room he remembered that there were no guards at the halfway house. He felt a little chill.

"Hey there. All ready?" he said, trying to look calm and enthusiastic.

"I guess," Stephen responded uncertainly.

Skip frowned. He had expected Stephen to be eager.

"Got all your stuff?"

Stephen shook his head. "A counselor cut the lock off my locker for an unannounced search this morning. Everything I had that was valuable was stolen while I was up front filling out my paperwork. All I have left is here in my laundry bag."

"I'm sorry," said Skip.

Stephen picked up the laundry bag and started to walk past his dad. But when he was a few steps away from the bunk, he walked back to a nearby trash can and picked out a piece of paper.

"What's that?" questioned Skip, still frowning.

"I'll tell you in the car," Stephen said stiffly and walked toward the door putting his chin up slightly.

Stephen's demeanor unsettled Skip. Today, the very day Stephen had surely dreamed about for years, he acted anxious and sad. Trying to fill the unexpected, awkward silence, Skip started to describe the house he had rented for Stephen. "You're really going to like this little—"

"You got the phone installed, right?"

"Yes." Skip said. "It wasn't easy finding a home telephone. They aren't sold at that many places anymore."

"And you got the phone service set up through the company that I gave you? You checked the phone and it has a dial tone?"

"Yes, Son. I did everything you told me to do." Skip knew that his last sentence had a little bite to it. Skip had expected Stephen to be a little more grateful for the work and expense that he put into getting the place ready for his son's arrival.

Oblivious, Stephen pressed on. "They are going to call the house at least once a day, every day. It may be at 2 a.m. It may be at noon. And I have to answer. I am required to stay at the house and not go anywhere except for when I call in and get approval to go somewhere. Then, I can only go to the appointed place and straight back."

Skip sighed.

When Stephen sees how nice this place is, perhaps that will cheer him up. He hasn't seen the inside of a house for eight years.

The house was in a neighborhood full of young professionals, Stephen's age. Skip had chosen it in the hope that his son might make friends with some of his neighbors and learn the habits of successful people.

As they walked up the front porch steps and through the front door, Skip began regaling Stephen with all the house's features. It was small, but spotlessly clean and comfortably appointed. Skip had filled it with a mixture of new and repurposed furniture. He had even placed family pictures on a ledge. He thought they would make Stephen feel more at home.

Skip had expected Stephen to race through the house experiencing the sheer joy of freedom. Instead, he sat on the bed, traced his finger gently over a fluffy pillow, and began to sob.

"What's wrong?" Skip croaked.

Stephen's spoke through his sobs. "Everything is overwhelming. I haven't sat on a real bed with a mattress like this for years." He looked up at his dad with tear-filled eyes. "I keep looking over my shoulder, expecting a guard to come throw me back in the hole and tell me to sleep on the floor."

"If you don't plan to violate the terms of your probation, why are you worried that you'll have to go back to prison?" Skip touched his son's shoulder lightly.

Stephen shrugged. "I don't know. In prison, you can get punished just for being associated with something bad that happens, things you have no control over."

Skip had no idea how to respond. He was sure anything he said would be wrong.

"They expect me to start looking for work right away. How am I to do that? I'm thirty-three years old. I haven't finished college. And I've never done anything worth listing on a resume. What, exactly, am I supposed to say to a potential employer? Sean told me that when he first got out, and he got a job offer, he was thrilled—until the probation officer turned up at the job site and told the supervisor that Sean was a felon and that he would have to be excused regularly for drug testing. Can you imagine how humiliating that will be?"

Skip wanted to show sympathy, but he was still dealing with his own pain and anger. He fought back the urge to say, "None of this would have happened if you'd taken my advice a decade ago and stayed away from drugs." Instead, he said, "We *have* to trust God to open doors." Skip was talking to himself as much as he was talking to Stephen.

Stephen held up the paper he'd taken from the trash can back at the halfway house. "I just got this from Mom."

Skip heard a bitter edge in Stephen's words. When he read the letter that Stephen handed him, he understood. Skip recognized Savanah's handwriting. Savanah's letter said that Stephen had stolen valuable years from their relationship and informed him that he would have to earn his way back into her trust. It didn't invite reconciliation. It seemed to create a wider chasm between them, putting conditions on Stephen that Skip knew his son was unlikely to be able to live up to any time soon.

Skip wanted to tell Stephen that his mother loved him and that she was dealing with the hurt and pain of Stephen's choices too, but he couldn't bring himself to say anything.

Stephen's shoulders shook, and Skip could see that dark thoughts of failure and guilt were consuming him. Skip felt he needed to do something to get Stephen's thoughts headed in a better direction.

Trying to lighten the mood, he said, "I bought some stuff to make hamburgers. And there's a small barbecue pit on the back porch. Do you want to make an early dinner?"

"Yeah. I think that'd be good." Stephen wiped his red eyes with his hands and looked away from his father.

They turned the TV to a sports channel for some background noise and went about seasoning the meat and chopping the vegetables. As they watched the burgers brown on the pit, they sipped iced tea on the back porch and talked about the upcoming college bowl games.

Eager to get Stephen thinking positively, Skip said, "I know you're going to have an amazing testimony one day. I could see you volunteering with a program that helps disadvantaged teenagers stay away from drugs. Wouldn't that be a great way to turn a bad thing into something positive?"

Stephen looked horrified. "You can't be serious! Who would ever take advice from me? I did everything wrong. Remember?"

Skip's heart sank. He'd said the wrong thing again. He tried to explain. "Right now, it feels that way. But when you get back on your feet, sharing your story will help so many people. It will give you purpose."

Stephen said, "Dad, I appreciate that you believe in me. I really do. But I had some messed-up thoughts and beliefs when I went to prison. Prison does not make your broken thought patterns better. In some ways it damaged me further. I don't know how I'm going to heal. I'm sitting here terrified because in a few hours you're going to leave and go back to your house in San Antonio and I'm going to be here alone for the first time. I haven't been alone for more than a few minutes in almost nine years. If I'm afraid to be alone, I don't think I'm ready to inspire someone else and I'm not sure I ever will be."

Skip hadn't anticipated this, but he was undaunted. "But you've come so far. You survived. There are so many people out there who need to hear that they are not too far gone, that God loves them no matter where they are."

Stephen shook his head. "I just don't see me doing that. I can't imagine a day when I'll feel comfortable talking to a stranger about what it's like to go to prison. I want to put that part of my life behind me as fast as I can. And I haven't been a Christian long enough to tell anybody about God. The only thing I know about God right now is that I need him."

Skip was crestfallen. He'd been positive that Stephen sharing his story was how God would make something good out of something so bad. Another idea came to him.

"Well, if you don't feel like you could talk about it publicly, perhaps you could write it down? Your story is very powerful. You could write a book."

Stephen laughed. "Me? I just learned how to read six years ago. Besides, what on Earth would I fill a book with? I can't think of one thing that happened to me that someone would find worth reading."

"I can think of lots of things," Skip said. "I kept a journal of all the things you told me. Most people have no idea what it's really like in there. Your story could give people hope, both people in prison and the people waiting for them. I kept all your letters. If I gave you my journal and your letters, I know you could do it." Skip felt his heart racing. He had imagined this conversation many times and Stephen always broke into a grateful smile, delighted at the idea of sharing his story to help others.

After a brief silence, Stephen said, "You kept all my letters?"

Skip nodded.

"Dad," Stephen said his name slowly, "I think you're the one who is supposed to write the book. You're the one with a heart for it."

Skip opened his mouth, but he couldn't find words. This thought had never occurred to him. Finally, he said, "What are you talking about? I didn't go to prison. What could I possibly share?"

"You're a survivor, too."

"What do you mean?"

"Your only son went to prison for almost nine years. Yet here you are. You survived the shame, the lost dreams. You loved a broken person and survived."

Skip had always tried so hard to be the strong one, to be the reassuring voice for his son. Now his son was reassuring him, telling him that he knew he was loved, and perhaps even admitting that his choices had cost them both dearly. Skip's carefully practiced composure faltered as hot tears stung his eyes. "Please don't call yourself 'broken.' You can heal."

"You're going to tell me that if I go to church everything in my life will be better. And maybe that's true. I don't know. I'm not sure what my faith will look like, but it probably won't look exactly like yours, Dad," said Stephen.

While these words were not what he wanted to hear, a peaceful feeling settled in Skip's heart and a voice in his mind told him not to argue this point. "Well," Skip said, his voice thick, "if you decide not to tell your story—our story—I just might."

"Fair enough," said Stephen licking mustard from the corner of his mouth, hamburger in hand. He was about to take another bite, but paused and said, "Just change my name." He brought the burger to his mouth again, and then added, "And leave out the stuff about Bear."

"Why?"

Stephen shook his head. "No one would ever believe it."

ABOUT THE AUTHOR

Lily Taylor is the chief legal officer for a national company and is a frequent speaker and lecturer on legal topics dealing with complex business transactions. But even attorneys cannot always save their loved ones from the consequences of their mistakes. She wrote *Unconfined* to shed light on the personal tragedy of incarceration experienced by over two million Americans annually and showcase the redemptive power of God's love even in the darkest circumstances. When Lily is not enjoying the peaceful beauty of the beach near her home, she enjoys teaching Bible study and encouraging young people to study law.

Printed in the USA
CPSIA information can be obtained
at www.ICGtesting.com
JSHW020544260923
49112JS00004B/309

9 781631 952999